DEBATING CHINA

DEBATING CHINA

THE U.S.-CHINA RELATIONSHIP IN TEN CONVERSATIONS

NINA HACHIGIAN

EDITOR

OXFORD
UNIVERSITY PRESS

OXFORD
UNIVERSITY PRESS

Oxford University Press is a department of the University of Oxford.
It furthers the University's objective of excellence in research, scholarship,
and education by publishing worldwide.

Oxford   New York

Auckland   Cape Town   Dar es Salaam   Hong Kong   Karachi
Kuala Lumpur   Madrid   Melbourne   Mexico City   Nairobi
New Delhi   Shanghai   Taipei   Toronto

With offices in

Argentina   Austria   Brazil   Chile   Czech Republic   France   Greece
Guatemala   Hungary   Italy   Japan   Poland   Portugal   Singapore
South Korea   Switzerland   Thailand   Turkey   Ukraine   Vietnam

Oxford is a registered trademark of Oxford University Press
in the UK and certain other countries.

Published in the United States of America by
Oxford University Press
198 Madison Avenue, New York, NY 10016

© Oxford University Press 2014

Library of Congress Cataloging-in-Publication Data
Debating China: the U.S.-China relationship in ten conversations / edited by Nina Hachigian.
pages cm.
Summary: "Experts from the U.S. and China engage in 'letter exchanges' that illuminate the multi-
dimensional and complex relationship between the two countries."—Provided by publisher.
ISBN 978-0-19-997387-3 (hardback) — ISBN 978-0-19-997388-0 (paperback)
1. United States—Foreign relations—China.
2. China—Foreign relations—United States.   I. Hachigian, Nina,
editor of compilation.
E183.8.C5D426 2014
327.73051—dc23
2013023099

7 9 8 6
Printed in the United States of America
on acid-free paper

For my mother and father,
who were always the wind at my back

CONTENTS

ACKNOWLEDGMENTS

The outstanding experts who contributed to this volume have my sincere gratitude. This book would not exist without them, and they impressed me repeatedly with their insights and convictions. That they were willing to take a gamble on an experimental approach is a testament to their open-mindedness. It was my privilege to work with such a stellar group.

I am very grateful to my fine colleagues at the Center for American Progress, especially Rudy DeLeon and Melanie Hart, for their support of this project as well as their general excellence and good cheer.

A few others deserve special thanks. The Luce Foundation provided critical financial support. Elizabeth Steffey first planted the notion of expanding an earlier published exchange into a book, and Jeff Wasserstrom pointed me in the right direction with my plan. Rebecca Friendly was an invaluable help with editing and organizing. Robert Kapp went beyond his call of duty as a translator, and Ken Sofer, Yao Lei, Philip Ballentine, and Luke Herman provided able research assistance. Greyson Bryan, Michael Schiffer, David Shorr, and Peter Scoblic's editorial input was enormously helpful. I am grateful to Jim Steinberg, whose views on foreign policy have consistently informed mine, for writing the conclusion.

My agent Andrew Wylie made it happen, and I want to thank David McBride and his team at Oxford University Press for embracing a new idea and then working hard to realize it.

I owe everything to my incredible parents who never failed to support me in every way. My brother Garo's common sense advice hit the mark. My wonderful children inspire me so much. And Joe Day, my husband, always had incisive feedback and encouraging words when I needed them most.

INTRODUCTION

NINA HACHIGIAN

On a wintry day in 2009, when new snowfall blanketed the grounds of a government-sponsored research center in Beijing, I had a lively exchange with an influential Chinese security expert, Dr. Yuan Peng. He and I debated the respective roles of America and China in global affairs at a small conference, along with other academics and former government officials. While our conclusions were radically different, we shared an understanding of the important questions to ask and a genuine desire to make the other understand why we held our point of view. Afterward, we published a version of our dialogue in the British foreign policy journal *Survival*. Later, a colleague suggested that our back-and-forth would make for a good book, and here we are.

The United States and China have the world's two largest economies and military budgets. They lead the globe in Internet users and greenhouse gas emissions. They are the biggest traders, investors in R&D, and consumers of multiple commodities. Both are nuclear powers and permanent members of the United Nations (UN) Security Council.

No bilateral relationship is more important to the future of humanity. How America and China choose to cooperate and compete affects billions of lives. We need to understand better how each side views the promise and perils of their relationship because steady, clear-eyed, workaday bonds can be a force for global stability and prosperity while intermittent, fear-based, and confrontational ties will lead to a darker future.

This volume offers a portrait of U.S.–China relations in ten conversations. In the chapters that follow, a Chinese and an American policy expert discuss the rich dynamics around a facet of the Sino-American relationship, writing letters back and forth. All are titans in their fields, highly respected in academia and policy circles, and many have played important formal and informal roles in steering bilateral relations. They converse regularly with their counterparts abroad, but rarely does the public get to listen in on these conversations.

You will now have that chance. I paired the experts on nine critical topics and offered them a series of questions (printed at the front of each chapter) to guide their dialogues—on economics, human rights, media, global roles, climate and energy, development, military affairs, Taiwan, and regional security. These represent the major issues, but Chinese and Americans interact on a growing list of policy questions. As Kenneth Lieberthal and Wang Jisi discuss in their overview, the relationship is expanding.

In one sense, these exchanges are discrete conversations between individuals who, unavoidably, bring their specific approaches and biases to the task. Yet because of their deep experience, frequent interactions with policy makers and attention to their government's positions, the authors' arguments often closely reflect those animating many official and unofficial policy dialogues. Different experts would have made for a different book, but probably not that different.

Taken together, the conversations offer grounds for optimism about the future of U.S.–China relations. They reveal genuine mutual respect between the writers, significant common interests between the two countries, and, as Yao Yang describes it in the economics chapter, a fervent appreciation that "[t]he world cannot afford to see confrontation between our two nations."

Still, distrust permeates the book. In the opening chapter, Lieberthal puts it baldly: China and America have failed "to develop trust in the long term intentions of each toward the other." His chapter partner Wang confirms that many Chinese "believe that the Americans have both the motivation and the means to 'create trouble' in China, as they are doing elsewhere," and that U.S. policies toward third countries, like North Korea and Iran, are "often interpreted as part of a grand strategy intended to weaken China."

Subsequent chapters echo Wang's observations. In the discussion of military developments, Christopher Twomey worries about self-perpetuating spirals that are pushing both countries to arm. Xu Hui disagrees, fingering "hostile U.S. intentions" and stating that "the main obstacle in the constructive development of Sino-American military relations is not so-called 'spirals' but American security conceptions and strategic intentions toward China." Xu writes that many Chinese analysts believe that the United States' "rebalance" to Asia was designed "to contain China's rise." In the last chapter on regional dynamics, Michael Green takes this accusation head on when he states, "There is no mainstream support in the United States today for a policy of containing China." His writing partner, Wu Xinbo, responds that he remains "less sure" than Green on that point.

No American counterarguments—from offering alternative explanations of American behaviors, to broadening the historical record, to recalling America's massive and ongoing efforts to integrate China—seem to persuade the Chinese authors that the United States does not seek to keep China down. As Wang writes, both nations "assume they are on the defensive rather than the offensive and deny any hostile intention toward the other side."

The essays offer various explanations for China's acute suspicion of American intentions. One is a belief in the determinism of the international order. Zhou Qi describes a common Chinese view in the chapter on political systems and rights: "[T]he second-most powerful country in the world will inevitably pose—or at least be perceived to pose—a challenge to the most powerful country in the world. Therefore, it is almost impossible to build mutual trust between them." She also suggests, as do others, that when the Cold War ended, China and the United States lost the strategic glue of a common adversary.

The media contributes to the cycle of distrust. Wang Shuo describes how social media is amplifying Chinese nationalism and predicts, "The Chinese people will support a more assertive China on the international stage, even demand it, and the government will happily oblige." Susan Shirk agrees and warns about the "steady drumbeat of officially sanctioned media messages about America's supposed 'containment' of China." "The precedents of pre-war Germany and Japan," she continues, "show how this kind of commercialized semi-controlled media, by creating myths and mobilizing anger against perceived foreign enemies, can drag a country into war."

China is no Nazi Germany—and a major power clash is less likely today than in the 20th century—but China has been growing so rapidly, its interests expanding so exponentially, that some Americans are concerned about how it may use its new found power in the future. Lieberthal argues that those looking to bolster their case for fulsome military budgets can play on this concern and that it stems in part from Americans' "innate distrust of authoritarian, one party systems." Zhou claims ideology is to blame for "persisting American perceptions of 'the China threat.'" Her counterpart, Andrew Nathan, suggests, in contrast, that American concerns are actually strategic: China would be more politically stable, and its intentions more transparent, were it governed by the rule of law and an open political process.

If the United States is trying to contain China, it is going about it in a peculiar way—with American help, China has been expanding along every conceivable dimension over the last 40 years. America does, however, want to shape Chinese behavior. As Green explains, the United States is seeking ways, for example, "to encourage China to become a net exporter of security" to the Asia-Pacific region.

America also wants to ensure that China's rise is not destabilizing, in part through encouraging its participation in the rules-based international order. Several American authors point out how much the system has enabled China's meteoric economic rise from a Gross Domestic Product (GDP) of $202 billion in 1980 to well over $7 trillion today.[1] In our new exchange on global roles, Yuan Peng, though he labels parts of the system "unreasonable," asserts that China is "integrating into the international system rather than trying to break it" and describes China's constructive contributions in areas such as peacekeeping and climate change. By contrast, Barry Naughton, in the dialogue on economics, writes that China "seems perpetually dissatisfied with the global system, and determined to extract as many benefits as it can from the system without, however, making any constructive proposals to change the system."

How can the relationship proceed amid such distrust? From Yuan comes the suggestion of "a new type of cooperation that deals with problems 'case by case' and 'step by step.'" This approach, I suggest, could build "tactical trust" that could aid in developing long-term, strategic trust, over time. But, I caution, China and the United States should broaden and deepen cooperation while still managing their competition and conflicts. As Alan Romberg writes, the American and Chinese leaders who opened the relationship in the late 1960s "wisely decided that even if they could not resolve [some] issues, they could manage them." To do that well, as he suggests, remains a challenge for leaders today.

Romberg is referring specifically to the political status of Taiwan, long a source of vehement disagreement. His exchange with Jia Qingguo shows how different American and Chinese perceptions can be. Similarly, Green concludes that he and Wu are "talking past each other" on North Korea policy (though, at times, Washington and Beijing cooperate productively on that issue). Nathan makes the same observation about his dialogue with Zhou, suggesting they disagree on "how to define the issue itself upon which we disagree." He writes, "International human rights law calls for political freedom and accountable government. These are not controversial values in China any more than they are in the United States. Chinese leaders have endorsed them, and Chinese people seek them." Zhou avoids criticizing America's human rights record, reluctant to engage in the tit-for-tat that Nathan thinks is exactly what the relationship needs. Wang Shuo sums it up nicely when he writes: "Better mutual understanding solves problems caused by misunderstandings, but not problems that have nothing to do with misunderstandings."

In some areas, common interests and assumptions offer hope that the United States and China can increase their cooperation. We learn in the chapter on climate and energy that China and the United States agree that global warming is an urgent problem, that they are the two biggest culprits, and that both must act boldly to forestall its worst effects. While there is not perfect harmony on who bears what degree of responsibility, it is clear, in Kelly Sims Gallagher's words, that "our shared interests...are greater than the issues that divide us," and that joint projects hold promise. Her partner Qi Ye calls for a "jubilant spirit" to continue their hard work and build on existing cooperation.

Similarly, in the dialogue on global development, Elizabeth Economy, though critical of Chinese actions, suggests that "adopting best practices and learning from each other" will allow the United States and China to "contribute to both the economic and social health of the countries in which they invest." Zha Daojiong agrees, observing "Competition between China and the United States in development need not be destructive nor inevitable." We can hope that Chinese and Americans' "common belief in pragmatism," as Yao Yang calls it in the economics chapter, will prevail.

The exchanges illustrate why the U.S.–China relationship is so consequential. China's decisions affect America's economic well-being, its sense of security, freedom of action, internal policy debates, foreign policy, and even its weather—and vice versa. China and 1.3 billion people are not going anywhere. Neither is America. The U.S.–China relationship is a showcase of globalization's essential truth: what I do affects you. That deep, persistent interdependence partly explains why Sino-American ties are so difficult. The United States and China need each other, and each needs the other to change.

The bolder America can be in tackling its own problems and investing in its own future, the easier it will find its relationship with China. The more China can push through needed domestic reforms, the less fraught its ties with America will be.

Several authors suggest the need for a shared vision to drive the future of the relationship. Xu Hui explains that "international relations are, in large part, mentally constructed." Wu Xinbo offers that "without a positive vision, the world will not improve and evolve." I suggest a future based on the idea of America, China, and other nations embedded in a matrix of international rules and institutions that help foster cooperation and bound their rivalries. Abiding by a common framework, with pragmatism as their guide, America and China can "move beyond dialogue to real achievements," as James Steinberg advocates in the Conclusion, to improve both their relationship and the world around them.

Importantly, not one author believes strategic confrontation between America and China is inevitable. None sees a relationship that is necessarily zero-sum—quite the opposite. The United States and China can both provide fulfilling lives for their people, at the same time, and can even help one another reach that essential goal.

AN OVERVIEW OF THE U.S.– CHINA RELATIONSHIP

KENNETH LIEBERTHAL
Brookings Institution

WANG JISI
Peking University

Framing questions: *What are the essential characteristics and dynamics of the U.S.–China relationship? What factors are driving China and the United States toward conflict, rivalry, and partnership? Has global power shifted toward China and has that affected the relationship? What domestic political dynamics in America and China influence the relationship? What interest groups and public opinion inform them? What are the significant obstacles to deeper understanding? From an American and a Chinese point of view, what is a plausible and optimistic scenario for the bilateral relationship in ten years? To what degree do these visions overlap? What forces shape the ability to reach each of these visions? What are the most important short- and medium-term steps toward a cooperative, stable relationship that benefits both countries?*

• • •

Dear Jisi,

I am both heartened and troubled by the situation at present in U.S.–China relations. I am writing now to explain the reasons for my unease even in the face of the enormous accomplishments since we established formal diplomatic relations in 1979.

As I see it, U.S.–China relations have four essential characteristics at present:

Mature. The key officials on both sides know each other and interact very frequently. Each knows the basic positions of the other side and how specific issues (such as the South China Sea, North Korea, U.S. arms sales to Taiwan, currency concerns, and so forth) have been handled over a period of years. Our two governments conduct more than 60 formal dialogues per year, and our presidents meet regularly at multilateral gatherings (such as the Group of Twenty (G-20), East Asia Summit, and Asia-Pacific Economic Cooperation (APEC) Leaders Meeting) in addition to frequently communicating by phone.

Both sides, moreover, have long been committed to preventing disagreements from dominating the relationship, as each seeks basically cooperative ties. Neither side feels it serves its own interests to purposely worsen relations with the other.

In short, our governments have developed wide-ranging, generally effective ties at an institutional and personal level. Each can more often than not anticipate the general position the other side will take as major issues come up, and we have proven ourselves able to manage—even if we cannot fully resolve—the many issues on which we do not have full agreement. On balance, the degree of success over the past 30+ years—despite changes of leaders in both countries and major changes on the world scene—is truly remarkable.

Dense. Our two governments and societies interact very extensively. Almost every U.S. cabinet department—not just State, Defense, Commerce, Treasury, and the U.S. Trade Representative, but also Housing and Urban Development, Health and Human Services, Environmental Protection, Transportation, Energy, Education, Agriculture, and so forth—deals with its Chinese counterpart every week.

Our economies have become interdependent to the point where neither side can take strong measures against the other without in the process seriously injuring itself. U.S. corporations are major investors in China, and the United States is China's largest single export market. China holds more

U.S. sovereign debt than does any other country, and Chinese investments in the United States are growing rapidly. While the two sides have serious economic and trade problems, each realizes that it cannot do without the other.

More students from China than from any other country are studying at American colleges and universities, and the U.S. government seeks to have 100,000 American students studying in China. The number of people who travel between our countries in any recent year tops 2 million.[1] And Chinese has become second only to Spanish as the most studied foreign language in American schools, while English is the most widely studied foreign language in China.

Thus, U.S.–China relations are not merely a diplomatic phenomenon. The relationship is grounded in dense ties that increasingly encompass the younger generation, too, on both sides.

Expanding. As China's global footprint continues to expand, regions of the world that previously played a marginal role in U.S.–China relations are becoming more central. For example, the United States has been the dominant external military power in the Persian Gulf for decades and has also been highly dependent on imports of oil from there. But as of 2013, less than 15% of America's imported oil comes from the Gulf, and that number should drop to virtually zero by 2015 or soon thereafter. While the United States will for many years remain the dominant outside military power in this region, it is less likely to get embroiled in a war over oil there than it has been in recent decades.

China's position is very different. As of 2013 more than 50% of its oil imports come from the Persian Gulf, and that number should grow to over 70% by 2020. Yet China will not have the military capacity to shape events in the Persian Gulf by 2020—or for a considerable time thereafter. But China's oil dependency will draw it ever deeper into the politics of the region in a way that Beijing has largely avoided heretofore.

The United States and China should, therefore, focus on the best mix of economic, military, and diplomatic stances in the Persian Gulf that will protect their overall interests, including America's ongoing interest in the free flow of reasonably priced oil out of this region. But China lacks people with a deep knowledge of both the Persian Gulf and the United States, and the United States lacks people with a deep knowledge of both the Persian Gulf and China.

U.S.–China relations will increasingly require finding ways to discuss and manage an expanding menu of issues in which the two sides lack needed expertise and experience. This applies both geographically (such as to the

Persian Gulf) and functionally (with new issues such as cyber-security). The expansion of the scope of issues that are key to U.S.–China relations will make this relationship more difficult to manage in the future.

Distrustful. The pioneers in U.S.–China relations assumed that greater familiarity would produce increased mutual trust. They therefore promoted increasing contacts, for example, among educators and scientists as well as diplomats and security specialists. But perhaps the greatest single failure in more than 30 years of formal diplomatic ties is the failure to develop trust in the long-term intentions of each toward the other ("strategic trust"). Arguably, indeed, distrust has actually grown in recent years.

Such distrust can be deeply damaging. It colors perceptions of motivations in ways that make sincere cooperation more difficult and that foster suspicion over even well-intentioned acts. It also increases the opportunities and power of those in each country who out of belief or interest promote skepticism about the intentions of the other side.

There are very good reasons why the United States and China should have trouble developing strategic trust. The two countries differ enormously in their respective histories, cultures, political systems, social structures, and economies. Both are continental-scale and extremely complex societies and thus are especially difficult to comprehend. Neither has a good "feel" for the domestic politics of the other, and thus each is inclined to see the other as more strategic, disciplined, and internally well coordinated than is really the case. This leads both sides to attribute strategic significance to various developments that in fact are not the result of intentional policy on the other side.

Within this context, strategic distrust on the Chinese side appears based especially on China's analysis of the past. China's international experience since the middle of the 1800s has convinced it that Western industrialized countries (including Japan) play to win and seek to prevent rivals from gaining sufficient power to knock them off of their perches. With the world's second largest GDP, China now foresees at some point overtaking the United States in total economic size. Many Chinese have apparently concluded from this that the United States must be so concerned not to lose its No. 1 ranking to China that it therefore is very likely engaged in a wide-ranging effort to delay, complicate, or even disrupt China's rise. This effectively frames overall U.S.–China relations in zero-sum terms.

I am very worried about this perspective, especially as it has developed despite the fact that the United States has worked hard to increase Chinese trust. Note that when the United States had extraordinary leverage in global affairs in the waning years of the last century, we did not block China's advance. For example, we welcomed tens of thousands of Chinese students to study at our universities, even before most of them could pay tuition. We worked hard to bring China into the World Trade Organization, and every modern president has resisted pressure to adopt protectionist measures as China has developed its export machine. President Obama encouraged a shift from the G-8 to the G-20 so as to bring China to the top table in global economic affairs. In short, at these and other junctures since the 1970s, the United States could have seriously obstructed China's rapid development, but Washington instead encouraged China's integration into the global economy and international system.

We, of course, have our own concerns. Americans have an innate distrust of authoritarian, one-party systems (especially if that party calls itself "communist"), as we are discomfited by the lack of transparency and slight regard given to civil liberties in such political systems. We see a more mercantilist approach to economic and trade policy in China than we are comfortable with and are especially concerned about failure to follow through adequately on Chinese government promises on protection of intellectual property, market access, and hidden export subsidies. The Chinese military's obvious reluctance to enhance ties with our forces worries us. And China-based cyber-theft of advanced American technology has been occurring on a truly unsettling scale.

Nevertheless, American policy makers still hold out the hope of developing a basically constructive relationship with China, one in which the two countries cooperate where they can and limit frictions where they must. But China's deep distrust of American intentions is itself corrosive, making Washington more worried about the need to adopt measures to defend U.S. interests if Beijing seeks to rise on the basis of weakening America in Asia and elsewhere. Can you suggest ways to avoid having this turn into a self-fulfilling prophecy of mutual antagonism? What would we have to do to significantly reduce China's distrust of America's long term intentions?

VISIONS OF THE FUTURE

America's vision of the world ten years from now bears strong resemblance to the world today. While acknowledging that global power is becoming more diffuse with the rise of the major developing countries, the United States seeks to maintain its role as the world's indispensable nation—the one country that can act on a global scale to maintain a fairly rule-based, open international system with democratic ideals and a constantly expanding global economy.

I believe China's vision has it playing a far greater role, especially in Asian affairs but also in global institutions, than it does today. It seeks a global system less dominated by the advanced industrial powers and especially by the United States. But it also recognizes the benefits that the U.S. role continues to provide to China and the instability that may increase—at times to China's disadvantage—if the American role rapidly diminishes. Yet as long as Beijing believes that America will ultimately seek to slow China's rise, I fear it will be inclined to try to erode American power even as it recognizes the ancillary benefits it derives from America's global role.

Three things stand out from these two visions. First, they are not in sharp conflict. China is not a revolutionary power with expansionist territorial ambitions, and the United States sees a large and legitimate role for China in the future international system. The conflicts and tensions need not produce fundamental antagonism and a zero-sum mentality in both capitals.

Second, each country's vision assumes that it will successfully manage its domestic affairs and thus maintain its national cohesion and vitality. But both America and China now confront deep domestic economic and social challenges, and there is some doubt as to how effectively each will muster the political will to deal with these. The shadow of the future looms large in U.S.–China relations, and the relative success of our respective efforts to implement needed domestic reforms will shape expectations of each country's future vitality and national mood. This can seriously impact our views of each other and visions of our respective roles in the world a decade from now.

Third, an antagonistic relationship will ultimately be hard to avoid if new approaches are not adopted to deal with the corrosive issue of strategic distrust. I welcome your views on what these should be. Clearly, efforts to date have not proven sufficient to address this issue effectively and the next few years can prove critical.

Sincerely,
Ken

• • •

Dear Ken,

Your characterization of the essence and dynamics of today's China–U.S. relations is well taken. As personal friends and colleagues for more than 20 years, we are naturally quite familiar with each other's viewpoints. As you may have assumed, I don't have any major disagreements with your analysis and forecast. The four adjectives—mature, dense, expanding, and distrustful—you used to describe how the two countries are interacting with each other are very balanced and comprehensive. However, I do want to add some other elements that I believe to be important in the China–U.S. relationship, and make a few more remarks following your four themes.

As you pointed out, our two governments have established a mature working relationship that has successfully managed a number of difficult issues and crises since Beijing and Washington decided to approach each other more than 30 years ago. As a senior official of the Clinton administration, you were personally involved in handling the political storm in China–U.S. relations after the deplorable NATO bombing of China's embassy in Belgrade in May 1999 during the Kosovo War. I remember you telling me afterwards that your counterparts in China's diplomatic circle took significant personal political risks to save the relationship from sinking, and I believe that you were among the few U.S. officials that made painstaking efforts to bring bilateral ties back into normalcy after the tragedy. Fortunately for the interests of the two peoples, Chinese and American national leaders and officials responsible for the bilateral relationship today have followed the long tradition of clearly recognizing its vital importance and investing much of their political capital in pushing it forward.

My worries about China–U.S. relations arise not from the degree of maturity of the government-to-government connection but from the new circumstances in both countries that complicate the decision-making processes. As you convincingly argued, our increasingly dense interaction provides an unprecedentedly broad basis for cooperation. However, the more interest groups, institutions, and individuals brought into the connection, the more chances for dissatisfaction, grievances, frictions, and conflicts of interest to rise and pull the China–U.S. connection in different directions.

Compare these circumstances with those around 40 years ago when Mao Zedong, Zhou Enlai, Richard Nixon, Henry Kissinger, and a handful of other decision makers in Beijing and Washington were determined to normalize their bilateral relationship. Although not totally immune from domestic factors, the momentum of the China–U.S. rapprochement was driven by single-minded national security considerations—the shared apprehensions about Soviet expansionism and the U.S. desire to extricate itself from the Vietnam War quagmire. At the operational level, the execution of their decisions was relatively unaffected by outside forces and their respective domestic political environments—and, at times, occurred in extreme secrecy.

This simple logic no longer applies to the nature and reality of the present China–U.S. relationship. Our two nations do not confront a common menace as we did with the Soviet Union, and it is hard nowadays to identify any organizing principle to guide the relationship or our policies toward each other. It is not an exaggeration to assert that this relationship is the most complicated one in international history. Your letter rightly referred to "an expanding menu of issues in which the two sides lack needed expertise and experience." Indeed, this menu of issues actually encompasses all the important issues the world faces today, and is still expanding.

The expansion of issues inevitably entails an expansion of interest groups and government agencies involved in China–U.S. ties, as mentioned above, which makes the decision-making processes in Beijing and Washington increasingly complicated. For example, more than two dozen ministerial-level government agencies on each side have been attending the annual China–U.S. Strategic and Economic Dialogue initiated (S&ED) by the two heads of state in 2009. It is easily imaginable that these government agencies have their own perspectives and represent different interests in society.

Pundits and historians in both countries often express nostalgic feelings about the Mao–Nixon/Zhou–Kissinger years and admiration for the top leaders' wisdom, courage, vision, and decisiveness in making diplomatic breakthroughs. These years are gone forever. The current and future generations of leaders in the two countries have to steward the relationship in completely different circumstances. Such issues as the currency exchange rate, trade frictions, carbon emission reduction, and individual human rights cases are all important in China–U.S. relations and often need to be passed to the top leadership for a decision. Some issues are highly technical and have to go through numerous layers of policy coordination. Therefore, the difficulty in making and implementing decisions is now more a reflection of bureaucratic politics than individual leaders' personal ability or preference.

Moreover, an increasing number of the issues between China and the United States are multilateral, that is, they involve a third or more other parties. For instance, Beijing is concerned about Washington's possible scheme to take advantage of China's territorial disputes with Japan, Vietnam, the Philippines, and some other neighboring countries. Many Chinese fear that the strengthening of U.S. security ties in the Asia-Pacific region is directed at China. On the U.S. side, there are expressed concerns that China lacks conviction about the denuclearization of North Korea or Iran and wants to protect undemocratic regimes in Myanmar, Sudan, Zimbabwe, and Syria at the expense of U.S. interests and wishes.

People usually suppose that more contact and cooperation between nations, as well as between individuals, generates more mutual understanding and friendlier feelings. This does not appear to be true in the current China–U.S. interaction. Your letter gave some compelling reasons that explain why. I suspect that the strategic distrust you described may not wither away any time soon and may indeed become more deeply entrenched in both societies, unfortunately. There is a tendency in each society to blame the other side for its own internal difficulties. The other side, in turn, deems this practice irrelevant and unreasonable. Some American politicians, for example, want to hold China responsible for the losses of American jobs due to bilateral trade and outsourcing by U.S. manufacturers. Many Chinese officials and media figures, meanwhile, accuse the United States of supporting separatist activities and violence in Tibet and Xinjiang. They reprimand Western correspondents and non-governmental organizations (NGOs) for creating instability in Chinese society by fueling anti-government sentiment and political dissension. This kind of distrust cannot be wiped out by bilateral dialogues, however sincere the participants may be.

Putting China–U.S. relations against a larger historical background, one cannot fail to note the rapidly changing power balance between the two nations. As recently as 2001, China's total GDP was only 12.8% of U.S. GDP. In 2011, China's GDP reached $7.3 trillion, amounting to 48.5% of U.S. GDP and surpassing Japan as the second-largest economy of the world. China has also made great progress in enhancing its military and technological capabilities. Statistics and assessments vary, but many economists predict that China will replace the United States as the world's largest economy between 2020 and 2025.

Relations between nations are defined largely by their relative strength, especially if they are great powers competing with each other. With the rapid growth of China's power, influence, and prestige in global affairs, its political elites have gained a great deal of national pride, confidence, or—as some outsiders put it—arrogance. If China's relationship with the United States in the past was based on an asymmetry of power in favor of the Americans, the relationship today should reflect the resurgence of China and increasingly be based on equality. According to most Chinese political analysts and officials, China's foreign policy in general and its policy toward the United States in particular should be more assertive. Some suggest that Beijing should no longer "tolerate" continued U.S. arms sales to Taiwan and should find ways to retaliate and "punish" such U.S. actions. Some advise the government to use military means to recover the Diaoyu Islands from Japan and many islands in the South China Sea from Vietnam and the Philippines since all these islands are China's territories. They strongly suspect that the Americans are quietly backing those competitors of China to weaken its international position. There are also proposals that China should try to establish its own security alliances in response to the U.S.-led security arrangements in the Asia-Pacific region, which are, to Chinese eyes, designed to contain or encircle China.

As for the American efforts you list to increase Chinese trust by welcoming China into the international community, a common Chinese response is that all those actions are in the United States' best interests—there is no altruism involved. The United States wants to integrate China into the so-called "international community" in order to change China and make it more pro-American, or more like America.

As you illustrated in your letter, "[t]here are very good reasons why the U.S. and China should have trouble developing strategic trust." I assume that the two of us will readily agree that one of the reasons for China–U.S. strategic distrust is the narrowing power gap between our two great nations. Most Chinese observers believe that the United States is a declining power and will try hard to prevent China from catching up with it. U.S. policies toward North Korea and Iran, Syria, and other Arab countries are often interpreted as part of a grand strategy intended to weaken China. American officials and commentators deny such intentions, and they tend to suspect that China's apparently uncooperative attitude in handling these regional issues reflects a systematic attempt to damage America's international position.

One asymmetry I note in the mutual distrust is that China seems more apprehensive about actual and possible American political penetration into its domestic affairs, whereas the United States is more concerned about

China's international challenges in the long run. In this sense, Chinese anxieties are more immediate and present, and American worries are based on projections of China's ascendance and its implications. Interestingly enough, therefore, both assume that they are on the defensive rather than the offensive and deny any hostile intentions toward the other side.

Another asymmetry I have discovered is between the leadership and the general public in each country, or between the "insiders" and "outsiders" of government-to-government relations. Top leaders, officials, diplomats, and policy advisors responsible for the relationship are reasonably well informed of its crucial importance, complexity, the countries' respective power positions, and each other's sensitivities. They also clearly recognize the danger of a China–U.S. confrontation. In comparison, the general public, the media, and a large part of the elites, officials, and politicians (including U.S. members of Congress) on both sides cannot be expected to understand the whole picture of the China–U.S. relationship, although they may pay close attention to it or even presume to know a lot about it.

This asymmetry of knowledge can have a significant impact on the bilateral relationship when the leadership (the "insiders") in both countries is increasingly susceptible to public and elite (the "outsiders") opinions and when this relationship gains more importance and relevance to the fate of each country. Already, there have been many suspicions in each country that their own government is "too soft" or even "selling out the nation's interests" to the other country. It is likely that leaders in Washington sometimes feel it easier to deal with their counterparts in Beijing than to convince the U.S. Congress or certain think tanks of their wisdom and vision in dealing with China. The same can be said of Beijing's dealings with Washington. In other words, the future of the China–U.S. relationship will depend, to a large degree, on how successfully the two leaderships can manage the diversity of interests and views in their own country related to the relationship.

I very much second the three conclusions at the end of your letter. Given the observations I presented above, I strongly believe that a healthy, strong China–U.S. relationship must be built on the prospects of two powerful, stable, and prosperous countries. The more successful our domestic transformations are, the more confident the two sides will become, and the less likely we will run into confrontation. As to your question about possible new approaches to dealing with the issue of strategic distrust, I don't think I have any good ideas. We may have to live with the issue for a long time to come. Paradoxically, a political crisis triggered by a deplorable incident might serve as a wakeup call, as some crises in the past did have a sobering effect and helped to clarify the nature of this relationship. But, of course, I don't want to see anything like that happen.

Sincerely,

Jisi

· · ·

Dear Jisi,

Thank you for your response to my letter. You raise three key issues: coping with an increasing array of interest groups on each side; dealing with the issues raised by a shifting balance of power; and devising initiatives that might reduce distrust of long-term intentions ("strategic distrust"). I'll contribute some thoughts on each in the hope of enriching this discussion.

Interest Groups

I fully agree that the expansion in the players involved in U.S.–China relations has made decision making more complex in both Beijing and Washington. But I think the Chinese and American situations differ considerably when it comes to the impact of interest groups on policy making.

In the U.S., interest group activity around China peaked[2] in the 1990s, when activists of all stripes sought to leverage the horrific visual images of the June 4, 1989, Tiananmen massacre to press their case with the American public. During that decade even advocacy groups with no previous serious interest in China (such as those focused on making abortion illegal) sought to portray the PRC as the worst offender in the world on "their" issue and then use this China connection to gain national prominence and increased clout.[3] This tactic had largely spent its force by the time of the terrorist attacks of September 11, 2001.

But even during this period, China policy was not wholly a captive of these activist groups. The U.S. government has long incorporated complex interests into its decision-making system. Policy toward China has tended to be concentrated in the White House more consistently than has been the case for other foreign policy issues, and China policy in other agencies is coordinated primarily through the National Security Council (NSC) structure. The Congress has in many ways made its concerns felt, but the White House under presidents from both parties has driven and shaped

China policy, and there is no indication of substantial recent deviation from this model.

In China, by contrast, the power of vested interests within and outside the Communist Party appears to have grown considerably in the past decade, and the rapid expansion of new communication channels such as social networking has greatly amplified the voices of public opinion. The Hu Jintao administration's consensus-based model of making important decisions arguably has enhanced the ability of interests to make their views count, though President Xi Jinping is apparently less inclined to follow this model than his predecessor. Despite its use of various interagency committees, moreover, Beijing lacks the well-institutionalized and powerful coordinating mechanisms embodied in the U.S. NSC system.

As the problem in Beijing of a more complex arena of bureaucratic and other actors will not go away, I believe the best approach may entail a step recently taken—enhancing the leverage of the very top leaders through a combination of reducing the size of the Politburo Standing Committee from nine to seven in November 2012—and moving away from the current consensus-based norm of decision making. With stronger leadership from the top, it may be possible to forge an NSC-type system to coordinate inputs and policy implementation.

Shifting Balance of Power

Significant changes in power relationships affect the psychologies and politics in each country, their concrete capabilities, and the larger diplomatic environment within which they operate. With so many factors in flux, it is not surprising that differing perceptions and reactions become a problem, with the shifting balance of power exacerbating U.S.–China distrust.

You focus especially on the changing ratio of the Chinese and American GDPs. What you say is both important and accurate. But two additional factors make the situation even more complex as we look to the future.

First, as I briefly alluded to in my initial letter, both China and the U.S. now face economic policy challenges that will require very strong leadership to resolve. The United States must adopt a set of fiscal policies that will keep America's national debt manageable while permitting ongoing investments in key areas that enhance national power—education, science, physical infrastructure, energy, and the military. China must vigorously implement the shift in its development model toward a more innovative, higher value-added, less resource-intensive, and more domestically driven economy that its leaders already have agreed is necessary for its sustainable development.

Neither country at this point has demonstrated that its leaders have the will and political capital necessary to make these changes. But the economic balance a decade from now will reflect the extent to which each succeeds in making these critical economic transitions. The gap between the two economies a decade from now is thus less certain, I think, than your letter implies.

Second, economic size is not by any means the sole (or necessarily the major) factor in determining national capabilities. The United States is as of now blessed with significant advantages across the board: abundant natural resources, a favorable overall population age distribution, only friendly countries on its borders, very extensive international alliances and partnerships, and arguably the world's most advanced and capable military, corporations, higher education system, financial system, judicial system, innovation system, and civil society. The United States is also a mature democracy that need not worry about the stability of its overall political system.

All of these important advantages can be frittered away if Washington fails to deliver the decisions and policies necessary for America's continued solvency and vitality. But these advantages are either impossible to create (e.g., natural resource base) or require many decades to build (most of the others). The real balance of power will, therefore, remain difficult to judge and prone to differing interpretations.

I regard China's future as remarkably unpredictable. Demographics, resource constraints, and popular attitudes alone dictate that it will not be a straight-line extrapolation from its recent past. It is, to me, the uncertainties about both the U.S. and Chinese trajectories over the coming decade that feed arguments in each country about how we should deal with the other.

Reducing Distrust over Long-Term Intentions

The coming few years may prove particularly important for determining the longer-term trends in U.S.–China relations, and there is ample room for worry. In China, the new leadership coming into power has such a massive set of domestic challenges on their plates that they may well seek genuine caution in foreign policy overall and in U.S.–China relations in particular so that they can concentrate on their domestic agenda. It is also possible, of course, that they will prove more assertive internationally in order to bolster their domestic political capital and divert attention from domestic failings. But my judgment is that this is less likely, unless circumstances force them to move in this direction.

In this context, recent developments in the United States may spell trouble. The U.S. Department of Defense is facing the most constrained budget environment since the turn of this century, and there is a tendency for key players to seek new rationales to bolster their case for maintaining or even enhancing past budgetary support. The biggest expenditures tend to be for major weapons systems, and such expenditures (unlike those for training and personnel, for example) often enjoy very strong backing from members of Congress who represent the districts where production facilities are located. This seems to be what is occurring in support of the relatively new "Air-Sea Battle concept," and creating the impetus to prepare for major war with China[4] is increasingly the major motivating rationale for this concept. There is simply no prospective military challenge other than China that might require the development of very expensive new military systems.

In 2013, the underlying contention over defense department resources in combination with having many new decision makers in major positions that shape policy toward China is creating at least a possibility of a tougher and more confrontational U.S. approach to China, just at the time when the new Chinese leadership is likely hoping to avoid problems in U.S.–China relations.

In this circumstance, the new Chinese leadership may feel compelled to push back hard against American initiatives in order to gain the political capital necessary to implement domestic reforms and also to demonstrate to the United States that its own tougher approach will prove very costly. At a military level, it is more than possible that vigorous U.S. pursuit of capabilities to implement the Air-Sea Battle concept will enhance the People's Liberation Army's (PLA) leverage in China's own internal budget debates.

This context highlights that it is more important than ever to develop some new initiatives that might move U.S.–China relations onto a more promising long-term trajectory. I appreciate your comment that you do not have any good ideas as to what might be done along these lines. I have two suggestions, each of which could be fleshed out in various ways.

First, if the two governments distrust each other's long-term intentions, we should structure some high-level, sustained dialogues about the long term. Currently, despite our very extensive bilateral contacts, none of our official dialogues look beyond the short run in any meaningful fashion. Key new dialogues might address: How does each military see its strategic posture in Asia ten years from now, including how does each side see the PLA relating to the extensive system of U.S. alliances and security partnerships throughout the region? What contingencies might occur on the Korean peninsula over the coming decade, and how does each side evaluate the threats and opportunities that each contingency contains? How might both sides reduce the U.S.–China military dimension of the cross-Strait issue over the coming decade? Having sustained dialogues about the longer term may improve mutual understanding and reveal ways to enhance mutual trust.

Second, we should look for opportunities to break the previous mold on the types of cooperative initiatives we undertake. For example, we might consider how our two navies can work together (perhaps along with the Indian navy) to increase security for shipping oil from the Persian Gulf. Lessons from the anti-piracy efforts that our two navies have participated in in the Gulf of Aden might provide useful insights as to how to bring this about.

In sum, we agree that U.S.–China relations are highly substantive and robust and that basically cooperative relations are in the interest of both countries. We also agree that there are serious challenges to keeping our overall relationship on a positive level as we move forward. I hope you find my preliminary thoughts about some new approaches to be helpful. I look forward to your comments both on these suggestions and on the underlying analysis in the rest of this letter.

Best,
Ken

• • •

Dear Ken,

Thanks for your very thoughtful comments. They have stimulated my thinking about a number of issues in China–U.S. relations, and I would like to make three points in response.

The shifting balance of power does not necessarily favor China in the coming years. It is a very commonly held Chinese perception that China has already become the No. 2 power in the world and should act, as well as be treated, as such. This perception is bolstered by a number of Chinese and international commentaries, including a popular book published in 2009 with the sensational title *When China Rules the World*.[5] This book, written by a British journalist, predicts China will overtake the United States as the world's largest economy by 2027 and double in size by 2050. Meanwhile, distinguished American strategists and scholars like former National Security Advisor Zbigniew Brzezinski, former Secretary of State Henry Kissinger, and former President of the World Bank Robert Zoellick have all advocated the concept of the Group of Two (G-2), as if it were already a reality that America and China were the two most important players in global affairs. Historian Niall Ferguson even coined the term "Chimerica" to describe the symbiotic nature of the U.S.–China economic relationship. Their expectations of China's international role, along with China's own efforts to cultivate patriotism at home, have reinforced the notion that China will soon catch up with the United States in terms of national power and global status.[6]

These expectations and descriptions, however, may be misleading. Your letter is very correct in cautioning against a hasty conclusion about the shifting balance of power between our two countries. My earlier letter to you did note the "rapidly changing power balance" and the fact that "many economists predicted that China will replace the United States as the world's largest economy." I also presented the pride and confidence held by China's political elites based on their assessment of China's newly gained power. However, I personally don't put great stock in these predictions or fully share this attitude. Instead, I completely agree with your opinion that if China fails to achieve its declared goals of changing its pattern of economic development and embarking on necessary economic and political reforms, its rapid progress thus far will be disrupted. In the decade ahead, China will face a lot of uncertainties.

The depiction of China as the world's No. 2 belies many facts. First, the European Union as a whole remains the world's largest economy, although it is undergoing a serious setback. The Europeans play a greater role than the Chinese in most international economic and political arenas. Second, by a few important measurements Russia is still militarily stronger than China. Finally, and more importantly, China still lags far behind the Western powers and Japan in terms of per capita income and technological innovation.

In addition to China's internal pitfalls, its international environment is not rosy. China can hardly take any pleasure from the American and

European economic slowdowns. China's continued resurgence is, to a large degree, contingent on a vibrant global economy and steady supplies of food, energy, and other natural resources from overseas at reasonable prices, none of which are assured. In Asia, China is facing the traditional "security dilemma," which means that as its military capabilities improve, its neighbors may become more apprehensive and attempt to develop counterweights, including moving strategically closer to the United States and strengthening security cooperation among themselves.

This is already conspicuous in the latest events regarding China's territorial disputes with Japan, the Philippines, and Vietnam. While Beijing definitely wants to see more unity within BRICS (Brazil, Russia, India, China, and South Africa) as a collective force to balance the Western world, these countries have their own interests and considerations that differ from China's. In short, the new global and regional balance of power may not appear to be as favorable as many Chinese observers have anticipated.

China's concept of national security is far broader and more complicated than that of America, and therefore a system akin to the U.S. NSC is not likely to take shape.

Your letter suggests the possible forging of "an NSC-type system to coordinate [foreign relations] inputs and policy implementation" in China's decision making. Interestingly enough, this idea has been floating around in China's think tanks for quite a few years, spurred on by what analysts see as insufficient inter-agency foreign policy coordination, especially in managing international crises.

Though I am sure you are well aware of it, it is not widely known to the outside world or even to China's general public that there exists a Central Foreign Affairs Leading Group (CFALG) responsible to the Communist Party's Politburo for deliberating and coordinating foreign affairs. This group also serves as the Central National Security Leading Group dealing with national security issues. Since the mid-1990s, CFALG has been led by the Communist Party's general secretary and China's head of state (Presidents Jiang Zemin, Hu Jintao, and Xi Jinping successively). Its other current members, around a dozen, include the State Councilor responsible for foreign affairs (Yang Jiechi at the time of this writing) serving as its general secretary, the heads of the Ministries of Defense, Foreign Affairs, Commerce, State Security, Public Security, Taiwan Affairs Office, the Communist Party's Publicity Department,[7] and International Department, and a few other government and party agencies related to foreign and national security affairs. The secretariat of CFALG is a substantive Party agency called the Central Foreign Affairs Office (CFAO), headed by Yang Jiechi.

Two characteristics make CFALG and CFAO different from the NSC of the United States. First, "national security" in China is much more broadly defined than in America. In addition to all the obvious issues related to national security and foreign affairs, separatist tendencies in Taiwan, Tibet, and Xinjiang and political dissenters like the religious group Falun Gong are all seen through the prism of national security. This makes China's policy coordination and implementation increasingly cumbersome. Second, since the number of CFALG's designated members is greater than the number of NSC principles who meet, and given its broader responsibilities, its meetings are probably less frequent. How Beijing will improve its foreign policy decision-making processes remains to be seen, but an NSC-type system is not on the horizon.

Beijing's domestic concerns continue to dominate its dealings with Washington, and may do so even more in the future.

We have discussed in our correspondence the close interaction between domestic politics in the two countries and the China–U.S. relationship. This is particularly true in the case of China. I would like to share with you a story I heard recently to illustrate how sensitive the U.S. connection can be to the Chinese.

At a bilateral meeting between some American and Chinese military officers on how to enhance their cooperation, an American officer tried to convince his Chinese counterparts of the wisdom of sending PLA officers to be trained in the United States. He referred to the Arab Spring in Egypt in 2011, saying that because a number of Egyptian army officers had been educated at West Point or other U.S. military institutions and had established personal connections with Americans, when the Hosni Mubarak regime was overthrown and the country was in turmoil, American and Egyptian military forces were still able to cooperate and share information.

This American officer had no idea how much damage his words might have caused the fragile U.S.–China military relationship. A revolt or social chaos like the Arab Spring is the very last thing the Chinese leadership wants to see happen in China. Furthermore, the PLA will spare no effort to prevent Americans from influencing the internal affairs of China, not to say the internal affairs of the Chinese military. The American officer's comments just confirmed the suspicion among many Chinese that military-to-military relations serve the U.S. purpose of penetrating deeply into the Chinese armed forces for ulterior motives. Therefore, the PLA only learned a negative lesson from that Egyptian story, not a positive one.

The larger moral of this story, seen from China, is that when many countries in the Middle East, Central Asia, and other parts of the world are undergoing political transformations, some of which have turned turbulent and violent, Chinese officials and elites must become even more vigilant against foreign—especially American—interference. Many Chinese believe that the Americans have both the motivation and the means to "create trouble" in China, as they are doing elsewhere.

The case of Bo Xilai, the former Party Secretary of Chongqing, is very illustrative. Wang Lijun, the former police chief of Chongqing, defected by driving several hours to the U.S. General Consulate in Chengdu to seek political asylum (but failed) after a fierce quarrel with Bo in early 2012. Gu Kailai, Bo's wife, killed a British citizen in Chongqing, allegedly for personal reasons involving her son, who is now a student in the United States. Although Chinese and American officials handled these episodes discreetly and, fortunately, they did not precipitate an outright diplomatic crisis, such events may foretell events in the future that connect sensitive Chinese domestic political issues to the United States, and vice versa.

This brings me to my response to the two recommendations you make in the letter. Both recommendations are well intended, and both involve the Chinese military coordinating or cooperating with the U.S. military. I think they might be technically feasible and strategically conducive. But I am honestly not sure whether the expected benefits would be great enough to outweigh the possible political risks in Beijing's calculation.

In any case, people like ourselves should continue to make efforts to strengthen ties between our two great nations and to avoid antagonism. Without these joint and coordinated efforts, the relationship may go adrift and bring about undesirable consequences to us all.

I hope our correspondence will continue in another venue, and look forward to your further thoughts about this most important relationship in the world today.

Best regards,
Jisi

THE ECONOMIC RELATIONSHIP

BARRY NAUGHTON
University of California at San Diego

YAO YANG
Peking University

Framing questions: *What are the main issues and concerns from a Chinese and an American point of view when it comes to bilateral trade and investment? Is China growing at America's expense? Or is America growing at China's expense? Is China taking jobs from the United States? What are the main issues and concerns with regard to the bilateral economic relationship? Will both countries be able to rebalance their own economies in the coming decade? Why or why not? What does rebalancing involve in each case? What forces constrain and help them? How will their success or failure to rebalance affect the relationship? To what degree are America and China playing a helpful or harmful role in the global economy? Do they play by the international economic rules of the road? How important is the role of international organizations like the G-20 and the International Monetary Fund (IMF), and how are they likely to evolve?*

•   •   •

Dear Yang,

No two countries have benefited more from globalization over the past 30 years than China and the United States have. For China in particular, its opening to the global economy and entry in the World Trade Organization (WTO) have been key parts of the Chinese economic miracle that has reshaped our world. By all rights, economics ought to be the area that brings us together, and mutual economic benefit ought to help us overcome the friction and inevitable misunderstandings that are being discussed in other parts of this book. But it just isn't that way. Economic issues separate us almost as often as they bring us together. Why is that?

Economic theory teaches us that international trade makes both parties (and the world) better off, but it also creates winners and losers. That's true for every country. In the United States, there were many people who gained from the deepening of economic relations with China. The winners were consumers of inexpensive Chinese imports, of course, and also American producers who benefited from new customers in China. Most striking of all, though, were the corporations that benefited from the opportunity to produce sophisticated new products—like an Apple iPad—at an unprecedented combination of low price and high quality by combining the resources of the United States and China. The world benefited from the creation of global production networks of incredible efficiency.

Yet this has come at a cost for some Americans as well. Recent work analyzing labor markets in individual cities over the past 30 years has confirmed what everybody suspected: low-skilled workers in the United States suffered significantly from the influx of cheap labor-intensive goods from China in the 1990s and 2000s. Their wages stagnated, while the rest of the economy grew. Of course, it's not China's responsibility to take care of the disadvantaged in the United States. That responsibility belongs to the United States, to our own people and policy makers, and to the gradual adaptation of markets. But this mixture of winners and losers highlights a simple fact: globalization and free trade can only work when there is a strong commitment to the overall process. When trade is free and fair, then each country will be better off as a whole, and can be sure it has the resources to take care of those hurt by the increasing exchanges. The mixture of winners and losers can be managed if these wrenching economic changes can be seen as the outcome of a fair process to which all sides are committed. Each side agrees to let the process of economic change—the working out of comparative advantage—take its course and accepts the outcome. In other words, both sides agree that they will maintain the commitment to free exchange despite the fact that there will be losers on each one's side.

Americans feel that they have made such a commitment in their relationship with China. American markets have been open to China. The United States is by far the biggest market for Chinese exports and has been a huge source of modern technology for China over more than three decades. Companies have poured investment into China that transferred hard and soft technologies to Chinese workers, managers, and engineers. U.S. universities have trained tens of thousands of brilliant Chinese scientists, many of them with full scholarships. It is no exaggeration to say that the astonishing growth of China over the past 30 years would have been inconceivable without the U.S. connection. So it is not unreasonable for Americans to ask China to make the same kind of commitment to the principles of free trade that we have made.

Seen in this framework, it's easy to understand why many Americans are dissatisfied with China's approach to the economic relationship, as well as why we attach so much importance to one apparently modest area that has divided us for years: the protection of intellectual property rights (IPR). The United States today emphasizes IPR protection in our own self-interest: no other economy has such a rich stockpile of contemporary intellectual property, and no economy is better at producing disruptive innovation in core science-driven areas and in bold new business models. But that's just the point. This truly is where the United States' comparative advantage lies. We are not really a traditional capital-abundant economy, exporting expensive machinery, like Germany or Japan. Rather, Americans excel at creating clever ideas and at structuring clever business models to stretch those ideas to maximum benefit: that is, in the sheer creation of intellectual property. So if we want to bring our comparative advantage into play, it is essential that we protect our intellectual property rights.

When China joined the WTO in 2001, it quickly brought its legal system into compliance with the WTO standards, including those of the associated TRIPS agreement (Trade-Related Aspects of Intellectual Property Rights). This was a huge step forward, but implementation since has been disappointing. At the heart of the problem are difficulties in enforcing judgments and legal rules that set ridiculously low standards of compensation: right now foreign firms can win judgments in Chinese courts, but the amounts are so small and the enforcement of judgments so slow and uncertain that they really do not deter pirates. This is a long-standing complaint of the United States, and a real concern.

Now the astonishing thing is that the great partner of U.S. businesses as they have developed their model of splitting up production and leveraging ideas into global networks has been China. Chinese companies on the mainland and in Taiwan are deeply integrated into the global production networks that were created based on the ability to securely use intellectual property across borders. Thus, the Chinese government's failure to seriously crack down on intellectual property pirates is doubly frustrating and ironic. These policies hurt American companies, but they also hurt Chinese development. They deter Chinese firms from investing in innovation and intellectual property, and they deter American firms from sharing knowledge with their Chinese partners, which is one of the most promising pathways upward for dynamic Chinese firms. Basically, they allow rip-off artists to profit at the expense of healthy, sustainable development in both China and the United States.

Another kind of intellectual property issue is becoming even more disturbing. Lately, the Chinese government has launched a vast program of promotion of high-tech industries. The program extends from support for Chinese technical standards (as in telecommunications) to financial support for Chinese producers in so-called "Strategic Emerging Industries." In the latter, China has outlined a list of 35 high technology industries in which it is determined to push Chinese producers to the global frontier by pouring money into investment. The policy documents of these programs are filled with rhetoric about seizing the "strategic heights" of the global economy. To Americans, it appears that the Chinese government has the announced intention of squeezing U.S. firms out of leadership in every conceivable cutting-edge sector: it looks like a concerted effort to deprive American firms of benefits in precisely those areas where they have the strongest competitive advantage. Further, if the allegations of Chinese government-sponsored rampant cyber-theft of American commercial information prove true, my concerns would be all the greater.

Please notice that I'm not arguing that China should refrain from competing vigorously and becoming a high-tech power. There's no reason that China should go on producing low-margin, labor-intensive stuff for the foreseeable future. More high-tech innovation from China will be good for everyone.

But anybody can see that that is going to happen anyway. Everybody can see that China is rising fast and will become a high-tech power, in many sectors, no matter what the Chinese government does. All you have to do is visit the laboratories of a top American university and see the Chinese doctoral students engaged in cutting-edge research with their American professors. China should and will move to the front ranks of world technology powers. But for this very reason, the Chinese government should see the obvious benefit in committing to a fair and well-regulated system of intellectual property protection, that will allow a fair, competitive outcome to the technology "contest" so that we can all benefit from the breakthroughs of ourselves and others. Unfortunately, Chinese government policy implicitly frames the issue as a zero-sum game for technology leadership (perhaps motivated by pecuniary concerns about technology royalties that are, in the final analysis, relatively meager).

The second major area where Americans find fault with China is in its pursuit of an unbalanced growth model, and especially an unbalanced trade account (see Figure 2.1). According to China's own statistics, China had a current account surplus in 2007 that was equal to 8.8% of GDP, a huge relative imbalance which, because China's economy is so big, translates into a huge absolute amount as well (about $400 billion). It's true that the surplus has come down to 2.0% of GDP in 2012, which is very welcome, and which means the issue is not as urgent as before. But the fact that China has amassed official reserves of over $3 trillion shows that large surpluses have been maintained for many years, and besides, it required the impact of major external events—including an unprecedented global financial crisis—to drive the Chinese trade account back toward balance. Now there is no particular reason to think that the surplus could not begin to widen again if Chinese growth slows, or if global demand picks up.

It should be obvious that the way that China sets its exchange rate is not working: the system is broken. Ever since 2005, the top Chinese leaders have been calling for a more balanced growth model, with a bigger share of domestic consumption, less investment, and a smaller external surplus, but all of those indicators are worse today than they were in 2004 (even with the welcome decline in the surplus). Everyone knows that this type of unbalanced growth model is ultimately unsustainable: former Chinese Premier Wen Jiabao himself said so many times, and current Premier Li Keqiang's comments amount to an even stronger assertion that doing business as usual won't work. Failing to address these imbalances means that

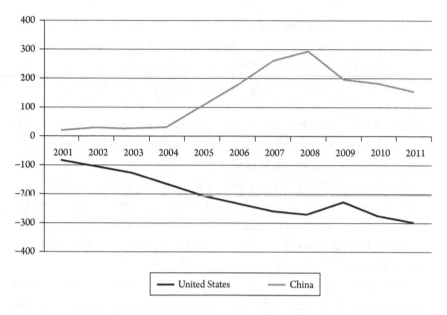

Notes: Calculated by USCBC. US exports reported on a free-alongside-ship basis; imports on a general customs-value basis.
Source: US Department of Commerce; US International Trade Commission (ITC)

FIGURE 2.1 Trade Balances in China and the United States ($ billions).

the Chinese people don't benefit as much from growth as they could. It also means that there is, in essence, a "bubble" in Chinese production of investment goods like steel, cement, and machinery. Excess capacity in these sectors could threaten global economic stability if the bubble bursts suddenly, and if surplus Chinese goods are dumped on the world market. It would have been far better if the Chinese government had followed through on its own proposed solution of moving toward a more balanced economy. The exchange rate should have been part of this solution: a stronger renminbi (RMB) gives Chinese households opportunities to consume more, and it gives American exporters an opportunity to serve those consumers. Of course renminbi valuation is not going to solve the problem by itself, but it's bizarre that the Chinese government keeps talking about stimulating domestic consumption while resisting the simplest single change that would contribute to that goal: letting the currency appreciate.

It should be obvious that part of the problem is the way the exchange rate is set. When the exchange rate can only be changed with the agreement of the top political authorities, it inevitably will become highly politicized. The default option will be to not adjust the exchange rate, and so it will do a bad job of reflecting the true (and changing) value of domestic and foreign goods. The exchange rate is a price. It is a very important price, but at the end of the day it's a price that must adjust when circumstances change.

Let's remember what happened in the mid-2000s. When people outside of China began to point out that China was running severe external imbalances and the renminbi appeared to be over-valued, what was the response of the Chinese government? It was to make it an even more politicized issue by insisting that foreigners didn't have the right to tell China what to do. But if a minor adjustment in the exchange rate requires a national discussion about sovereignty, is there really any chance that the exchange rate can be set rationally? I don't think so. And therefore there is also no assurance that China will not reproduce conditions of external imbalance in the near future, either accidentally or in pursuit of economic stimulus. The argument about imbalance is too long and complex to go into here, but for the United States, struggling to emerge from recession, it is not unreasonable to call on China to adopt policies that will restrain the size of its surpluses and allow market forces to influence the value of its currency.

This brings us to the last area of concern, which is the direction of reform in China and the role of state enterprises. For 25 years, China made enormous progress in reforming and opening up its economy. Whenever problems emerged, friends of China could truthfully point to the fact that China was more open and market-oriented than ever before, and that all the movement was in the right direction. That made many difficult issues relatively easy to resolve. But in the past five years or so, most of the movement has been in the wrong direction. Most troubling has been the increased support and protection given to state-owned enterprises. Right now, state-owned enterprises are treated as ordinary commercial entities in the United States, even though they are unpopular and provoke suspicions—sometimes unreasonable suspicions. But increasingly, Chinese government officials seem to expect their state-owned enterprises to act like national champions, and they seem to give them special preferences. This also threatens to undermine the basis for mutually beneficial cooperation and fair competition across businesses in both our economies.

In the end, you would think that China, as such a huge beneficiary of globalization, would emerge as a champion of the globalization process, a defender of the rules and norms of a system from which it benefits. From the U.S. perspective, that would mean giving U.S. firms—and private Chinese firms—access to a level playing field, so that competitive economic forces would determine the economic outcomes and the distribution of winners and losers in each economy. Under those conditions, both sides would be able to recommit to the economic relationship, and many economic issues would fade in importance. So far, China has resisted, and instead seems perpetually dissatisfied with the global system, and determined to extract as many benefits as it can from the system, without, however, making any constructive proposals to change the system. This is unfortunate, because the existing rules, free economic interchange, and growing sophistication would lead all of us to be better off. It would strengthen the economic relationship between us, and it would, not incidentally, accelerate China's rise into the top tier of global players.

Your friend,

Barry

• • •

Dear Barry,

I appreciate your candid and engaging discussion on what China has done wrong when it comes to Sino-American economic relations. Let me reply by telling you first what I agree and disagree with in your analysis and then offering my opinion on what Americans fail to take into account when they think about the U.S. economy and Sino-American economic relations.

I agree with you that China has benefited from the world system created and supported by the United States. The rapprochement of the United States and China in the early 1970s opened the door for China to return to the international community, and the decade after China and the United States established formal diplomatic ties in 1979 was a honeymoon period for Sino-American relations. On the economic front, the United States not only granted China Most Favored Nation trade status, but also tolerated China's mercantilist approach to international trade and finance. Notably, this included a dual-track exchange rate regime that allowed the coexistence of both a market determined rate and an official rate. Certified exporters were allowed to retain part or all of their foreign earnings and sell them in swap markets where they could buy the yuan for much cheaper than the official rate. At the same time, approved importers had to buy foreign currencies from the government at the official rate. As a result, this system subsidized exports over government-approved imports. In the 1990s, the economic ties between the two countries continued to expand, but on a more realistic basis. By that point, the United States no longer treated China as a potential ally, but believed that economic engagement was the only viable way to transform China. U.S. support for China's integration into the world system culminated with China's accession to the WTO in 2001. Since then, China's total exports have grown by more than a factor of five.

I concur with your criticisms about China's protection of intellectual property rights. As you have pointed out, weak IPR protection not only hurts American firms but Chinese firms as well. In fact, it may hurt Chinese firms more. Thanks to the advancements in modular production, American firms can produce key technologies back in the United States and export the finished components to China for final assembly with other parts. By doing this, American firms can avoid the complication of trying to protect their intellectual property in China. In terms of the allegations of cyber-theft of commercial information, though, China is equally, if not more often, hacked by foreign actors. The problem is to define what is strictly commercial, which is actually difficult. Both sides need to sit and talk seriously about this problem.

I also agree with your criticisms of Chinese state-owned enterprises (SOEs) and the Chinese government's support of national technological champions. This approach is not going to work well for two reasons. First, privileged companies will use government money carelessly; waste will be unavoidable. Second, taking this approach involves gambling against the odds. The success of high-tech innovations is a random event that follows the law of large numbers. With a sufficient number of tries, the frequency of a random event will converge to its natural mean (think about tossing a penny for many dozens of times: the number of times it's "heads" will approach half of the tosses). Suppose that the odds of a successful innovation are 5%. Then if the government supports five companies, the overall probability that one of them will produce a successful innovation will only be 25%. When innovations are left to the market, though, there are many more firms and individuals trying to innovate, so the overall probability of success will increase dramatically. If there are 100 firms and individuals trying to innovate, then it is almost a 100% chance that five of them will succeed. The market allows the law of large numbers to work, whereas concentrated government support of a few companies does not.

I disagree, however, with your analysis of global imbalances and your criticisms of China's approach in dealing with them, including its exchange rate policy. Long-term and structural forces that shape countries' growth trajectories are probably what cause global imbalances. For example, the United Kingdom maintained roughly a century of current account surpluses before the First World War, and the United States did that for about 80 years before 1980. Neither country managed to do so because they manipulated their exchange rates. It is also worth noting that the economies that managed to increase their standards of living substantially after the Second World War, notably Germany, Japan, Korea, Singapore, and Taiwan, ran current account surpluses in their periods of fastest growth.

These experiences contradict the conventional wisdom held by American economists that fast-growing countries should borrow today against their larger future shares in the world economy. One possible explanation is that the relationship between the GDP growth rate and a country's current account position is not linear. Unlike countries with very slow growth rates, countries with reasonably high growth rates should borrow. However, when a country's growth rate continues to increase, its savings rate will increase faster than its investment rate. That is because the investment rate increases proportionally with the GDP growth rate whereas the savings rate increases more than proportionally with the GDP growth rate because personal consumption tends to grow less than proportionally with income (think about the difference between Bill Gates' consumption as a share of his income and an ordinary American's consumption as a share of his or her income). Thus, this country will be more likely to run a surplus in its current account. In addition, for developing countries, fast growth is often accompanied by fast structural change that moves factors of production, labor in particular, from low productivity sectors to high productivity sectors. This, in turn, also generates surpluses by increasing the profitability of firms. In the 2000s, the Chinese economy grew by double-digits and the country experienced drastic demographic transitions and structural change. The overall supply of labor increased and there were large waves of migration from the countryside to the city. Therefore, China fits well into historical patterns.

China's approach to the exchange rate may be problematic, but for reasons other than its effect on global imbalances. The problem with the fairly fixed exchange rate is that it has forced China to accumulate a huge pile of wasteful foreign reserves. The People's Bank of China—China's central bank—has to buy one to two billion U.S. dollars every working day to stabilize the yuan's value against the dollar. Over the years, China has accumulated some 3.5 trillion dollars of foreign reserves, most of which are used to buy U.S. Treasury bonds and other low-yield dollar assets despite high returns to capital inside China. The reluctance of the Chinese government to allow faster appreciation is perhaps because of its aversion to unforeseeable fluctuations in the yuan's value. Given that the Chinese government is determined to make the yuan an international currency, it is unlikely that it will allow the yuan to experience large changes.

Now that I have addressed your comments on China, I will turn to my analysis of economic problems in the United States. Frankly, I have been struck by how reluctant many American economists are to discuss the structural problems that caused the 2008 economic crisis and hindered the American recovery. Most of them seem to believe that the crisis was a result of bad interest rate policy and lax regulation of the financial sector. Some more radical economists blame the excessive liquidity caused by the burgeoning savings from Asian countries, China in particular. The second group may be correct about the immediate causes of the crisis.

In my opinion, however, the crisis is deeply rooted in the American version of capitalism, or "high capitalism," as I like to call it. This version of capitalism aims at high innovation, high salaries, high returns, and a high level of competition. High capitalism has helped the United States become No. 1 in many areas in the world, but it has also caused structural problems in the American economy.

My first critique has to do with the American labor market. To sustain high innovation, the United States has maintained the most flexible labor market among the mature economies. Indeed, a flexible labor market has been cherished by many American economists as one of the most important factors allowing the United States to stay at the frontier of technological advancement. However, this flexibility comes with costs. American companies will lay off a whole department of scientists in order to shift to a new product. The destruction is not limited to human capital in the abstract, but extends to individual human lives.

Further, a flexible labor market can lead to very confrontational labor relations in the United States. The system is different in Germany and other northern European countries where a social contract exists among labor, capital, and the government. Their labor markets are not as flexible as that of the United States, and as a result, they are not as innovative as the United States. However, their economies and societies are more resilient than those of the United States. A paradoxical consequence is that jobs are forced to stay at home instead of being outsourced to low-cost countries.

My second critique is about the crown jewel of America's high capitalism, the financial sector. This sector caused the financial crisis and is still contributing to America's current account deficit. Even a casual glance around the world would tell you that, setting oil exporters aside, countries running current account surpluses, such as China, Germany, and Japan, have a stronger manufacturing sector relative to their financial sector, and that countries running current account deficits, such as the United States and the United Kingdom, have a stronger financial sector relative to their manufacturing sector. Why? Because of comparative advantage: countries tend to specialize in what they are relatively good at. The United States is an extreme case of a country with a very strong financial sector. The American manufacturing sector is not small, but it is dwarfed by America's super-efficient and super-profitable financial sector.

On top of that, the U.S. dollar is an international reserve currency accounting for 60% of world trade, and the United States has the strongest military in the world. All of this makes the United States a safe haven for global investors. Whenever a non-U.S. market shows signs of decline, investors flee to dollar-denominated assets. This is a blessing but also a curse for the United States. Large inflows of capital reduce the cost of capital, but also tend to cause current account deficits. A lower cost of capital has an inflationary effect on assets because people take the opportunity to borrow and invest more than usual. The "wealth effect" then kicks in, people assume that the value of their assets will continue to appreciate and tend to consume more than they earn today, causing the United States to have to borrow from abroad. Indeed, Wall Street regularly trades on future gains that may never be realized. To a large extent, the financial sector is detached from the real economy and has become an island creating its own wealth.

Consistent with the spirit of high capitalism, the American educational system is not designed for ordinary people, but for geniuses. This is my third critique. There is an assumption in American society that everyone has the potential to excel at something, and the educational system is supposed to encourage that to happen. This belief is the fundamental reason for the failure of the American educational system and has led to the bifurcation of American society over the last 40 years. While the elites are enjoying more and more benefits brought about by globalization, ordinary Americans have lagged behind because their education is inadequate. Economists believe that the reason behind America's growing income disparities lies in America's constant shift toward a more knowledge-based economy. Some of them also believe that the market will drive more Americans to get a better and better education. But in a large country like the United States, not everyone should expect to get an education that would allow him or her to take a job at the commanding heights of globalization.

Unlike physical capital that can be created almost instantaneously, it takes a much longer time to accumulate human capital, and at the personal level there are huge heterogeneities depending on a person's innate abilities, aspirations, experiences, wealth, family background, and social context. In the end, decisions about what education to get are always "sticky"—that is, they fall behind changes in market signals about what sorts of workers are actually needed. That is why there are "high-paying" and "low-paying" jobs. What high capitalism is doing, though, is forcing the United States to ship "low-paying" jobs to countries like China. Those jobs are not really "low-paying" for ordinary Americans because they are manufacturing jobs that pay better than many low-level service jobs. As a result, a deep ditch has been created between low-level service jobs and high-level global jobs. This disparity discourages people in low-level service jobs from becoming more educated because no matter how hard they try, they are not going to be able to jump over that ditch.

In summary, American high capitalism is a winner-takes-all form of capitalism. It makes the United States No. 1 in many areas, but it does not necessarily improve the lot of ordinary Americans. It is also the root cause of the financial crisis and America's persistent current account deficit. The policies adopted or discussed by American policy makers and scholars such as quantitative easing, fiscal stimulus packages, and government deficit reduction will only cure the symptoms, not the underlying economic disease.

What does all of this mean for Sino-American relations? It means a lot. First and foremost, it means that most of the ways that the United States has proposed to balance the country's trade with China—faster appreciation of the yuan and more consumption in China, among others—are not going to work. This partly explains why China has stubbornly refused to bend to the pressures from the United States. It is also one of the sources of mistrust between the two countries. From a Chinese perspective, American proposals are merely aimed at finding a scapegoat. In return, American officials take China's position as a sign that China has become "arrogant," a tendency that, to them, needs to be corrected. (Some of the United States' recent diplomatic and military moves in the Pacific region are widely believed by observers in China to be part of the United States' efforts to achieve that goal.)

While China needs to do more to contribute to rebalancing the economies of the two countries, real changes also have to come from inside the United States. As a first step, the United States has to reform its financial sector. As Lenin once pointed out, financial capitalism is the highest form of capitalism. That is, financial capitalism is the end state of capitalism. The logic from which Lenin derived this proposition might not be valid today, but it may hold for another reason: financial capitalism forces a country into indebtedness, which is unsustainable in the long run. Unfortunately, financial reforms under consideration in Washington are half-baked at best. America has a long way to go to make real reform happen.

The United States and China are the two most important countries on the globe in the 21st century. The world cannot afford to see confrontation between our two nations. China is a newcomer to the world stage and faces daunting challenges on its way to catching up to developed countries. However, many of these challenges can be dealt with by continuous growth and a collective resolution to pursue a better life—precisely because China is still a developing country. That momentum and commitment are much weaker in the United States. "Reform" used to be a word reserved for China; it seems that the time has come for the United States to think about reform too.

My personal regards,

Yang

• • •

Dear Yang,

Many thanks for your thoughtful and insightful response. It challenges me and requires me to think about my own country in fresh ways, which is difficult, but rewarding. I agree with many of your comments about American capitalism. Let me first discuss the American system, and then turn back to U.S.–China economic relations.

My delving into the American economy creates some difficulties for our dialogue. While writing my first letter to you about China, I was reasonably confident that I could represent the mainstream of American economists, but when we turn to the United States, this confidence evaporates. There is no consensus in the United States about the U.S. system or its future, so I cannot claim to speak for a large fraction of American economists. But since I was willing to criticize aspects of the Chinese system—and, as you point out, many U.S. economists are reluctant to discuss the structural problems of the U.S. economy—it is only fair that I try to respond to your criticisms of the American system.

I agree with you that the United States has a distinctive system—you call it "high capitalism"—that is characterized by flexible labor markets, breaking up and relocating (sometimes outsourcing) the stages of the production process, and dominance of the financial sector. I also agree that this is in some respects a "winner-takes-all" form of capitalism, with benefits and costs that are not often discussed. I was particularly struck by your analysis of how the "winner-takes-all" system interferes with efforts to improve the U.S. educational system because those in the lower and middle segments realistically judge that their chances of moving up through education are slim. What can we say about this system?

First, most Americans seem to like the system overall. The United States is a nation of immigrants and strivers who have had numerous opportunities to elect politicians proposing radical changes, and they only rarely do so. Even President Obama's health insurance plan, moderate and relatively modest, has been subjected to bitter attack. As a result, the United States has a very unique social contract—different from Germany, or even the United Kingdom, to say nothing of China—and one that is quite stable. Personally, I believe that there are many reforms that would improve the American system and the quality of American life, but frankly there is not much likelihood that the fundamental features of the American system are going to change in the near future. This underlines the fact that our challenge is to devise rules of engagement that will permit our very different political economies to interact in peace and to mutual benefit.

It seems to me that the problem facing the United States today is not so much the basic nature of the system, but rather that we seem to have lost sight of ways that we can improve our system, building on its strengths and minimizing its weaknesses. For instance, since many agree that labor market flexibility is a key U.S. advantage, you would expect agreement on measures to strengthen it. We should decouple health insurance from employment, for example, so that job loss would not be catastrophic and people could easily search for more lucrative, more rewarding, and higher productivity occupations. Following this logic a step further, we should begin to lower or eliminate payroll taxes—such as income tax and social security tax which are deducted from paychecks—where possible, and compensate by increasing taxes on carbon emissions. This would shift the burden of taxation from a good (work) to a bad (greenhouse gases), while also reinforcing one of the United States' core advantages.

But instead of debating alternatives, our political system has become polarized and paralyzed. The slow growth of a mature economy and the setbacks caused by the financial crisis limit our vision, while anger and anxiety caused by high unemployment and the loss of household wealth embitter the discussion. I was struck by the contrast between the United States today and the China you describe in your closing comments, a China that can deal with many of its challenges through continuous growth and collective resolution. This is a fair contrast.

Yet the current American gridlock may be temporary. The American system has an enormous amount of resilience. Once the electoral process settles the struggle for power, the discussion may shift into a more productive mode. This has happened before, and Americans are a lot less divided than they appear. To be sure, the future movement of policy will be incremental, compared to the big changes in some areas of policy in China, but Americans will regain the sense that we are going in the right direction.

Let us return to the question of U.S.–China relations. I very much accept your point: organizational changes in American capitalism accelerated the outsourcing of jobs to China. Although you don't explicitly say so, I think you also mean to point out that the imbalances of the past decade are not simply the fault of China. Again, I agree. The American model of capitalism, combined with overly expansionary policies of the Federal Reserve Board, and unnecessary budget deficits during the George W. Bush era, contributed to those imbalances.

This leads into your argument about exchange rates. You point out that China's rapid income growth naturally leads to high saving rates (since consumption growth inevitably lags behind income growth), and therefore that a prolonged period of current account surpluses is to be expected. This is true. Indeed, we might even add that a historic boom of the magnitude of China's boom creates massive productivity growth and also attracts capital, creating a natural "bubble," which can be hard to manage.

In all these points, I take it that your basic argument is this: exchange rate misalignment—the undervalued RMB—is not by itself the cause of global imbalances. There are powerful, long-running structural factors in both the United States and China that also contribute to imbalances. Therefore, we should not expect simple changes like letting the RMB appreciate to solve all the world's imbalances, and it is unfair for American commentators to harp incessantly on China's exchange rate as if it were the root of all evil. I accept this argument, and I am deeply impressed by your ability to frame these complex issues in terms of the really big picture.

However, I'm not convinced by the implication that there is somehow symmetry between U.S. and Chinese interests and policies; or that exchange rate flexibility is less necessary because it must be instituted in a world of powerful structural forces. Though U.S. institutions are partly responsible for shipping jobs to China, China benefits; and when U.S. macroeconomic policies created extraordinarily rapid growth of demand for Chinese exports, China benefited. Do these facts give the United States less right to urge welfare-improving policies on China, or more? I think more.

Similarly, your argument about the structural causes of imbalances is, in a way, an argument for greater exchange rate flexibility. There are strong structural and macroeconomic forces contributing to imbalances. Why, then, should the exchange rate also contribute to large imbalances? If market forces are allowed to work, the exchange rate will play a role in mitigating the imbalances; it won't eliminate them, but it will make them less severe. Exchange rates matter precisely because they are part of an equilibrating process. Because the world is uncertain and it's hard for us to predict these changes, it makes sense to let the price system play a greater role, and this includes a more flexible exchange rate.

Moreover, I disagree that the real cost of the fixed exchange rate policy is the accumulation of low-return assets by China. In fact, the accumulation of those assets (U.S. Treasuries) is precisely the cost being paid for a suboptimal policy. The Chinese government accumulated those assets because it was intervening to prevent the currency from appreciating (as you well know). A better policy would have allowed the market to steer savings toward higher return investments, and a more realistic exchange rate policy would have been a critical part of that better policy. Again, the exchange rate is a crucial part of the adjustment process that needs to be depoliticized.

All the issues we have been discussing are transforming, because we are entering a new and uncharted zone. China is entering a period of unprecedented economic uncertainty as it transforms into a middle-income country. The super-high growth era is ending, but as GDP growth slows down, the transformation of Chinese society may become faster and more profound. China is leaving behind centuries of poverty and becoming a society where individuals have the resources to shape their own destinies. This transition requires new skills, new institutions, and better-functioning economic regulations and procedures than ever before. There is a widespread feeling—both inside China and outside—that the measures and policies that were so successful in China during the past 30 years will no longer be suited to the new challenges.

From the United States' perspective, as we observe these massive and inspiring changes, one simple truth stands out: the policy changes that will smooth U.S.–China economic relations are also those that are best suited to make China a great and prosperous country. Economic policies that make China less nationalistic and more market-oriented are better suited to the emerging high-skill and innovative China, to the creative, prosperous, and powerful China of the 21st century. Consider just the financial system: China needs a system that allows capital to flow freely in and out, so that Chinese firms can become truly global. China needs to be able to attract foreign investors and financial market participants so that Shanghai can emerge as a global financial center. Both these objectives can be achieved by a policy shift that treats foreigners and Chinese investors equally, strengthens the rule of law, and eliminates the privileges given to state-owned enterprises. That will bring Americans and other foreigners into the project of a steadily rising China. It will show that in economics, we really do benefit from each other's success, much more than we compete for limited resources. Finally, by reducing these conflicts, we make it more possible for each of us to move forward with reforms of our own domestic systems that we each urgently need.

Your friend,

Barry

• • •

Dear Barry,

I enjoyed reading your thoughtful reply. I am pleased you agree with many points in my analysis of the economic challenges that the United States faces. However, you suggested that these issues might be temporary and would be corrected after the 2012 presidential election. The election is over but there is no sign that President Obama will do anything to reform what I called American "high capitalism." The reason for this inaction is likely that Americans are satisfied with the current system, as you suggest. But their opinions may be exactly what will drag the country down.

Take for example the shooting in Newtown, Connecticut. Twenty-six people, twenty of them little children, were killed by a crazy young man with guns legally bought by his mother. To an outsider, the solution to these kinds of mass killings is crystal clear: Ban guns! But many Americans think differently; they believe strict gun control is a violation of their constitutional rights. Because of this attitude, more than 30,000 people die from gun violence every year in your country. These casualties are higher than those America suffered during many wars.

American individualism is unique in the world. It has helped the United States to become the most innovative country in the world, and the world has benefited tremendously from American innovations. But innovation is not enough; social harmony is equally important for a well-functioning human society.

In a sense, individualism has hampered the United States' ability to adopt a rational approach to its relations with China. Before the financial crisis, America's foreign policy toward China was one of engagement, though the objective was to induce China to "play our game." But when China showed signs of playing a different game, America's policy immediately changed to one of confrontation. It seems that there is no middle ground between "one of us" and "the enemy" in American foreign policy.

You emphasized that China's exchange rate policy was one of the key obstacles for Sino-American trade relations. I still disagree. I do not think that the exchange rate plays a large role in creating imbalances between our two countries. Like I argued in my last letter, the imbalances are created by more fundamental and structural differences between our two countries. I also do not think that it is fair to blame China for manipulating the exchange rate while failing to mention the Federal Reserve's loose monetary policy. The Chinese monetary authorities buy foreign currencies, mostly American dollars, to maintain the yuan's value. In contrast, the Federal Reserve issues more American dollars (in what the Fed calls "quantitative easing") to suppress the dollar's value. If China is manipulating the exchange rate, the Fed is doing the same, albeit with a different method.

As I acknowledged in my last letter, I agree with your analysis of the issues that China needs to address in order to rebalance the economies of our two countries. I am glad to find that China's new leadership has already shown a strong desire to bring the country back on a path of reform. Let me briefly introduce several reform initiatives that people are discussing widely in China.

The first is *hukou* reform. The *hukou* system was introduced in 1958 to restrict people's mobility from one place to another, and it limits where in China individuals can legally reside. Today the system is widely regarded as obsolete and in need of reform. In fact, a government policy announced in February 2012 allows migrants in small cities to obtain legal permission to stay once they have found a stable job and place to live. This reform will not only restore social justice, but it will also make the Chinese economy healthier by boosting domestic consumption. At present, migrants from rural areas save quite a bit of their earnings to use when they return home. Giving them permanent residential rights in cities will stabilize their expectations and encourage them to consume more. *Hukou* reform will also expedite urbanization, and thus boost the growth of the service sector. The share of manufacturing in the Chinese economy will likely begin to decline at some point between 2015 and 2018, and the service sector will have to fill that gap.

The second area ripe for reform is finance. China's financial and banking systems are not fully open to domestic capital. For example, private domestic investors cannot start a commercial bank, though foreign investors can. The government needs to expedite the "Wenzhou experiment" it started and come up with a concrete reform plan for the country's banking sector soon. If the time is not right to allow private investors to open commercial banks, then the regulatory authorities should at least allow more shadow banking—that is, investment or lending not made through regular financial vehicles such as banking deposits—while strengthening supervision of it. The crippled financial system is one of the key reasons why China has a large current account surplus. Because the financial system is not capable of processing domestic savings, China is forced to export capital to other countries.

The third priority is to reduce subsidies to producers. The government heavily subsidizes producers by suppressing the cost of inputs and providing monetary incentives to select industries. Interest rates are tightly controlled and a comfortable profit margin is guaranteed to banks on their loans. Land is sold to investors at below-market prices, or even given to them for free, and tax exemptions are still common. For instance, the municipal government of Xi'an, my home city, gave Samsung 5 square kilometers of land and tax concessions for 15 years—worth 3.2 billion dollars by some estimates— so that the company would set up its largest overseas manufacturing facility, worth 7 billion dollars there. Also, local governments enforce environmental and labor laws loosely so that enterprises save money. A study by Huang Yiping, of the China Center for Economic Research at Peking University, shows that the total amount of subsidies through suppressed input prices could be or has been as high as 10% of GDP. This is equivalent to a high and regressive tax that transfers income from ordinary citizens to capital owners. And this is one of the reasons why the share of household income in national income is falling and income distribution is worsening.

None of these reforms will be easy to implement. The *hukou* reform faces strong resistance from both local governments and residents. Local governments argue that migrants are a drag on public resources, while local residents worry that migrants will narrow their chances of finding employment and reduce the education options available to their children. When it comes to government subsidies, interest groups strongly oppose any cuts to the assistance that they currently enjoy. Moreover, many government officials believe that government subsidies are still necessary to accelerate China's "catching-up." Financial reform seems to be the least controversial although the uncertainties that would come with a more open financial system could stall progress.

It will thus take great courage and political wisdom on the part of the new leadership to push forward these reforms. But I have reason to be hopeful. The 18th Party Congress has already sanctioned portions of the above reforms, in particular the *hukou* reform.

Continuing to implement institutional and economic reforms is one of the best ways for China to sustain its economic growth. In the past 30 or so years we have seen three 10-year cycles of reform. The first phase of reform was launched in the 1980s when China opened its economy to the world. The second phase began in 1992 and lasted until 2003, during which time swift reforms were carried out in the cities. While these reforms greatly improved the efficiency of the Chinese economy, they also left the social safety network shattered and millions of workers jobless. The third phase occurred during the Hu Jintao–Wen Jiabao era. One of the achievements of this period was the rebuilding of the social security system both in cities and rural areas. These leaders also abolished many of the policies that were discriminatory to migrant workers. But the government's intervention in the economy also increased and the pace of reform somewhat slowed. With this history in mind, the new leadership's resolution to bring the country back to the reform track deserves support. Over the long term, the Chinese government is likely to run the country by this pattern we call the "middle way"— ten years of market reforms, ten years to handle the societal consequences of reform, and then back to reform again.

In contrast, I would have to say that the American government is moving too slowly to reform the American system. One thing that Chinese and Americans share is a common belief in pragmatism. In fact, the United States introduced the philosophy of pragmatism to China. Pragmatists believe that there is no ultimate truth. In the same vein, there is no perfect system that can suit a country forever. The American version of capitalism has helped the United States become very successful, but it also has intrinsic drawbacks that need to be remedied through serious reforms.

My best regards,
Yang

POLITICAL SYSTEMS, RIGHTS, AND VALUES

ZHOU QI
Chinese Academy of Social Sciences

ANDREW J. NATHAN
Columbia University

Framing questions: *What role do "values" play in the relationship? Is U.S. foreign policy ideological? Is Chinese foreign policy ideological? How are American and Chinese conceptions of human rights and democracy similar or different? Are Chinese and American values different in these areas? If so, how should such differences be treated? What do Chinese people think motivate U.S. interests in human rights, religious freedom, and democracy in China? Do the Chinese consider their political system to be democratic? Would further political pluralism and greater individual political rights be a positive development for China or not, and why? How would that change Sino-American relations? What are the pitfalls of the current Chinese system, from a U.S. point of view? What are Chinese assessments of American democracy? From a Chinese and U.S. point of view, are Chinese citizens growing freer?*

•   •   •

Dear Andy,

I'm sure you would agree—values play a crucial role in Sino-American relations. But values are only one significant factor in the relationship. Another factor is mutual interests. The interplay of values and mutual interests is evident in a brief review of Sino-American relations.

During the Cold War, the United States refused to recognize the newborn People's Republic of China under Communist leadership because of its fundamental differences in values and political systems after the Second World War. Meanwhile China, following Mao Zedong's instruction, carried out a foreign policy of "leaning to one side" by building an alliance with the Soviet Union and close relations with the Soviet-led socialist bloc.

The famous U.S. National Security Council document No. 68, issued on April 14, 1950, identified China as a springboard for the expansion of communism into Southeast Asia. Immediately after the outbreak of the Korean War, the U.S. Seventh Fleet blockaded the Taiwan Strait, and the United States began to view Taiwan, under Chinese Nationalist control, as a potential asset in what the United States called its "island chain strategy." The United States restored its military and economic assistance to Chiang Kai-shek's regime in Taiwan, blocked the new Communist government in Beijing from taking the seat for "China" in the United Nations, and imposed a comprehensive embargo on China that was more stringent than the one imposed on the Soviet Union.

After the end of the Korean War, the United States quickly established a mutual defense system against China in Asia. From that point up until the late 1960s, the United States saw China as a serious threat in Southeast Asia, and containing China was considered essential to preventing Southeast Asian countries from falling into Communist hands.

However, the differences between their values and political systems did not lead to full-scale confrontation between China and the United States because of the interests they shared. By the late 1960s, China and the United States found common ground in the view that the Soviet Union's "social imperialism" was the most dangerous threat.

This strategic congruence continued throughout the Cold War. With the demise of the acute U.S.–Soviet strategic rivalry, the common interests of China and the United States became less clear. Differing ideology and political systems once again led to deep divergences. China's human rights record, which had not been the focus of American attention previously, emerged in the 1990s as one of four major areas of disagreement (the other three were Taiwan, trade, and weapons proliferation). Currently, deep differences in values, ideologies, and political systems lie at the root of persisting American perceptions of "the China threat."

Among Chinese, on the other hand, there is a view suggesting that the rivalry between China and the United States is ultimately insoluble because it is "structural" in nature. According to this notion, the second-most-powerful country in the world will inevitably pose—or at least be perceived to pose—a challenge to the most powerful country in the world. Therefore, it is almost impossible to build mutual trust between them. But history suggests that this fatalistic assumption may not be valid. The United States once overtook the United Kingdom as the world's dominant power, and Japan was once the second-largest economy, yet neither of them had as much difficulty reconciling their differences with the United States as China has had. This suggests that values, ideology, and political systems are, in the end, key causes of strategic suspicion.

The world has now entered the era of globalization, in which humankind faces common challenges from the proliferation of weapons of mass destruction, terrorism, drug trafficking, environmental destruction, climate change, humanitarian crises, and the negative effects of economic development. The United States, as the world's strongest power, and China, as the fastest growing developing country, share an interest in meeting these dangers.

Overall, therefore, while differences in ideology and political system continue to alienate and separate China and the United States, their common interests have nevertheless enabled the two parties to bound their disputes within a controllable range.

Americans rarely admit that they have an ideology because they see their country's behavior simply as a reaction to someone else's hostile ideology, like communism.[1] However, there is no doubt that the United States' foreign policy is informed by ideology. Perhaps the first central theme of American ideology as it relates to foreign policy is the concept of America's "special destiny" and national mission. American ideology combines the belief in a domestic American destiny with a conviction that the United States is uniquely endowed with a special mission abroad as the agent of human progress.[2]

Indeed, Americans almost universally accept "American exceptionalism." It assumes that God chose to place Americans in the New World, and that the

United States was thus a "City Upon a Hill," a shining example to the world. Americans believe they have the responsibility to spread the values of freedom and democracy and democratic institutions to every corner of the world.

"American exceptionalism" has been the intellectual starting point of both the idealist and the realist tendencies in American foreign policy since the establishment of the United States. It has served as the justification for both isolationism and liberal-internationalist interventionism. Because of these contradictory consequences of exceptionalism, though, exceptionalism itself seems contradictory. On the one hand, it might help feed the altruistic and humanitarian motives of U.S. foreign policy, but on the other hand it legitimized the bloody territorial expansion of the United States on the American continent in the mid-19th century, guided U.S. foreign policy into imperialism as the United States grew in the late 19th century, and justified the pursuit of global dominance in the aftermath of the Second World War. Americans have never understood why people outside the United States are unable to perceive any essential difference between "assuming leadership of the world" and seeking world hegemony.

Another important ideology of the United States is classical liberalism. Its fundamental tenets are a belief in democracy and individual freedom and an assumption that the primary purpose of government is to protect individual rights. The government pursues these policies domestically, but American exceptionalism also connects liberalism to American foreign policy by supporting the U.S. government's pursuit of democracy internationally.

China, of course, has its own values and ideology. The People's Republic of China was established in 1949 during the Cold War, and China pursued an ideologically driven, revolutionary foreign policy committed to the liberation of mankind. However, as the Soviet Union became more threatening to China in the late 1960s, Mao Zedong chose to cooperate with the most dangerous enemy's enemy—the United States. Moreover, at the end of the 1960s and again at the end of the 1970s, China engaged in military conflicts with the Soviet Union and Vietnam, countries that shared the same fundamental Marxist-Leninist political ideology. After the end of the Cultural Revolution, the new Chinese leader Deng Xiaoping started to implement the policy of "Reform and Opening," shifting China's priority from revolution to modernization, and placing greater emphasis on economic development. Ever since, China's focus on ideology in foreign policy has largely been replaced by the imperative for domestic economic growth.

Thus, in the post–Cold War era, China's foreign policy has been far less ideological than that of the United States. Whether China can modernize as much as it wants to depends on whether China can maintain a stable and peaceful regional and world environment, in which the U.S. role is essential. China's economic development needs the U.S. market, as well as U.S. investment and technology.

Because of its enduring memories of exploitation during the "Century of Humiliation," China is convinced that non-interference in the domestic affairs of other countries is morally correct. China is simply not interested in imposing its will on other nations. Americans find this nearly impossible to fathom. But Chinese are not inclined to imitate the U.S. political system, nor do they think the system is bad for Americans and needs replacement. U.S. policy toward China, on the other hand, seems keen on helping the Chinese change their political system. This is another sign of the ideological nature of U.S. foreign policy.

I want to turn now to human rights. Many scholars have made efforts to demonstrate that Confucianism—the most prominent strand in China's rich heritage of political and social thought—contains elements similar to Western ideas of human rights. Nevertheless, there are two major differences in Chinese and American conceptions of human rights. One concerns the state's role in the protection of human rights and the other is differing priorities within the overall idea of human rights.

On the first point, the notion of human rights in Western thought rests on the premise that human beings possess rights that the state or government may not violate.[3] This view assumes that only the power of the state is strong enough to suppress human rights.

The Chinese have never understood human rights in this way. Let me explain why. A central value of Confucianism is rites—elaborate and minutely prescribed codes of ritual behavior to be applied in a vast range of specific social interactions. For example, "*junjun, chenchen, fufu, zizi,*" or "A monarch behaves according to the norms for a monarch, a vassal behaves according to the norms for a vassal, a father behaves according to the norms for a father, and a son behaves according to the norms for a son." More specifically, "The monarch dominates, vassals are subordinate; fathers dominate, sons are subordinate; husbands dominate, wives are subordinate." Such hallowed behavioral codes might help facilitate beneficial customs within a community, but their ultimate purpose was to realize the ideal of political stability and social harmony at all levels, rather than to protect individuals from the tyranny of the ruler. Rites defined all individuals' duties in their relationships with others in the community, but they did not catalogue the rights of individuals beyond defining what treatment individuals should receive if they properly carry out their ritually defined roles.

In fact, in Chinese society and East Asian society as a whole, the emphasis is placed not on the rights of individuals but on their duties. If everyone does his or her duty and performs his or her proper function in the community, the relationship between members of the society will be effectively mediated, and political order and social harmony will be maintained.

However, a rites-based political order lends itself to authoritarian rule and to conformity, rather than to individual freedom. Thus, Confucianism has not produced liberal democracy, mass political participation, and the freedom of thought, speech, and association that form the core of Western conceptions of human rights. The Chinese system of values and social relations is "incompatible with the vision of equal and autonomous individuals that underlines international human rights norms."[4] As for the differences in values between East Asian society and the North America and Western Europe, Tu Weiming, a Harvard University professor, draws a conclusion: "The Confucian insistence on the importance of equality rather than freedom, sympathy rather than rationality, civility rather than law, duty rather than rights, and human-relatedness rather than individualism may appear to be diametrically opposed to the value-orientation of the Enlightenment."[5]

On the second point, about the contrasting order of priorities within the overall idea of human rights, contemporary Western scholars often describe two basic categories of human rights:

1. Civil and political rights are regarded as negative rights because they require restrictions on the activity and power of the state. The rights of personal security, freedom of thought, religion, speech, rally, association, the press, and political participation are defined as both defenses against and immunities from the repressive power of government.
2. Economic and social rights are defined as positive rights, because they involve the state's positive action. These rights include fulfilling such vital needs as food, shelter, health care, and education.

When the U.S. government speaks of human rights, what it tends to mean are civil and political rights. Human rights, as defined in American foreign policy, strongly stresses personal security as well as freedom of speech, religion, association, and so on. Little reference is made to social and economic rights. This preoccupation is also evident in the Department of State's annual country reports on human rights.

Having created a miracle of rapid economic development in the past several decades, the Chinese government and most Chinese people operate from the assumption that political stability is a fundamental prerequisite for further raising living standards. That belief has consolidated the focus in China on economic and social rights rather than political and civil rights. Nevertheless, with China's increasing prosperity and gradual establishment of rule of law, political and civil rights are also increasingly regarded as important.

Generally speaking, the Chinese like the idea of democracy. It is always referred to by Chinese official documents as a positive term, as in the Constitution of 2004. Democracy is also usually connected with socialism as in the term, "socialist democracy," or the phrase, "to build China into a democratic socialist nation." Former President Hu Jintao said, "There is no modernization without democracy," and in a late-2012 meeting President Xi Jinping observed that "the road to a politics of socialist democracy will continue to broaden." According to Yu Keping, a Chinese scholar and official, "Democracy is a good thing. This is true not only for individuals but also for the entire nation and for all the people of China."[6]

Yu confesses that democracy is not a panacea. Democracy often increases political and administrative costs, creates unnecessary and wasteful negotiations and discussions, delays decision making or policy implementation, and reduces the efficiency of management. Moreover, democracy may also cause the social and political order to spin out of control, leading to domestic divisions, or even bringing dictators to power. However, according to Yu Keping, among all political systems humankind has attempted, democracy is the best one, and political democracy is the inevitable trend of all the countries in the world.

Yu emphasizes that democracy requires certain economic, cultural, and political conditions, however, and that rapid, reckless pursuit of democracy will bring disastrous consequences. Democracy requires enlightenment, development, and authority; it may even demand coercion in order to maintain social order. Yet it cannot be developed through undemocratic methods. People's choices must be respected. Nor can democracy be imposed or borrowed from the outside. In the process of its democratization, Yu argues, China's "construction of political democracy must be closely integrated with the history, culture, traditions, and existing social conditions" in China.[7]

Li Junru, one of leading theorists of the Chinese Communist Party and the retired vice president of Communist Party School, has developed the concept of "consultative democracy," arguing that China's democracy should combine this idea along with electoral democracy, and "negotiation democracy." In "consultative democracy," which he argues has deep roots in Chinese traditional political culture, leaders are chosen and major decisions made through consultations between existing rulers and their subordinates.[8]

Li looks to the beginnings of 5,000 years of Chinese history to show how the tradition of political culture in China diverges from that of the West. He argues that at the dawn of China's written history, in the era of the "Sage Kings," public affairs were organized differently from those in ancient Greece. All major decisions were made by the leader and a gathering of tribal chiefs through a process of consultation. Thus, according to Chinese legend, the sage ruler Shun was "selected" as a new leader through a consultative meeting between Yao, the sitting ruler, and the assemblage of tribal chiefs. This manner of orchestrating political succession became known as "chan-rang," or "to resign and yield position to a younger wise and able person."[9] Coupled with the philosophy of "harmony with diversity," Li argues that Chinese history has led to a higher degree of popular comfort with the relatively harmonious form of consultative democracy than with the competitive democratic forms that took root in Western societies, particularly after the 18th century.

A related view about consultative democracy holds that consultative democracy now applied in China is even more democratic than competitive democracy, because the consultative democracy can permeate a whole political process, rather than just the electoral phase. Those who hold this idea are convinced that China's political system is even more democratic than that of the United States.[10]

Another justification for China's political process is that "consultative democracy in China pays more attention to the democracy in essence, tending to ensure that people in all occupations, areas and ethnic groups are all represented in the structures of national decision making,"[11] in contrast to the procedural emphasis in Western electoral democracy.

Chinese who are more familiar with the United States tend to believe that under America's political system ordinary people enjoy considerable democracy. However, they have two reservations. First, American democracy may fit American society very well, but it does not necessarily fit Chinese society. Since the outbreak of the financial crisis in 2008, the "Washington Consensus"—the template of a politically liberal market-based economy and society—has come into question. Chinese are asking: now that the American system does not run well even in the United States, how can it be successfully applied to other nations? Second, the Chinese see many shortcomings in American democracy, such as congressional paralysis, decision making inefficiency, bitter partisan conflicts, and the increasing flow of money in American elections. Violations of human rights in the United States, exposed by the Chinese government's own annual White Papers on American Human Rights, now receive greater attention as well.

My conclusion is this: Progress in the democratization of China along American lines could certainly bring about a dramatic improvement in U.S.–China relations. It is very likely that if China were to adopt American-style democracy, the United States would no longer fear the "China threat" so strongly, since Americans are convinced that democratic countries do not go to war with each other.

But because China's cultural and political traditions differ so widely from those of the United States, such an outcome can exist only in the imagination. In any case, the United States and China will be better off in the future if the United States steps away from the impulse to remold China in the American image, and from its expectation that history will inevitably turn China toward the Americanization of its domestic affairs.

Sincerely,

Qi

• • •

Dear Qi,

It's so nice to hear from you again. And it is a privilege to exchange views on such an important topic, which I agree is a source of misunderstanding, not only between the two governments but even among independent intellectuals like ourselves.

You are right that the West pays more attention to civil and political rights violations in China than to violations of economic, social, and cultural rights. Why? Let's look at a few cases that have caught the attention of the West.

- Wei Jingsheng: sentenced to 15 years in 1979 for the crime of counterrevolutionary agitation and a fake charge of leaking classified information after he put up wall posters that called for more democracy and accused the top Chinese leader, Deng Xiaoping, of enforcing dictatorship; re-imprisoned in 1994 after he met in Beijing with a U.S. State Department official; sent into exile in the U.S. in 1997.
- Liu Xiaobo: sentenced to 11 years in prison in 2009 after he led the Charter 08 movement calling for the Chinese government to respect rights granted in its own Constitution. His alleged crime was the publication of six articles critical of the government on Internet sites outside of China; awarded the Nobel Peace Prize in 2010.
- Chen Guangcheng: a blind activist who helped local women protest the practice of coercively aborting and sterilizing them when they were found to have unauthorized pregnancies; sentenced to four years in jail for the trumped-up crime of interfering with traffic; after release, subjected to illegal house arrest by non-uniformed thugs who beat him and his wife, their lawyers, and anyone else who tried to visit them. Chen escaped in 2012 and found his way to the U.S. Embassy in Beijing; the government allowed him and his family to leave the country and come to the United States.[12]

As such cases illustrate, violations of civil and political rights are dramatic and clear-cut. By comparison, economic, social and cultural rights, as defined in the International Covenant on Economic, Social\ and Cultural Rights (ICESCR), are mostly what are called "positive rights," which a government is supposed to "achiev[e] progressively" as state capacity permits. It's not fair to say that the U.S. government and civil society don't focus on these rights in China. In fact they have done a great deal to promote their advancement, through numerous government, foundation, and NGO programs in the areas of education, public health, environmental protection, and others. From a broader perspective, the United States has contributed to the advancement of these rights in China by providing access to U.S. markets, investments, and technology, which helped make it possible for millions of Chinese to lift themselves out of poverty. It is hard to say that a particular economic, social, or cultural right is being violated when progress is being made, except when there is discrimination in access to benefits on the basis of age, gender, sexual orientation, ethnic or racial status, or disability— issues which do indeed exist in China, and which some Western-based human rights groups do work on. Economic and social rights issues often surface as civil and political violations: as you see in several of the cases I listed above and in footnote 12, abuses of civil and political rights often occur when citizens try to use these rights to fight for their economic, social, and cultural rights.

Compared to economic, social and cultural rights, civil and political rights as defined in the International Covenant on Civil and Political Rights (ICCPR) are mostly "negative," meaning that the state's No. 1 obligation is to refrain from violating them (although it is also obligated to take actions to protect them). Violations tend to occur when the state punishes people for speech, deprives them of their freedom without due process, has them beaten up, subjects them to an unfair trial, and so on. Such acts are clear-cut, and the remedy is simple: Stop carrying them out.

Violations of civil and political rights offend Westerners' cultural values, but that is not what makes them wrong. They are wrong because they violate international law, a body of law that the Chinese government recognizes. Beijing has expressed its intent to follow the Universal Declaration of Human Rights, has acceded to many of the core international human rights treaties including the ICESCR and has signed although not yet ratified the ICCPR. They are wrong also because they violate the Chinese Constitution, which has an excellent chapter on citizens' rights and duties, and because they violate Chinese laws, such as the Criminal Procedure Law.

Perhaps most importantly, such acts violate the Chinese people's sense of fairness when they learn about them (which they often don't because of censorship). That is why such cases are almost always brought to the international community not by Westerners, but by Chinese victims and *weiquan* (rights-protection) lawyers who cannot find justice at home; and why they are most often publicized internationally by Chinese-founded and Chinese-staffed human rights organizations like Human Rights in China, Chinese Human Rights Defenders, China Labor Watch, and China Labour Bulletin.

To be sure, these groups have some Western financial support, but that is because they are banned in China. Inside the country there is a rising number of civil society groups that function without foreign financial support. To be able to do so, however, they have to work on issues that the government permits like the environment, women's rights, public health, and educational discrimination, and stay within the rhetorical and action red lines defined by the authorities.

Rights violations of the kind we are talking about are not scattered incidents in a political system that is generally fair—they have structural causes. As you know, every level of government in China—the province, the municipality, the county, the township—is ruled by a "Party secretary" (the top official in the Chinese Communist Party at that level) who controls all the levers of power in that locality—the police, the prosecutor's office, the courts, the media, the women's association, the economic development agencies, and the banks. With these tools the Party secretary is supposed to achieve a set of performance targets: most importantly, to grow the economy, control population growth, and maintain social order. In many cases— like that of Chen Guangcheng—it is the local Party secretary who decides to abuse a victim's rights because the person has gotten in his way as he tries to achieve these goals.

In other cases, like those of Wei Jingsheng and Liu Xiaobo, abuses are carried out by the security agencies that operate at every level of the political system, which include the regular police, the political police, the Internet police, and the state security ministry. These agencies, too, have unchecked power to carry out their mission, which is "stability maintenance." Their professional judgment about what they need to do to protect the regime is subject to no second-guessing or oversight—not by the courts, the media, academia, the foreign ministry, or independent civil society. Instead, all agencies are required to cooperate with them. The courts have to convict, and the media have to denounce, those whom the security agencies decide to silence.

Abuses, of course, also happen in the West—all the time—but the response is a constant pushback from independent courts, independent lawyers, independent media, and civil society groups. In China that balance of forces does not exist and the government prevents it from taking shape by beating, jailing, or exiling those who try to create it. Pervasive and unchecked human rights abuses continue because of the lack of independent power centers that can reveal and resist them.

To disapprove of a government that abuses people's rights is hardly a West-versus-China issue. It is an issue being fought by Chinese, in which Westerners play a supporting role. For us on the outside, refusing to support those fighting for their rights on the inside would not be to stand neutral. It would be to take sides against them.

Nor is my analysis of these issues distinctively Western. Among those who have said that the overconcentration of power generates rights abuses are Deng Xiaoping, who talked about it in his famous "political reform" speech of August 18, 1980; the late party secretary and premier, Zhao Ziyang, who discussed it in his taped memoirs published in the West as *Prisoner of the State*;[13] the former premier Wen Jiabao, who often talked about the need for political reform and "universal values;" and the scholars and commentators whom you mentioned in your letter, like Yu Keping.

Thinking about such people—and many others who are silenced—perhaps we need to refine your statement that "China...has its own values and ideology." Chinese people, like people everywhere, are diverse, and they have a range of views. But in my experience—and based on some survey research I have seen—support for such core ideas as justice and transparency are in the mainstream of the Chinese tradition and of society today. If anyone has "their own" values and ideology that are at odds with these values, it is not ordinary Chinese but those in power who abuse rights.

Human rights are not Western. The international body of experts that drafted the Universal Declaration of Human Rights, which included a Chinese jurist, intentionally framed its principles in a broad manner so as to achieve universality and leave room for different cultural interpretations. For example, the Declaration says: "Everyone has the right to freedom of opinion and expression." It does not demand a U.S. First Amendment–style interpretation of freedom of expression.

As to the form of a political system, the Universal Declaration provides a minimal definition in Article 21. It says, "The will of the people shall be the basis of the authority of government; this will shall be expressed in periodic and genuine elections which shall be by universal and equal suffrage and shall be held by secret vote or by equivalent free voting procedures." This obviously refers to democracy (although it does not use that word), but it does not require a U.S.-style two-party system, a separation of powers, or a two-house legislature. All it requires is the right of ordinary people to debate freely political issues and influence the distribution of power. And yet these rights are ruled out in principle by the official ideology of China's ruling party. Calling a non-democracy "consultative" or "negotiated" does not make it a democracy.

The Universal Declaration of Human Rights and other international human rights laws and norms leave plenty of room for the distinction you point to between Confucian and liberal concepts of democracy. A rites-based political order may indeed be conducive to a more consensual political process, as you say. But there is no reason why it has to lead to blatant violations of individuals' rights. I do not accept the claim made by some that China lacks the conditions to protect its citizens' rights because of "national conditions" or its stage of development. China today is by a long-shot sufficiently wealthy, well-organized, literate, and cosmopolitan for its officials to stop ordering the illegal beating and jailing of innocent people.

You do well to point to an ideological strain in American foreign policy. However, I don't share your view that ideology was the cause of the Cold War; I see it as a strategic confrontation over the balance of power, with China as a chess-piece in play between the main rivals, the United States and the Soviet Union. But let's save the history of the Cold War and its implications for international relations theory for a separate exchange of letters.

There are so many American voices speaking out about human rights that I'm sure some of them fit your description. However, if we focus on the organized human rights movement and foreign policy makers, who are the most important actors in the field and seem to be the ones whose actions your letter is referring to, I would say that they are not motivated by a sense of manifest destiny or the idea of a "city on a hill," but by a desire to create a better world by promoting universal norms. That is why this community of advocates and policy makers in fact opposes American exceptionalism: they want the United States to endorse these universal norms in order to strengthen them, not exempt itself from them selectively.

Promoting universal human rights norms makes sense to many activists and foreign policy professionals for sound strategic reasons. First, we will feel safer as businesspeople, scholars, and tourists when China has rule of law. You'll recall that a number of foreign citizens, often of Chinese descent, have been detained and abused in violation of their rights when visiting China. Second, China's strategic intentions will be more transparent if they are shaped in an open political process, and this will reduce suspicion directed toward China by all of its neighbors as well as by the United States, which will also be good for China itself. Third, China will be more stable politically once the regime is grounded in the consent of the people, and a stable and prosperous China is in the interests of the rest of the world. Finally, a world with a robust set of international norms and institutions that regulate fields like trade, investment, the environment, arms control, and human rights will be a more predictable and peaceful world, where conflicts of interest can be sorted out and common interests advanced in reliable ways. This is the strategic vision that world leaders formed at the end of the Second World War and that gave rise to the human rights regime in the first place, and as time goes by, it makes ever more sense.

This is why—and not for some arbitrary reason of Western preferences—you are right to say that if China were to adopt the rule of law and a more legitimate, stable set of political practices, a major source of suspicion between the United States and China would disappear. The United States would be more comfortable not for ideological reasons but for strategic ones. So would China's neighbors.

Like you and many other contributors to this volume, I'm optimistic that in the long run China and the United States are going to be friends, not competitors. My coauthor Andrew Scobell and I argue in our recent book, *China's Search for Security*, that the two countries' strategic interests are compatible.[14] But on a more personal level, I am always encouraged by the openness and honesty of conversations with Chinese friends like you, over even the most difficult issues like these. To be able to talk like this we must share some key values. My Chinese friends are individualistic, enterprising, and curious; they are loyal, sensitive, and affectionate; they are truth-loving, justice-loving, and generous. These values are neither exclusively Confucian nor exclusively Western. They are among the core values that the international human rights regime tries to protect. What stands in the way of their fuller realization in China is not culture or tradition, but the current structure of power.

Sincerely,

Andy

• • •

Dear Andy,

I am delighted to join you in exploring more deeply our perspectives on values, political systems, and human rights. My understanding was that the focus of our assignment was not to judge the human rights practices in

China and the United States, but rather to discuss how and why Americans and Chinese have different perspectives on human rights in their own and other countries. Thus I will refrain from responding with an inventory of past and present American abuses of human rights.

You do raise a whole list of problems in China's present-day human rights record, and explain that Westerners are particularly concerned about citizens' political rights in China because conditions in this area are so wretched. You go on to say that the United States is also concerned with Chinese social, economic, and cultural rights, and offer a set of concrete examples by way of illustrating American diligence on these questions, even going so far as to suggest that U.S. economic cooperation and trade with China is evidence of America's compassionate concern for China's economic, social, and cultural affairs, though it is clearly in the United States's own economic interest.

The arguments you present simply fail to address my two main points, and thus fail to refute them: first, comparatively speaking, Western countries, including the United States, place greater emphasis on political and civil rights, while developing countries, like China, place a higher priority on economic and social rights. Second, given the deeply rooted belief in "American exceptionalism," Americans wish to "spread" (to use that familiar American jargon) their own values and systems to the world at large. It seems to me, the fact that you list so many of China's violations of human rights, but fail to mention China's performance on economic and social rights (possibly your implication is that China does better in economic and social rights), is indicative of the first point. The fact that you are so profoundly concerned about and fiercely critical of China's political human rights record proves the second.

It is easy to cite examples that show how the United States places less of a priority on economic, social, and cultural rights. In retrospect, during the United Nations debates on the two International Covenants on Human Rights,[15] the United States' attitude was unmistakable: the U.S. argued that freedom of speech, religion, and association, and freedom from government interference, are the highest-priority human rights, while economic, social, and cultural rights are simply not as fundamental, even though they reflect the thinking behind Franklin D. Roosevelt's memorable formulation of the "Four Freedoms," including "freedom from want."

In 1952, right-wing conservatives in Congress battling to prevent American ratification of the proposed international covenants on human rights threatened to pass the so-called "Bricker Amendment," which would have limited the power of the executive branch. They forced a trade-off with the Eisenhower Administration under which Congress refrained from passing the amendment in return for the White House's abandoning its push for ratification of the international human rights covenants, and they won.

Only in June 1992 did the United States finally ratify the ICCPR (International Covenant on Civil and Political Rights). Then, in 1998, only six years later, the United States demanded that China sign the covenant on political rights as a precondition for the United States to drop its campaign for a United Nations Commission on Human Rights resolution condemning China's human rights record.

As for the International Covenant on Economic, Social and Cultural Rights, the United States has still not ratified it. Nor has it joined the American Convention on Human Rights and other important international human rights conventions, such as the UN Convention on the Elimination of All Forms of Discrimination Against Women and the UN Convention on the Rights of the Child. China joined the former in 1980, and ratified the latter in 1990. Because of this record, it does not sound convincing when you claim that Americans criticize China's human rights record not because those violations "offend Western cultural values," but because China's conduct violates international human rights standards.

Political rights are sometimes the subtext of U.S. economic relations as well. When the Clinton administration sought to obtain Permanent Normal Trade Relations (PNTR) status to advance China's entry to the WTO, it argued that only after China became more open to the world would ordinary Chinese people have the information and "contact with the democratic world" that could support the kind of Chinese political development the United States hoped for.

It is undeniable that along with China's "Reform and Opening" and rapid economic development since the end of the 1970s, Chinese have come to a much clearer understanding of the meaning of political and civil rights, and their demands for these rights are more vigorous than before. However, one thing has not changed over recent decades. Compared to the United States, China remains a developing country, in which economic and social rights are still the greatest concern for the majority of its people. This explains why those Chinese human rights activists that you list in your first essay, who receive so much attention in your country, are of concern to so few people within China.[16] In 1999, *The New York Times* published an article on this very point that still rings true today:

> Americans here [in Beijing] sometimes have a hard time understanding how many Chinese can simultaneously appreciate the freedom of the West...and readily dismiss the dissidents as foolish idealists. The vast majority feel they are finally getting a chance to savor freedom in their personal lives and work, and they want to enjoy the fruits of modern society. The last thing most of them want is upheaval.[17]

Andy, I hope you can understand that most ordinary Chinese people feel very strongly about official corruption, which is a daily topic of conversation, but at the same time most of them acknowledge that their country has made clear progress in respecting human rights and developing the rule of law. While many Chinese people affirm that the American system has numerous virtues, they do not want to live their lives under this system or any other Western country's system.

When I said in my first letter that the concept of American exceptionalism was one of the sources of U.S. human rights-related foreign policy, I was suggesting that American foreign policy on human rights is not, as many Chinese people misunderstand it to be, solely aimed at China. It applies to the entire globe.

On the other hand, as a number of American scholars have conceded, in executing its human rights policies abroad, the United States displays distinct double standards.[18] President Ronald Reagan, denouncing the Soviet Union as the "Evil Empire," embraced the views of his ambassador to the United Nations and former Georgetown University professor Jeane Kirkpatrick that "traditional authoritarian governments are less repressive than revolutionary autocracies; that they are more susceptible to liberalization, that they are more compatible with U.S. interests."[19] Kirkpatrick argued that the United States ought to align itself more fully with traditional authoritarian regimes and be more patient with respect to the evolution of their political systems. This policy, Kirkpatrick held, would support the overarching American goal of blocking Soviet expansionism and obstructing the Soviet Union's strategic interests.

While in power, the Reagan administration adopted policies that evidenced blatant double standards. The United States launched virulent attacks on human rights grounds toward countries, such as Cuba and Nicaragua, which maintained good relations with the Soviet Union. But toward pro-American right-wing authoritarian regimes, the United States was tolerant and protective. That list is long and includes brutal regimes in Cold War–era South Korea, South Africa, the Philippines, and Haiti, as well as a whole set of Latin American authoritarian regimes in places such as Chile, El Salvador, and Guatemala.

Before the end of the Cold War, even during the Carter administration's human rights–focused foreign policy, the United States did not pay much attention to China, despite widespread, egregious human rights abuses as China emerged from the Cultural Revolution. The American target at the time was the Soviet Union, and the Soviet Union's alliances. Only after the Cold War ended—when, as you put it, China was no longer "a chess piece in play between the main rivals, the United States and the Soviet Union," and China was no longer strategically useful for the United States in combating the Soviet Union—did China become a focal point of U.S. human rights attention. I predict that you might respond by saying, "that was only the result of the Tiananmen Incident," but please consider whether the United States would have shifted the focus of its human rights criticism to China if it had still been wrapped up in its bitter conflict with Moscow? I doubt it.

In spite of all this, I still believe that many Americans, including you, Andy, are sincere in your concerns over human rights in China, both because of deep-seated American values and American exceptionalism, which I have already discussed.

China has been undergoing "Reform and Opening to the Outside World" for 30 years—a blink of the eye against the background of 5,000 years of continuous cultural and political history. In this process, we welcome criticism from our friends. Nevertheless, to expect China to solve, in that short span of time, all of its outstanding problems—economic development, social equality, and protection of human rights—is simply unrealistic. Massive changes in philosophic outlook, social customs, and institutional systems require time—even more so in China's case, because the development model applicable to China is still being painstakingly constructed day by day. Political reform in a country as gigantic as mine is not something to take lightly. In fact, the depth and the speed of change in China in recent decades have already been very difficult for many Chinese people.

In such a short exchange, we do not have the space to discuss the extremely complex question of the causal relationship between economic development and political development. On this topic I can only say that in the process of its development, China has many, many pressing problems crying out for resolution, including those of human rights. But, for now, China's economic development, the improvement of the lives of its vast populace, and the undeniable enhancement of its international status have given the Chinese people grounds for even greater confidence in the Chinese model of development, particularly nowadays, when the once-vaunted "Washington Consensus" model of development has been so seriously called into question because of the 2008 financial and economic crisis.

To those Americans who are truly concerned about and truly care about China, I would suggest they return to the words of the eminent American historian Michael E. Hunt:

> Our own immoderate expectations of China's fitting the American mold and our surprise and overreaction to China going her own way have thus contributed to the general instability that has characterized our bilateral relations. The lesson seems clear. Our dealing with China needs to take account of not just our own preferences and experience but China's as well.[20]

Sincerely,

Qi

• • •

Dear Qi,

We seem to be talking past each other, which is a common problem when people discuss important and complicated issues. It's not so much the facts we disagree about as the question of how to define the issue itself upon which we disagree. You criticize U.S. government policy; I do not defend it. I criticize the human rights performance of the Chinese government; you do not defend it. The core issue for you seems to be whether U.S. human rights policy is political, and therefore self-interested and inconsistent; I agree that it is. The core issue for me, however, is something I think we honestly do disagree about, and that makes it worth discussing. That issue is whether Chinese people want human rights and, relatedly, whether the non-governmental human rights movement in the West—which is a more important outside force in this field of work than the U.S. government—does the right thing when it supports Chinese human rights activists.

I agree that human rights is political. Although the human rights idea draws from many historical sources and many people contributed to its formation, human rights in its modern form—as a body of international law that identifies rights owed "universally" to all people—was crystallized in the United Nations Charter in 1945 and the Universal Declaration of Human Rights in 1948. This took place under a large degree of American influence. The aim of American officials and non-governmental persons who promoted human rights—but also of people from many other countries who were also involved—was to help create a post–Second World War world order that would be more stable and peaceful. This was considered a strategic interest of the United States and its allies. There followed a period when the human rights regime hardly developed at all. This stagnation, too, was political in origin: it was due to the Cold War stalemate between the Western and Soviet camps. Starting with the Helsinki Accords of 1975, the international human rights regime entered a period of rapid growth that has continued to the present. This process was yet again political: it was propelled by the interests of various actors. Civil society activists in the Soviet bloc used human rights to advance their pro-reform cause against the resistance of their regimes; activists in the West used human rights to put pressure on both socialist and right-wing dictatorships that they opposed; the U.S. government used human rights to increase support at home for an active foreign policy and to build up American soft power abroad; UN officials got involved partly to build up the institutional profile of the United Nations. Today the human rights regime is under debate, with the Chinese, American, and other governments as well as non-governmental actors working to shape it in ways they consider to be consistent with their own interests.[21]

This process was inherently and inescapably political. To me, that is normal. It shows that there is a lot at stake in how human rights are defined and implemented. Those of us who support the idea of human rights as—to use the words of the Universal Declaration of Human Rights—"a standard of achievement for all mankind" believe that we must stay in the political game and keep promoting human rights, or else those who have an interest of one kind or another in defeating these norms will have their way.

Whether the Chinese government has actually violated some of the existing human rights norms also seems not to be a point of debate between us. If we didn't talk about specific cases, however, it would be hard to be sure which norms we agree Beijing has violated. That's why I gave examples in my first letter of cases in which violations were clear-cut, were committed by the Chinese government or its agents, and violated norms that the Chinese government has pledged to respect. When it comes to cases like these, I feel safe in saying that not only are universal norms violated, not only are international laws violated, not only are foreign values violated, not only are the laws of China violated, but the values of most Chinese people are violated. After all, I have never met or heard of a Chinese person who wants to be unfairly jailed, tortured, disappeared, or abused by officials or to see other citizens subjected to such injustices. Unfortunately, however, censorship ensures that these abuses remain hidden from most Chinese.

It is impossible to be equally clear about economic, social, and cultural rights because these rights are, by definition, supposed to be achieved progressively. I heartily agree with you that China has made great progress in providing access to these rights as its economy has grown. On the other hand, you would probably agree that there are problems of discrimination in access to these rights in China. Access to education, jobs, social welfare programs, and other benefits is often denied to citizens on the basis of their household registration, HIV/AIDS status, hepatitis B status, sex, height, age, and sometimes even physical attractiveness. Practices like these violate the international human rights principle of non-discrimination, as well as the Chinese constitutional principle of equality before the law. Some Chinese lawyers and civil society groups are fighting against such forms of discrimination.

Third, we agree that the United States also violates human rights. That view is shared widely across the American human rights movement. For example, Human Rights Watch, where I used to serve on the board, has a robust program of research criticizing the flaws in U.S. human rights policy at home and abroad.[22] Some of the biggest rights organizations here, like the American Civil Liberties Union (ACLU), focus exclusively on human rights problems in our own country. Activists in China who have tried to form organizations like this have been jailed or exiled.

Fourth, I share your criticism of American double standards in the application of human rights principles in its foreign policy. That, too, is a target of constant criticism by U.S.-based human rights groups. I agree with you that

Ronald Reagan's government supported a lot of rights-violating regimes. Human Rights Watch and other groups struggled against this and eventually forced Reagan to change his positions on Guatemala, Chile, South Africa, the Philippines, and several other countries, so that the policy later in his administration was more human rights–friendly than at the beginning. And not all presidents shared Reagan's views. Most other presidents have been more pro–human rights than he was. U.S. policy varies (as does Chinese human rights policy) across time, across issues, and across branches of government.

One place where I think we disagree is with respect to a view that you seem to hold, although you don't say it explicitly: that violations of civil and political rights have to be endured until a given country—in this case China—gets richer, so that economic, social, and cultural rights can be achieved. I do not believe that any such trade-off exists. A government does not need a high level of economic development to stop abusing civil and political rights. Such abuses don't do anything to benefit economic development, social order, or any of the other legitimate goals of government. Even if they did, such violations are not justifiable, because rights like freedom of speech, freedom from torture, and the right to life are obligatory for governments to respect at every level of development. To protest against violations of these rights is hardly the same as "expecting China to solve all of its outstanding problems in a short span of time," any more than protesting U.S. violations of rights amounts to expecting the United States to solve all of its problems in a short span of time.

Finally, I have no problem with your point that China should not, as you put it, "live under any Western country's system" or, as Michael Hunt says, "fit the American mold." This is a false issue for the mainstream of the American and international human rights movements, although there may be some Americans who advocate such things. International human rights law calls for political freedom and accountable government. These are not controversial values in China any more than they are in the United States. Chinese leaders have endorsed them, and Chinese people seek them. International human rights instruments say nothing about specific American-style institutions like the separation of powers, the multiparty system, federalism, or the Electoral College.

In my opinion, the logic that flows from the view you and I share, that both China and the United States have human rights problems, is not that Americans should criticize Chinese human rights violations less, but that Chinese should criticize American human rights violations more. A robust two-way dialogue on human rights would be a great thing. It is too bad that it does not exist. I am glad we have engaged in a small-scale version of it here.

Sincerely,
Andy

THE MEDIA

WANG SHUO
Caixin Media

SUSAN SHIRK
University of California at San Diego

Framing questions: *What role do traditional and social media in both countries play in the U.S.–China relationship? What important effects have the Internet and social media had on American and Chinese domestic politics? How does the exponential expansion of the amount of information available to the public change the political game in China? In the United States? What important effects have the Internet and social media had on American and Chinese society? What role do they have in Sino-American relations? Why does the Chinese Communist Party (CCP) believe it needs to still exercise control over content? Does censorship have its desired result or does it undercut support for the CCP? Why is freedom of expression so important to Americans? From China's viewpoint, why is Chinese censorship such a politically potent issue in the United States? What is useful or destructive about U.S. funding of technologies that allow Chinese and other citizens to circumvent their government restrictions on the Internet?*

• • •

Dear Susan,

What would come to the mind of an ordinary American if we asked about the Chinese news media? Perhaps he or she would think of the government news agency Xinhua's ad in New York City's Times Square. Back in Beijing, the government has touted Xinhua's conquering of a premier electronic ad display as a symbol of China's rise and its increasing soft power: now we have Americans' attention.

Americans are paying attention to China, but not because of Xinhua's ad. All Xinhua did was buy time slots for the display at a very high price, nothing more, nothing less. In a way, this venture is worse than Japan's purchase of Rockefeller Center 30 years ago. Theirs was a bad investment. Ours is bad consumption.

The news media can only build influence, never buy it. Xinhua pretends otherwise, and those supporting its endeavor pretend to believe it. This game of China's official news media reaching out to an international audience will continue, until they run out of money. Then it will have to stop.

The truly important shift in the industry is happening elsewhere.

When we met several months ago in Beijing, I said that never before has such a powerful tool been put into Chinese people's hands: information sharing, opinion generation, and action coordination all integrated into a single platform. I speak, of course, of Weibo, a godsend to the Chinese people.

The Chinese did not invent Weibo; it is China's copycat version of Twitter. The Chinese government blocked access to Twitter, as well as Facebook, in 2009, the same year Weibo caught fire in the country. Since then, the leading Weibo service provider, Sina Weibo, has gained more than 300 million users.

There was doubt at first: Do you really want to put every detail of your life on Weibo? If you did, would anyone care?

People do care. It is the same question people asked when Twitter first arrived: What can I do with it? The answer is that you can do whatever you want with it. You can still find more than enough details about other people's lives on Weibo, but you also find discussions of every important issue that matters to today's China. With unprecedented information-sharing capability, Weibo has evolved to have very strong social and political dimensions.

Let me offer an example. In 2012, a highway accident occurred in Shaanxi Province. Several dozen travelers perished in the tragedy. The provincial head of the safety regulatory agency visited the accident site. Idiotically, he let someone take a photo of him smiling. The photo went viral on Weibo. While they were infuriated by the official's indifference, Weibo users noticed something even more damaging. He was wearing a luxury watch worth way beyond what he could afford on his legal income. Weibo users dug into the official's history, compared notes on Weibo, and eventually found many photos of him wearing watches, more than a dozen of which were as expensive as the first one. An official investigation found him guilty of corruption.

The *biaoshu* (a pun that means "uncle" in Chinese and also "watch official" (character by character), episode shows that on Weibo people choose for themselves what they care about without input from the government. They use Weibo to share information; support fellow users' appeals; set their own agendas; build pressure groups; and call for action when necessary. It is not the news media as we know it. It is public opinion on steroids: the opinion of the people, by the people, for the people.

This is not unique to China. Similar episodes must have happened on Twitter. The difference is that in China, it has had a much more radical effect. To China's fragile news media industry and government media regulatory system (I am not doing justice to the word "regulatory," and you know what I think of this system, but let's indulge ourselves with this description), Weibo is a bull in a china shop.

China's news media landscape is structured according to how distant a news media outlet is away from the government. At the inner circle is *dangbao* (government news media), or news media outlets directly controlled by the government. *Dangbao* has a matrix system. At the central level are the Xinhua News Agency, *People's Daily*, CCTV, Central People's Radio, China Network TV, and so on. The system extends both down and sideways to every level and line of the government. For each ministry in Beijing and each municipal government across the country, there are *dangbao* branches. *Dangbao* are *shiyedanwei* (government-sponsored institutions). Their budget depends on the government. Their employees enjoy ranking and perks like government officials and are frequently transferred to other government posts. *Dangbao* are furthest from being independent and closest to the government.

One step farther away from the government are news media outlets affiliated with and operated by *dangbao* groups. *Dangbao* began to create these in the 1990s to exploit business opportunities in the mass market. They run on their own budgets, usually without government support. A few of their employees are seconded from *dangbao*, but most are recruited from the market. *Dangbao* maintain their influence by nominating individuals to the top positions in these outlets, and retaining the power to hire and fire. These news media outlets are a hybrid of *dangbao* and the market. How independent they are depends very much on where they operate and how open-minded the local government leaders are. On one end of the spectrum, many metropolitan newspapers focus on satisfying local readers' appetites for sports and entertainment news. On the other end of the spectrum, there are newspapers like *Nanfang zhoumo* (*Southern Weekend*) with nationwide influence and a consistent pursuit of more independence.

Furthest away from the government are the independent, or professional, news media organizations. They emerged at the end of the 1990s. They do not rely on any government support. They have their own budgets and make their own staff decisions. The government still controls their license to publish, but that is all.

Independent news media outlets and a few *dangbao*-affiliated news media outlets like *Southern Weekend* represent emergent professional journalism in China. You and I both know that the professional news media in China have a long way to go before they are as independent as *The New York Times* or *The Wall Street Journal*. But Chinese professional journalists have the same burning aspiration to be independent. With this goal in mind, they are on the right track to truly professional journalism.

The professional news media have been very successful in China in the past decades. It is easy to understand why: Chinese people are thirsty for the truth and independent viewpoints. Chinese professional news media have gained national influence, become opinion leaders, and along with this, enjoyed business success, which in turn attracts more investments into professional journalism.

With success has come a curse. The government's regulatory pressures have weighed heavily on the independent news media, and the more successful the outlet, the stronger the pressure. *Dangbao* are trusted to self-regulate. But the government applies heavy-handed pressures on the professional news media, deciding what story topics are off-limits, what government policies can be scrutinized, and so on. As with everything else in China, it's not a one-way street; the sequence of tightening and loosening of controls depends on the overall political atmosphere. I don't want to go into detail here, but suffice it to say that Chinese professional news media do not enjoy the best regulatory environment today.

Weibo's sudden rise surprised both the news media industry and government regulators. Its instant success also poses serious challenges to the Chinese professional news media, already handicapped by heavy government regulations.

The technology challenge is not the problem. Chinese professional news media were among the first to embrace and exploit new media technologies worldwide. I don't know any professional news media outlet in China today that does not subscribe to a full media strategy. This means high-quality journalism through any medium (text, photo, audio, video, cartoons, etc.), on any platform (print, desktop, mobile phone, tablet, etc.). Chinese professional news media have gone through not one but two revolutions in the past decade, the first time with the Internet, then through social media.

The real challenge is the immediacy of Weibo and other forms of social media. Journalists everywhere are asking themselves the same question: Will society decide it needs fewer professional journalists to dig, identify, sift, and package facts and provide a neutral viewpoint? Will it rely instead only on information and opinion of the people, by the people and for the people, empowered by social media?

For the American professional news media, my answer would be a firm no. I would be less confident when answering for the Chinese professional news media, because in too many cases government regulatory pressures prevent them from doing their jobs.

Weibo is by no means a regulation-free zone. But government regulators, who are rushing to catch up with Weibo, are still way behind on the learning curve. Also, importantly, the government agency overseeing the Internet media is a little bit more open-minded than the one regulating the professional news media.

The asymmetric regulation of the professional news media and social media would concern no one outside the news media industry if the impact were only felt inside. But it is not. The asymmetric regulation of the professional news media and social media has had an impact across society.

In the United States, professional news media like *The New York Times* firmly established themselves as opinion leaders in the pre–social media era. Though social media have empowered individuals to compete for opinion leadership, professional new media in America retain significant influence today. This competition, therefore, is beneficial and healthy to society because the professional news media act as anchors against the vicissitudes of public opinion. Social media has thus improved, not impaired, the richness of social dialogue.

The story is different in China. Our social dialogue is losing its anchors. With heavy government regulation, it's become increasingly difficult for Chinese professional news media to contribute its uniquely valuable offerings, like investigative stories and independent viewpoints, to social dialogue. In contrast with the situation in the United States, Chinese social media represented by Weibo is replacing the professional news media, not complementing it.

The important question is whether Weibo, as a complex adaptive system, through interactions of hundreds of millions of users, will find and create new anchors for the social dialogue. Possibly. But I would suggest that it would be much better if professional news media also acted as anchors in the new game. Social dialogue needs high-quality information because without that, people do not know what to believe and will believe whatever they want to believe. The way out is simple but not easy: a freer press.

Susan, you may be asking yourself: What does this have to do with the U.S.–China relationship?

Weibo is reshaping the way the government and the people in China interact, putting people and the government face to face. And Weibo usually magnifies, not moderates. So when the government's objectives and public opinion conflict, the conflict becomes more violent. These are not surprises to us anymore.

The opposite is also true. When the government's objective is compatible with public opinion, then the government tends to take a more populist policy stance than it needs to. The U.S.–China relationship will feel this impact. A populist approach in international relations becomes nationalism.

Chinese people care about what happens in the world. In a way, the entire modern history of China is a very long-term reaction to outside shocks.

An index of the U.S.–China relationship would show a slow upward trend on a chart, interrupted repeatedly by crashes. Since the 1971 Nixon-Kissinger reopening of China, U.S.–China relations have moved between a limiting line and supporting line. The supporting line, before the collapse of the Soviet Union, was the strategic interdependence of the U.S. and China in the U.S.–Russia–China triangle. Today it is the interdependence of the United States and China in globalization, most importantly economic globalization.

More interesting is the limiting line. Three factors are at work here: great power politics, natural suspicion between authoritarian and democratic regimes, and communism-capitalism antagonism. The latter has been fading out of the picture. The second one is a really big factor for Chinese government, but much less so for the Chinese people. However, the first factor, great power politics, offers a very powerful argument. Most Chinese people find it convincing.

According to the Chinese understanding of great power politics, the reigning hegemon, the United States, intends to contain China's rise. East Asia is the major theater of the U.S.–China global competition. Japan is a proxy for America in the region and a tool of U.S. strategy. Sino-Japanese confrontation, be it over the Diaoyu Islands or other issues, must be interpreted with this understanding in mind. A similar logic applies to quarrels between China and its other neighbors: Vietnam, the Philippines, and South Korea.

Whether this logic is valid is beside the point. What's important is that the Chinese people universally subscribe to it. The Chinese people have split feelings toward the United States; they love it as a democratic capitalistic powerhouse, but they are suspicious of it as the reigning hegemon.

Let's return to Weibo. Public opinion on that forum centers on three major themes: people's livelihoods, democracy, and nationalism. A lot of people call for more equitable development. Many citizens are also asking for democratization and to introduce competition into the political arena. But almost everyone wants China to be stronger and wants it to reclaim its rightful place in the world. Dr. Sun Yat-sen's *Sanminzhuyi* (Three People's Principles, which not coincidentally mirror these three major themes: people's livelihoods, democracy, and nationalism), 100 years later, still dominates Chinese people's aspirations. Because communist ideology has lost its appeal, in the next decade, these themes will be reliable sources of political capital. Successful politicians will need to deliver the right mix of them, but I would say that nationalism would have to figure prominently. Look at what happened after the Diaoyu Islands confrontation in 2012 when ordinary Chinese took to the streets to protest Japan and boycotted Japanese products. If nationalism is not the only adhesive uniting the whole nation, it is clearly the strongest.

Moreover, nationalism offers the government and the people the most common ground. More equitable development will require sacrifice by the rich and powerful. Democratization means sharing political power. In both these cases, Weibo tends to magnify the conflict between the people and the government. But with nationalism, the government and people tend to converge. It is the natural choice of least resistance and will likely result in more populist policies.

China will be more assertive in the U.S.–China relationship, not only because it is getting stronger but also because the way that the government and the people interact is changing. The Chinese people will support a more assertive China on the international stage, even demand it, and the government will happily oblige. This has happened in many countries. What differentiates today's China is that the independent news media will be less influential than it should be, which means fewer anchors to offset public opinion's tumultuous waves.

Welcome to a brave new world.

Wang Shuo

• • •

Dear Wang Shuo,

I couldn't agree with you more that Weibo has produced a quantum leap in the information environment in China. By enabling citizens, including influential public intellectuals, to disseminate news and opinion pieces to millions of others with a speed that (so far at least) surpasses the ability of the monitors on the microblog platforms to delete them, Weibo has dramatically expanded the scope and openness of political dialogue in China. The diversity of opinion being articulated online nowadays is extraordinary. Weibo is creating a marketplace of ideas that is a healthy sign of social progress.

But, as you point out, Weibo has its downsides as well. Unlike foreign social media, Weibo servers remain very much under the thumb of the Communist Party headquarters in Beijing. And while Weibo is enabling a lively pluralistic conversation about China's problems and solutions, the medium does have an unfortunate tendency to stimulate intemperate venting rather than dispassionate, thoughtful discussion. Professional journalists in China have an important role, as you suggest, in "anchoring" these online debates.

I can well understand why you and other journalists are feeling discouraged about your current situation. Party censorship tightened in the lead up to the 2008 Olympics and never relaxed after that. Reporters and editors have to tiptoe around taboo topics, including anything regarding high-level national leaders. I remember once asking you about who you thought would be selected for the Politburo, and you replied, "I don't pay attention because I know we can't report about it. That's for the foreign media." Not only are newspapers and magazines hamstrung by what you euphemistically call "government regulation," but they also must compete for readers with the comparatively less fettered information on Weibo.

Though I agree that professional journalists operate under serious constraints, you shouldn't be so modest about what they have achieved over the past decade. Exposés by Chinese journalists about issues that their readers care deeply about, such as the safety of food and medicine and environmental pollution, have led to positive policy changes just as American journalistic muckraking did a hundred years ago, and still does today. Journalists like you at *Caijing* magazine and *Southern Weekend* newspaper and the brave Dr. Jiang Yanyong's leaks to *Time* magazine helped break the story of the SARS epidemic in 2003.

There are many other examples of watchdog journalism, such as a local newspaper in Gansu province reporting a horrific case of melamine-tainted milk and infant formula in 2008. The magazine, *Caixin*, that you and Hu Shuli founded, recently exposed bribe taking by the people at the highly respected Securities Regulatory Commission, which decides which companies can go public. At least some senior officials recognize that the media provides valuable feedback to the CCP and the government about problems, especially at the grassroots level, that they can try to remedy before they provoke active political opposition.

Let's also acknowledge that competition from the commercial media and the Internet also has forced the official media to change. The state media has to provide more timely and reliable information to the public in order to salvage its own fraying credibility. Xinhua News Service reported casualties from the 2008 Sichuan earthquake in real time, and has since started to report some protests.

Even the party mouthpiece, *People's Daily*, is striving to shore up its credibility by posting from a critical perspective on its Weibo account. Hard-hitting criticism of the government may help the newspaper improve its image and attract new readers, its editors appear to think. In February 2013, the *People's Daily*, and other state media led the charge against the refusal of the Environmental Protection Ministry to release the findings of a soil pollution survey it conducted several years before. "Covering this up only makes people think: We're being lied to," complained the Weibo of the newspaper that once was the epitome of Communist Party orthodoxy.

The commercial media—and its challenge to the credibility of information provided by the official media and of the government itself—also drove the CCP to embrace the norm of transparency, which is articulated in the Open Government Information Regulations that were enacted in May 2008. Although that promise of transparency hasn't been fully delivered, citizens now have an opening to demand more information on government budgets and the assets of officials.

One perverse effect of the information revolution is that the propaganda bureaucracies have aggrandized their power and resources by arguing that media commercialization and the growth of Internet sources make their job harder and more essential to the survival of the Party. The propaganda czar sits at the apex of power as one of China's top seven leaders in the Politburo Standing Committee. His decisions are rarely questioned, much less overruled by other leaders.

I'm sure you would agree with me that the Propaganda Department's expensive effort to censor content is self-defeating. I made this point to a room full of propaganda officials at the U.S.–China Internet Industry Conference in Beijing a couple of years ago and was surprised that a few of them privately complimented me for my speech. I argued that online censorship in particular was undercutting public support for the Communist Party. People may not realize that the newspaper they read or the television news shows they watch have omitted certain news events. But the hand of the censor is highly visible to netizens reading news stories online. When readers see a piece of news or a critical opinion suddenly disappear, it reveals the weakness of the Party by showing what innocuous information the Party leaders fear. Netizens mock the censors with deliciously clever humor, including cartoons and spoof videos. This covert resistance further erodes the moral authority of the CCP, and over time may lead to outright opposition to Party rule.

Social scientists are starting to study the patterns of censorship to figure out what topics the Communist Party establishment most fears. Preliminary results indicate that they tolerate much criticism of the government. What the censors insist on deleting is any call to mobilize collective action or any criticism of censorship itself.[1]

So far, the propaganda cops have taken a relatively light hand to Weibo content. The central government sees it as a useful safety valve for citizens to let off steam and a mechanism to monitor and discipline corrupt officials especially at the local level.

One Internet company executive told me that shortly after Weibo took off in 2011, the propaganda bureaucrats called a meeting of government ministers and provincial leaders with the companies to discuss what to do about it. "Just shut it down!" cried the ministers and provincial leaders, who were smarting from online criticism of their performance. The State Internet Information Office, the propaganda agency responsible for managing online information, paradoxically was its greatest defender; it reminded everyone in the room that shutting down Weibo would infuriate hundreds of millions of netizens who might rise up against the Party, and that a managed opening would be better.

The central leaders have decided that Weibo microblogs, while creating an illusion of freedom, can serve as an effective weapon for heading off threats to Party rule. Sina.com and Tencent, the major microblog platforms, are monopolistic private companies completely dependent upon the patronage of the Communist Party. Their servers are located in Beijing, not outside the country where the Twitter, Google, Facebook, and YouTube servers reside. That's why some media critics take a much less sanguine view of Weibo than you do. Chinese blogger Michael Anti describes Weibo as an advanced tool of communism to channel public opinion to control local governments and to track networks of political critics, reminiscent of George Orwell's dystopian novel 1984. When the authorities ordered Sina to strengthen its monitoring capabilities and enforce real name individual registration that would help the internal security police apprehend "trouble makers," the company didn't dare say no.

Today, Sina is struggling financially under the burden of these costly requirements; Weibo provides an expensive public service that the company hasn't figured out how to commercialize. Website managers can make money under the table, however. *Caixin* recently published an expose of how desperate local politicians hire public relations companies to bribe the website managers to delete information that sullies their reputations.

Let's now turn to the question of how the media impact Sino-American relations. It's very tempting for leaders who are insecure about their support at home to deflect criticism and bolster their popularity by using all types of media to divert anger to foreign targets. Moreover, your analysis of how Weibo magnifies opinion when it coincides with government interests rings true to me. Your predictions of how this dynamic will increase nationalist foreign policy jibe with my own views.

Chinese nationalist emotions have genuine roots in the society's bitter historical experience with Japan and in its experience of living in a rising power that is breathing on the heels of the dominant superpower, the United States. Much nationalist resentment, however, is manufactured by the commercial media—exciting stories about foreign threats sell papers—and by the CCP authorities. The propaganda bureaucracies have demonstrated their ability to shut down ultranationalist anti-Japanese websites and to moderate media rhetoric against Japan and the United States when they want to—they did it often in the 1990s.

But over the past several years, Americans have noticed with apprehension a steady drumbeat of media messages about America's supposed "containment" of China that have undoubtedly been officially encouraged. The precedents of Germany and Japan show how this kind of commercialized semi-controlled media, by creating myths and mobilizing anger against perceived foreign enemies, can drag a country into war.

China's leaders certainly understand this risk. Several Chinese foreign policy experts have told me that former president Hu Jintao, after returning from a very successful state visit to the United States in January 2011, ordered the Propaganda Department to tone down the containment rhetoric against the United States. But the popular revolutions of the Arab Spring that erupted the following month so alarmed Party leaders about the possibility of contagion to China that no one enforced the order, and the containment drumbeat continues to foment popular suspicions of American intentions toward China.

Some Chinese citizens, however, are starting to question whether the overheated anti-foreign nationalism that dominates the media and Internet isn't just a Communist Party ploy to distract the public from the domestic problems in their own backyard. I was in Shanghai and Beijing in September 2013 when the Japanese government purchased several of the tiny islands in the East China that are claimed by Japan (which calls them the Senkakus) and China (which calls them the Diaoyus). The commercial media played up the crisis with shrill, bellicose rhetoric and images of fishing boats and law enforcement vessels steaming toward the islands to contest Japan's actions. Government spokesmen signaled approval of consumer boycotts of Japanese goods and other forms of protest that might create leverage on the Japanese government. During a weekend of violent protests, a couple of students told me they didn't join in because they felt manipulated by the government. Compared to the traditional media, the Weibo discussion actually appeared milder and more critical of the smashing of Japanese cars and shop windows.

Do you see other hints of nationalism fatigue among well-educated Chinese? My students tell me that Weibo criticism is increasingly targeted on corruption, pollution, and other domestic failures as much or more than on Japanese or American affronts. One harbinger is that the official media is using its Weibo to distance itself from unthinking nationalism. One February 2013 *People's Daily* Weibo complained about the steady diet of television shows on the anti-Japanese war and their caricatured treatment of both sides.

Hu Xijin, the editor of *Global Times*, the commercial newspaper under the *People's Daily* media group that built a huge audience over the past 15 years by dramatizing foreign threats, has become a lightning rod for the Weibo debate over government-sponsored nationalism. On the day in February 2011 when he opened his Weibo account, he noted, "Right now people are attacking patriotism. They equate patriotism with 'loving the government.'" Perhaps to improve his image and that of *Global Times*, Hu has started posting Weibo criticisms of the government on domestic problems. For example, Hu posted on the environment ministry's hiding of data about water pollution: "China has too many secrets, and secrets become bombs in the end…. The government should be unswerving in its pursuit of greater transparency."

How do you think this nascent debate over nationalism will evolve? Might the skeptical minority serve as an effective check on the "tumultuous waves" of nationalist public opinion that could sweep away foreign policy restraint? Are professional journalists able to provide balanced analysis to anchor the debate? Or will censorship and their commercial interests keep newspapers and magazines publishing exciting stories about foreign threats that appeal to most readers? Will the Communist Party establishment have the confidence to lead public opinion toward the United States and Japan in a more moderate direction or will it continue to orchestrate the media and school textbooks to cultivate popular suspicion of Japan and the United States?

As you aptly observe, nationalism is the strongest adhesive uniting the whole nation, and it offers the government and the people the most common ground. That's why I argued in my book *China: Fragile Superpower* that China's insecure politicians bolster their popular support by stoking anti-foreign nationalism in the media despite the international risks. A mass media that is market oriented but still controlled by the government is a recipe for nationalist pressure on decision makers. The views expressed in newspapers and the Internet blow back on the leaders, creating the impression that everyone is a passionate nationalist. That's why one Chinese foreign policy expert I know has advised the government to do regular surveys of public opinion on international issues instead of relying on the distorted picture provided by the media and Internet. A more fundamental solution would be to eliminate the Propaganda Department and decontrol the marketplace of ideas to allow people a broader range of information, which will in turn give China's leaders more accurate information about public opinion. Loosening their grip on the media will also make the leaders look more confident and gain them legitimacy at home and abroad.

Of course, we might argue that the American media also "demonizes" China. It's certainly true that except for the positive reporting on the business pages, American headlines on China are dominated by political repression, social unrest, and cyber-attacks. Fox television and partisan online media build their audiences by taking slaps at China. But their negative slant is driven by commercial considerations not official dictates. If Washington could control the news about China, it would be a lot different!

The increasingly porous information environment in China is aggravating the threat perceptions between Chinese and Americans. Now Chinese citizens have access to criticisms made of their country by American politicians and media; and Americans read what the Chinese are saying about the United States. As a result, both of us feel defensive and unfriendly. Our diplomats try to highlight how well our governments are cooperating, but most media voices are telling another, more hostile story.

I wonder what you think about whether U.S. government support for media and Internet freedom has positive or negative impact inside China. Americans cherish their own press freedom and wish the same for the Chinese people. When our Department of State funds groups developing technologies to help Chinese citizens climb over the Great Firewall or members of Congress try to restrict American companies from selling Internet surveillance technologies to China, do the Chinese people welcome these actions or resent them as outside meddling? How could U.S. policy toward Chinese media promote positive political change in China without creating a public backlash?

Susan

• • •

Susan,

March in Beijing is *lianghui* season, a good time of year to observe Chinese politics. The *lianghui*, or coinciding meetings of the National People's Congress and Chinese People's Political Consultative Conference, was more significant than usual in 2013: Xi Jinping was elected president of the People's Republic of China, and Li Keqiang became premier, thus finalizing the every-ten-year leadership transition. A new chapter officially starts.

The spokesperson for the *lianghui* usually attracts a lot of attention. That was true even more so this year because it was Fu Ying, a vice foreign minister. Fu has been overseeing Asia affairs since 2009 and was China's ambassador to Britain before that. She is cosmopolitan and candid, belonging to the moderate wing of China's international policy-making circle. She is so welcomed by international observers that some suggest she is a part of a Chinese diplomatic "charm offensive."

She was not so charming, however, when a Japanese reporter asked this question during a press conference: Will China's diplomacy become even more overbearing?

She replied: "Didn't you notice that the Chinese journalists smiled when you asked [that] question? You [will] hear entirely different opinions inside China. Most Chinese, including Chinese journalists here today, want China to be stronger [on international issues]. It's a fact we must recognize: international observers feel the Chinese government is too aggressive; ordinary Chinese people believe the Chinese government is not aggressive enough."

Fu Ying continued: "China pursues peaceful diplomacy. But it will act decisively when provoked by a certain country on territorial and sovereignty issues." She concluded: "China prefers solving its dispute with Japan through dialogue. But one hand doesn't clap. If Japan chooses to be unreasonable and acts tough, China will return the favor."

Fu's remarks received universal accolades on site, on TV, and later in newspapers.

Susan, we both worry about the consequences of China's rising nationalism. You worry more about the government's manipulating hand during the process. While sharing your concern, I would argue that the Chinese people as a nation are becoming more nationalistic, with or without the state's help. There is danger in not recognizing China's nationalism as an inherent, organic political phenomenon and thus hoping for a quick fix. But there is no silver bullet.

I have three terms to frame my thoughts: asymmetric, positive feedback, and marginal.

By *asymmetric* I mean that a lot of Chinese people believe that the government has been too strong on too many domestic issues, but most Chinese people believe that the government has been too weak on the international issues. Fu made a valid point in her response. The asymmetry that Chinese people think they find between the government's internal and international behavior actually reflects the Chinese people's own asymmetric view of international and internal affairs.

Let me explain.

Most Chinese liberals who demand a smaller, less interventionist state and more individual freedoms also demand a stronger, more assertive China on the international stage. They are keenly aware of the potential hypocrisy, but proudly keep both convictions anyway. To them, if things like fairness and justice exist only inside one nation but not among others, too bad.

This is nothing new. Master Zuo's *Spring and Autumn Annals*, one of China's oldest and most respected classics said: those who are not our kin are sure to be of a different heart.

This thinking is not unique to China. Pericles, in his famous tribute to fallen Athenians in the Peloponnesian War, said these immortal words: "Having judged that to be happy means to be free, and to be free means to be brave, do not shy away from the risks of war." But freedom was not a universal principle for the Athenians. Decades later, when the Melians argued that they were fighting for their freedom, the commanders of the invading Athenian navy responded this way: "The strong do what they have the power to do and the weak accept what they have to accept." These words have also become immortal.

Yes, these views are very much pre-United Nations, pre-WTO, pre-World Bank, and pre-IMF. They are out of fashion, run counter to global trends, and present a very unpleasant view of the world where only power prevails. Yet, they are eternal, very easy to understand, and require only instinct to follow, whether for the Chinese, the Japanese, or the Americans. Americans call it realism or Rooseveltism; the Chinese call it *badao* (hegemony). Modern nationalism is a much younger movement, but they find good company in each other.

Realism is by no means the only view of international politics; today liberalism is at least as strong, if not stronger in China. For Americans, both liberal internationalism and realism are alive and well. For the Chinese, to balance one's moral influence and hegemonic power well is a superlative strategy. However, there is also an asymmetry in the competition between liberalism and realism. Liberalism prevails only among its believers. Realism prevails if one of the competing nations adopts it.

Thus, the third asymmetry: mutual trust is hard to build, but much easier to lose. And it is easier to build trust among your own people, but much harder with other people.

These asymmetries are very susceptible to positive feedback loops. One person's hard feeling toward another makes others feel negatively toward him. One country's tough policy begets another's tough reaction. The situation spirals downward easily and quickly. When Fu said China would return the favor, it was a most natural reaction and also an ominous warning.

This happens not only between two states, but also between two peoples. A senior Japanese diplomat told me that the dispute over the Diaoyu/Senkaku Islands was entirely different from disputes over shrine visits and textbooks. "This time it is about territory; this is a real issue. The Japanese people discounted the shrine visit and textbook issues, but not territorial issues. They are firmly supportive of the Japanese government's tough policy." He was most likely telling the truth. Sadly, it is also true for the Chinese government and the Chinese people.

Susan, you asked whether, in the face of China's rising nationalism, professional journalists would be able to provide balanced analysis to anchor the debate. My answer is yes, but with a caveat.

Professional journalists, like my colleagues at *Caixin*, are doing our job by providing in-depth reports and balanced views on international topics whenever the opportunity presents itself. And yes, these do help.

But, looking at the whole picture, I have to say that news media can only play a marginal role in checking China's rising nationalism.

The media reflect the people they serve. If the Chinese people as a nation, emboldened by their newfound economic power, are determined to be more visible on the international stage and more aggressive on issues they deem vital, then the media, as a whole, will usually encourage it. Adopting a nationalistic editorial policy is appealing to audiences, politically safe and, most importantly, sound from a business point of view. So why not? Particularly if the majority of journalists, like their fellow countrymen, truly subscribe to this nationalism. Chinese journalists are, first of all, Chinese.

There will still be liberal leaning media, going against the tide, preaching bravely to the people, but do not overestimate how effective they will be. They will work only on the margins. I would say enlightened nationalism is the best result we can expect.

Truthful, well-balanced reports will dispel many misunderstandings between two nations. There is no question about this. But they will also make irreconcilable differences clearer. Better mutual understanding solves problems caused by misunderstandings, but not problems that have nothing to do with misunderstandings.

Weibo is an extremely powerful technology empowering Chinese people with huge information flows and instant interaction. It is far ahead of other developments a healthy, dynamic, and balanced society should have, like the rule of law, civil society, and democratic institutions. Weibo is great, but without these developments, Weibo will not check the rise of China's nationalism, but help it, strengthening the asymmetries, nurturing the positive feedback loop. Without mediation and institutional buffers, Weibo becomes a great platform for a populist agenda. As Yu Keping, a leading political scientist in China, said, populism appears patriotic, but usually leads to extreme nationalism.

China's nationalism is rising and will most likely continue to rise. Its tide is coming in. The answer is not turning the tide, but preempting its potential floods. This means deciding how not to let it spiral out of control and cause unnecessary military conflicts.

I hope I am wrong.

Wang Shuo

• • •

Dear Wang Shuo,

Every time I write a blog post or speak at a university about the dangers of xenophobic nationalism in China, Chinese students accuse me of implying that they have been brainwashed by the Chinese Communist Party instead of feeling an authentic emotion. In the same spirit, you say to me that "There is danger in not recognizing China's nationalism as an inherent, organic political phenomenon, and thus hoping for a quick fix."

I assure you that I don't believe that Chinese anti-foreign nationalism is entirely constructed by Communist Party propagandists; I understand that much of it is the spontaneous emotion of a proud people who are reviving their national strength after a long period of humiliating weakness.

But on the other hand, wouldn't you agree that nothing is completely spontaneous in China? People's views have been molded by the anti-Japanese Patriotic Education Campaign of the 1990s, by the school textbooks that ignore post-war Japanese history, and by the censored media that frames Japan, and increasingly the United States too, in a negative light. The government built the Great Firewall to keep people ignorant of alternative interpretations of international affairs and Chinese domestic affairs. Just months after *The New York Times* started an online Chinese-language edition published in Beijing, the Chinese government blacked it out so no one in China can read it unless they have a VPN.

Xi Jinping laid down a clear nationalist line for his new administration in one of his first acts after coming to power at the 18th Party Congress in 2012: he took the new leadership team (and the television cameras) to the national history museum, which depicts China's modern history as a story of victimization at the hands of imperialist foreign powers. Xi used the media event to articulate the guiding motto for his reign—"national rejuvenation."

I do believe that government censorship of the media is at least partially responsible for nationalism and an assertive foreign policy. Greater freedom of the press and a more pluralistic open debate about foreign and domestic policy would improve the odds for China to rise peacefully. Yet I recognize that freedom of the press is no ironclad guarantee of a restrained foreign policy. In late-19th-century America, the sensationalist reporting of yellow journalism drummed up enthusiasm for the Spanish American War. Much later, however, American newspapers and magazines intensely debated our misguided wars in Vietnam and Iraq.

But if China had a free press, wouldn't there be at least a few articles questioning whether the tiny islands in the East China and South China Seas were worth fighting over? Or discussing various compromise solutions to the maritime territorial disputes? And wouldn't there be a lot more exciting exposes of domestic scandals to help sell newspapers and magazines without hyping foreign threats? I'll take an increment of enlightened nationalism over know-nothing nationalism any day.

Although anti-foreign nationalism is on the rise, it needn't dictate Chinese foreign policy. I don't buy the argument that I've heard from Chinese officials that because of enflamed public opinion they had "no choice" but to take coercive actions over the Diaoyu/Senkaku Islands or Scarborough Shoal in the South China Sea. Sending government ships and planes to break Japan's administration of the Diaoyu/Senkaku Islands and roping off entry to Scarborough Shoal to keep out fishing boats from the Philippines are risky behaviors that could escalate into military confrontations. Policy makers could have avoided them by suppressing instead of encouraging anti-Japanese demonstrations. And in the future they can avoid being dragged into fights over territorial disputes by opting for more active diplomacy or even international legal mediation.

True, China's leaders feel very politically insecure and are highly responsive to nationalist public opinion. They are well aware that nationalist revolutionary movements brought down the Qing Dynasty and the Republic of China and don't want the same fate to befall them. Still they can manage or ignore public opinion when they want to. They should be held responsible for their policy choices. Popular nationalism doesn't doom China to act aggressively.

Look at how insulated Taiwan policy has been from public opinion even though reunification with Taiwan has always been a popular nationalist cause. No PRC leader has ever allowed mass demonstrations over Taiwan even when the island's democratic politicians moved in the direction of independence. (The possibility of the protests turning against the CCP may have looked too dangerous for the PRC leaders to risk them.) Over the past decade, Hu Jintao did an impressive job of protecting Taiwan policy from the overall trend of greater assertiveness. Hoping to go down in Chinese history as a national unifier, he pursued a benevolent policy of winning the hearts and minds of Taiwan people by offering economic benefits and a measure of international respect. Media rhetoric toward Taiwan was accordingly muted. And no one called Hu too soft on Taiwan.

Past Chinese leaders also orchestrated the media to reduce acrimony with important countries when they felt it was in China's interest to do so. Deng Xiaoping and Hu Yaobang promoted friendship with Japan to get its support for market reforms in the 1980s. In the 1990s, when Jiang Zemin enjoyed his role as a statesman on the world stage, the media dialed down its criticisms of the United States and started talking about win-win solutions.

Of course the media landscape has changed since then. Today's mass media are more competitive and market-oriented than they were in the past; and Weibo spreads news throughout the country with unprecedented speed.

But if the Propaganda Department wanted to encourage greater balance in the news about Japan and the United States, don't you think it could? Even if such an official effort weren't entirely successful, it would send a positive diplomatic signal that the Chinese government was trying its best to do so. I am not advocating for censorship, but I did want to make the point that China's leaders are not helpless in the face of popular nationalism.

So while I agree with you that the media alone cannot check the rising tide of nationalism, I am less convinced than you seem to be that this nationalism is inexorable. Such fatalism lets China's leaders off the hook. China's authoritarian leaders hold levers that they could use to dampen nationalist pressures on foreign policy. We should urge them to revise textbooks and expand access to diverse sources of information including from abroad. Let's also call on them to give groups like private business that benefit from peaceful interdependence a greater voice in the foreign policy process.

Sad to say, it's bound to become much harder to manage anti-foreign nationalism if and when China makes the transition to electoral democracy. Politicians campaigning for votes in new democracies find the temptation to play to nationalist emotions almost irresistible. Once democratic governments mature, however, the voters' reluctance to see their sons and daughters risk their lives in combat tempers their enthusiasm for international fights and restrains their elected leaders.

In our conversation about the dangers of excessive nationalism we seem to have drifted beyond our concentration on the media. To circle back, both of us worry that China's media environment is providing fertile soil for the growth of anti-foreign nationalism that could push the country into confrontations with the United States and its neighbors. But you see nationalist public opinion as a volcano erupting spontaneously on the Weibo platform and only marginally tempered by professional journalism. I attribute more responsibility to the CCP's management of media content, even on Weibo, to bolster its popularity by creating myths about foreign threats.

I look forward to continuing our conversation over some good Chinese food in Beijing.

Susan

GLOBAL ROLES AND RESPONSIBILITIES

YUAN PENG

Chinese Institutes for Contemporary International Relations

NINA HACHIGIAN

Center for American Progress

Framing questions: *How do the United States and China each view their own relationship to the current international system? What dilemmas do they face in following and respecting international norms? How does the United States see its role in the world? How does China? Are those roles compatible? To what extent do shared global challenges push the United States and China toward cooperation? How do their approaches toward intervention in crises in other countries differ and how does that relate to the debate about global responsibility? Which international organizations are most critical for solving global problems? Can the United States and China work within these organizations, separately and together? What are the signs that China is ready to help solve global problems or is not? Does it have a responsibility to do so? What are the signs that the United States is or is not genuinely ready to share leadership?*

• • •

Dear Nina,

It's nice to speak with you again about U.S.–China relations. Given that strategic distrust between our two countries is still a big problem, it's a good idea to clarify some of the issues that concern our countries the most. I'd like to present my understanding of U.S.–China relations and the roles our countries play in our current international system.

From the Chinese point of view, the current international system is experiencing the fourth historical transformation in modern history. The first was the emergence of the Westphalian system in 1648, the second was the Versailles-Washington system starting in 1918, and the third was the Yalta system beginning in 1945. There are four signs of this new transformation. The first is the rise of emerging powers and the shift of gravity in world power from the West to the rest. The BRICS countries (Brazil, Russia, India, China and South Africa), VISTA countries (Vietnam, Indonesia, South Africa, Turkey, and Argentina), Next-11 (populous countries like Indonesia, South Korea, and Mexico), and more are becoming major players in the world.

Second, the dominant forces of the Western world, including the United States, Europe, and Japan, all face economic difficulties, political problems, and a synchronous decline in their overall strength, something that has not happened in memory. Third, non-state actors, such as terrorists, transnational corporations, NGOs, civil society groups, and Internet players (such as netizens, hackers, and others), are playing a key role in international politics and economics for the first time. Fourth, the world is now concerned with global problems like climate change, energy, natural resources, and demographic changes in a way it has not been before. Those four signs show that we are going through a historic change of the international system. We are in an era of great transition.

In the context of the transformation of the international system, the United States, the leader of the Western world, and China, a representative of the emerging powers, are undergoing great shifts with respect to the balance of power, their international roles, their own ideas, and their internal and external strategies.

In China's view, although the United States is still expected to be the only superpower for the next 20 years (based on its natural resources and military, scientific, strategic, cyber, cultural, geopolitical, intelligence, and alliance powers), America's ability to control the international system is already decreasing. For example, its domination of the WTO, IMF, and

World Bank is diminishing somewhat, and its right to manage other international institutions is weakening. Since the United States has withdrawn from the Kyoto Protocol and failed to join the United Nations Convention on the Law of the Sea, its influence on climate change, international maritime disputes, and many other areas is constrained. On such global concerns as cyber-security, nuclear proliferation, and weapons in space, America is still debating the solutions with other countries, which also limits its influence.

As for China, opportunities and challenges coexist. From the opportunity perspective, as an emerging power, China can take advantage of the transformation of the international system by engaging actively to modify unreasonable international mechanisms (including international or regional organizations, regimes, and laws) and constructing new ones with other countries. From this perspective, China will have greater influence in the international arena than before.

However, the current era poses three challenges for China: first, the transformation of the international system may result in a chaotic non-polar system or even disorder, which would disrupt China's process of modernization; second, new problems and frictions in the U.S.–China relationship will inevitably emerge in the new international system. If not handled properly, the whole situation could easily slide into the historical model of a clash between the status quo power and the emerging power.

Third, due to its unique national characteristics, China itself has not yet made adequate psychological and strategic preparations for changes in the international system. This is because China's total GDP is the second largest worldwide, but its per capita GDP is 88th in the world; China's economic influence in the world is expanding, while its military, political, and cultural influence is still quite limited, and its soft power even less developed. It has become the first country to be immersed in information technology without yet being fully industrialized. China has become the first poor country with the title of second largest power in the world. It has become a reluctant "No. 2."

Therefore, in the next 20 years, even if China's economy surpasses that of the United States in the 2020s, China will still be a developing country. Also, China is unlikely to change its socialist system in the foreseeable future. Subsequently, the mainstream view in China is that China is a "developing socialist emerging power." China's economic and energy interests are global, but for two reasons, for the next 20 years it will be "an Asia-Pacific regional power with some global reach." One reason is that territorial issues like Taiwan, disputes in the South China Sea, and the Diaoyu Islands have not been resolved.

Another reason is that China's ability to affect events overseas is limited. China will have to mainly focus its energy and resources on domestic affairs to achieve the ambitious goal of "establishing a well-off society in an all-around way" in 2020 and becoming a middle-level developed country in 2050. And historically speaking, China has long been an inward-looking country, with no tradition of expanding its power overseas.

China is especially looking forward to participating in the reconstruction of the international order and becoming a full stakeholder. Yet China will not be the great influential power that the United States and other countries expect it to be. Former U.S. Secretary of State Hillary Clinton criticized China for being a "selective stakeholder."[1] This critique is actually partially correct, for every country can be considered a "selective stakeholder" by other countries. Just as the United States will not stop selling arms to Taiwan, intervening in the South China Sea, and growing its military alliances in the Asia-Pacific region in accordance with the requirements and expectations of China, China will not take global responsibilities in accordance with all the requirements of the United States.

In the future, China will continue to play an appropriate role and assume appropriate responsibilities based on the norms of international law, on its own strengths and capabilities, and on the expectations of the international community. In practice, China has been playing a special, influential role in the world arena. China has adopted a constructive posture and tried to achieve more international cooperation with the United States in the following ways.

First, China is achieving a peaceful rise by integrating into the international system rather than trying to break it. In today's era of economic globalization, a country can develop through orderly international competition and mutually beneficial cooperation. It is no longer necessary or possible to take the old path of challenging either the existing international order or other countries. The more developed China becomes, the more it needs a peaceful and stable international environment. For these reasons, China will continue to play the role of a constructive participant and gradual reformer in the international system.

Second, China has pushed past some traditional limits and taken substantial steps forward in meeting its international responsibilities. To take just the example of UN peacekeeping operations, China has dispatched about 21,000 personnel on 30 UN peacekeeping missions, which is the highest contribution of personnel among the permanent members of the UN Security Council. China always plays a constructive role in dealing with regional hotspots, such as the Darfur conflict and the rebuilding of Afghanistan. China also takes an active role in international cooperation, anti-terrorism, and non-proliferation. It provides humanitarian aid, dispatches rescue teams to countries hit by disasters, and has deployed naval escort fleets to combat piracy in the Gulf of Aden and off the coast of Somalia—an unthinkable step a decade ago.

Third, China is becoming an important engine of the international economy, but also a significant contributor to the international economic system. Statistics from the World Bank show that China has contributed over 10% to world economic growth every year in recent years. In 1997 when the Asian financial crisis caused a dramatic devaluation of currencies in countries and regions close to it, China succeeded in keeping the renminbi exchange rate basically stable, which contributed greatly to regional economic stability and development.

Since the international financial crisis erupted in 2008, China has taken an active part in the G-20's efforts to build a global economic governance mechanism, promote reform of the international financial system, and facilitate multicountry macroeconomic policy coordination. China has also participated in international trade financing schemes and financial cooperation, making significant efforts to help develop a stable world economy.

Fourth, China has actively participated in international systems, formulating international governance rules and addressing global issues. China is a member of over 100 intergovernmental organizations, is party to over 300 international conventions, and always abides by international law and generally accepted principles. China is the first developing country to implement the National Climate Change Program.

China is also one of the countries that has made the greatest efforts to promote energy savings and emission reductions and that has made the fastest progress in developing new and renewable energy sources in recent years. Facing the challenges of global resource scarcity, China has chosen the strategy of promoting technology innovation, blazing a new path beyond resource grabbing and becoming the leader in green economic growth and green development around the world.

Fifth, China has not only settled historical land boundary issues with 12 neighbors through dialogue and negotiation, but has also made a constructive proposal to "shelve disputes and seek joint development" in the South China Sea, East China Sea, and the surrounding seas. China is doing its utmost to uphold peace and stability in these areas.

Cooperation during the transition of the international system should be the new basis of Sino-American relations. As stakeholders, the two countries once worked well together during the "Versailles-Washington system" and the "Yalta system," and we do so today. Building and reforming the current system has great potential to become the new foundation of cooperation and source of mutual trust in the Sino-American relationship.

China and America faced a common threat during the Cold War, which formed the strategic basis of their cooperation. Common interests made us interdependent. As we look forward to the future, although these two pillars of the Sino-American relationship are weakening, managing common challenges can become the new foundation. Both countries have to deal with the same problems, such as terrorism, climate change, nuclear proliferation, and energy. Not only can we find broad common interests by resolving common problems, but we can share more and more common ground in areas of the global commons such as cyber, maritime, outer space, and others.

We are entering into a new era where the United States will no longer be able to "call the shots" alone, as its power in an increasingly multipolar world begins to wane. China, seeking to be a regional power, has no intention of challenging American dominance either globally or in the Asia-Pacific area. As the Obama administration noted, it's time for the United States to build a multipartner world. China and the United States should work together to achieve the shared goal of making the international system better, which is the only correct choice that the two countries could make. I am very pleased that President Xi Jinping's idea of seeking a new type of major power relationship has been echoed by U.S. President Obama and former Secretary of State Hillary Clinton. This shows that decision makers in both countries want to work together to pursue a bright future in bilateral relations.

History has proven that only when countries cooperate can international problems be solved. The global anti-terrorism cooperation regime and the G-20 mechanism are widely considered to have benefitted by Sino-American cooperation. Frankly speaking, Sino-American cooperation cannot solve all international problems; however, nothing can be solved if we fail to cooperate. The "C2" theory raised by China during the fourth round of the Strategic and Economic Dialogue (our large, annual bilateral talks) should be a good model to frame the transition of the international system and the future cooperation of the two countries. Former State Councilor Dai Bingguo outlined this idea of China and the United States as "two [nations] in coordination bent on more communication, coordination and cooperation." Both countries should update their thinking according to this frame.

Here are some pieces of advice:

For the U.S. government, the biggest question is whether it will accept China's peaceful rise. In other words, is America willing to share power with China, especially in the Asia-Pacific? Washington needs to be open-minded and have a strategic vision to make the right choice. As the old saying goes, actions speak louder than words. Real actions are required to show sincerity.

For the Chinese government, the key point is whether it will share responsibility with the United States. This will require a revolutionary change of the traditional Chinese mindset and existing principles. For example, should "non-interference in others' internal affairs," China's long-standing diplomatic principle, be updated to keep pace with the times? Does China need to overcome its Middle Kingdom mentality (inward-looking, low-profile, reluctant to engage in international affairs, etc.), to become a more active participant in international affairs?

Both countries should respect each other's core interests and major concerns. History shows that if we properly handle these, Sino-American relations will grow smoothly. Otherwise, there will be trouble. If the U.S. government continues being problematic on sensitive issues, it is obvious that China will not devote itself to international cooperation with the United States.

Both countries should try to follow a new type of cooperation that deals with problems "case by case" and "step by step," rather than by working within a larger framework. Mutual trust can only be established gradually after a period of sustained cooperation. It is impossible to accomplish the whole task with one stroke.

I welcome your comments.

Sincerely,
Yuan Peng

• • •

Dear Yuan Peng,

It is truly a pleasure to be writing with you again. After all, it was our earlier published exchange that sparked the idea for this book.

I agree with a number of your observations, especially about the changing nature of international relations. Power is indeed growing more diffuse. Multiple nations are becoming influential, vocal actors on the world stage. Individuals and non-governmental entities are newly potent. Many challenges that face humanity—financial crises, nuclear proliferation, climate change, pandemic disease, terrorist attacks, food insecurity—are global to a degree they never were before and, as President Barack Obama has often noted, no one nation can solve them. Nations are now becoming interdependent for security as well as for economic growth. Unfortunately, interdependence is no guarantee of peace.

In the face of these complex trends, the fundamental questions Americans ask about the world remain simple: How are we going to solve these newly virulent global problems? How can we improve the lot of Americans and citizens everywhere? Solutions to global challenges depend upon three essential ingredients—leadership, contributions, and a rules-based architecture that fosters collective action. Let's look at each of these.

America has been leading in the international sphere for two generations: first in the Cold War and then as a superpower in a unipolar system. Even during this more recent period, America rarely acted on its own, generally preferring to share power by developing a consensus in the international community. But it was able to "call the shots," as you say, or at least many of them.

Though the way America chooses to exercise its leadership is changing, I would not expect it to fade anytime soon. There are three primary reasons for this. First, American decline is not as certain or likely as you may suppose. Of course American power is decreasing relative to other nations, like China, which are growing fast. But the United States retains some critical assets that ensure it will remain influential for a long time to come. These include some sources of power you mention, like our unparalleled military capacity, and some you do not. Among these is our flexibility—our system does self-correct, albeit slowly. Though we are stuck in a political quagmire, I see signs that Americans will do what we need to get back on a successful path. Moreover, America has a history of bouncing back from tough times including the Civil War, the Great Depression, and Vietnam. Neither China's fast rise nor America's inevitable decline are as certain as they seem to many. Political scientists have had a miserable track record of predicting the fate of nations, and I doubt they have gotten any better at it.

Second, there is still a firm political consensus in Washington that America *should* lead. Though Democratic and Republican politicians disagree on a wide variety of issues, they are united in believing that America can and should be influencing world events in ways that contribute to peace and prosperity. Problems need to be solved and without American focus and motivation, it is not clear they will be. From around the world, other nations welcome American leadership and will not join attempts to usher it out. As former Secretary of State Hillary Clinton said, "The world looks to us because America has the reach and resolve to mobilize the shared effort needed to solve problems on a global scale, in defense of our own interests, but also as a force for progress. In this, we have no rival."[2] America has a distinguished position in many corners as "the least distrusted" big power.

Even China is ambivalent about the prospect of American leadership diminishing, as you suggest, because what would come next? It's not clear that any one country or group of countries can or wants to step into the breach, leaving open the possibility of a zero-polar world where problems fester and deepen. Even though America may grow relatively less powerful, it is still the only nation that has the will and the ability to motivate a wide range of actors, forge a consensus and drive action.

As I said, though, America is altering how it leads to adapt to the times. Washington is encouraging leadership in others (despite prophecies of doom from vocal domestic critics). European nations and the Arab League were out in front in the diplomacy and military action to help the Libyan people rid themselves of Colonel Qaddafi, for example. South Korea and Mexico have hosted G-20 meetings. As Secretary Clinton said, "part of leading is making sure you get other people on the field."[3]

One of the reasons Washington wants other nations on the field is so they can contribute to a central purpose of American leadership: solving global problems and creating public goods—like a clean environment or safe sea lanes—that we all share. America cannot do it alone and should not have to. In a whole host of ways, from inducements to disincentives, Washington is asking others, China included, to give funds, time, and ideas. [4]

But the reason China should contribute more to solving global problems is not because America is asking. It's because as a major power, China will benefit more than most from the stability that comes from addressing threats. China should also want to sustain the system that has allowed it to convert the ingenuity and work ethic of its people into rapid economic growth. China is probably the No. 1 beneficiary of the existing international system.

China is also more able than most other nations to act. Its incredible growth rate, astronomic cash reserves, and track record of making successful investments in its national priorities show it has the capacity to contribute to the needs of the global order. China should set a positive example to those on the development path, showing that success means paying your share to give others the same opportunities. China's responsibility also flows from being a major contributor to at least two of the central challenges the world currently faces in macro-economic imbalances and global warming.

The existence and health of the system is not a permanent condition—it has to be nurtured in the face of multiple threats. Violators have to be punished, lessons learned, new frameworks adopted, and capacities strengthened. You assert that America's ability to control the international system is decreasing—that might be true in certain ways. But if it is, that is all the more reason that China has to contribute.

The last ingredient to global problem-solving is a rules-based system. Since its founding, the People's Republic of China (PRC) has integrated itself increasingly in the international system of rules, norms, and institutions. This is tremendously welcome. It helps China, the United States, the U.S.–China relationship, and the system. China is active in many international organizations, especially the United Nations. A Chinese national is the deputy managing director of the IMF. When a WTO decision goes against China, Beijing corrects the problem. At the G-20 leaders' forum, China is contributing constructively as a founding member.

These institutions, along with international laws and norms, are key to solving global problems. They spread out the burden of cooperation, ensure transparency in the problem-solving process, give stakeholders a voice, help nations develop habits of cooperation and attach a cost to breaking the rules. And only central nodes can coordinate dozens of countries acting at once. It's good news that China is using these institutions.

Thus, in some areas, China already is the "responsible stakeholder" America has encouraged it to become. I agree that China's contributions have been substantial in peacekeeping, in resolving the Darfur crisis, and more.

But in other areas, China is either not fully abiding by international rules and norms or playing as helpful a role as it could in handling violations of the rules by others. For example, it has focused on blocking action on Syria at the United Nations as opposed to ending the bloodshed. It could be putting more pressure on Pyongyang to find the path toward a lasting peace. On Iran's nuclear ambitions, Beijing has been quite engaged, but it has tended to want the international community to decrease rather than increase pressure on Tehran. When it comes to climate, China is to be commended for the impressive progress you cite, but as the world's largest carbon emitter, its pledges still do not amount to the decreases in emissions the science says are necessary to prevent the worst ravages of global warming. China's claims in the South China Sea appear to violate the UN Convention on the Law of the Sea. It does not protect intellectual property in accordance with international law. And, as China's leaders have admitted, China's human rights record also has a long way to go before it conforms to international treaties that China has signed.

In the economic realm, China is already more than just a stakeholder. It is a systemically important player because China's domestic economic policies affect the globe. So the pace at which it makes a critical transition from its export-driven growth model to a more domestic-consumption based, innovation economy is a critical component of China's global role. To the outside world, it seems painfully slow.

From China's point of view, there are good reasons for all of these positions. But from the point of view of the United States, or of any observer looking at the health of the international regimes of non-proliferation, human rights, climate, economic growth, and others, China's inaction, or lack of sufficient action, risks weakening and undermining the system. The unavoidable quandary of public goods is how to get all who enjoy them to contribute. Every country will be tempted to free-ride. China is too big for that now.

Let me be clear that I am not suggesting that China has to sacrifice its own interests. Countries act in their self-interest, period. Rather China should consider its own interests in light of others' and realize them in ways that make the international system stronger, not weaker.

You explain Beijing's choices to act robustly in some areas and not in others by saying that "China will not take global responsibilities in accordance with all the requirements of the United States." But these are not the wishes only of Americans. People in Rio, Sydney, and Seoul are just as passionate about climate change; residents of Berlin, Mexico City, and Cairo are similarly concerned about human rights. Many Asians are just as concerned about North Korea's nuclear weapons and many in the Middle East are just as concerned about Iran's nuclear ambitions as Americans are. People the world over want a global economy that can reliably raise living standards. America might be the one asking China to do more, but it asks on behalf of many.

You cite Taiwan arms sales and the South China Seas as two issues where America is acting as a "selective stakeholder" because we are not abiding by China's requirements for responsibility. You go on to warn, "If the U.S. government continues being problematic on sensitive issues, it is obvious that China will not devote itself to international cooperation with the U.S." I realize that Taiwan is of the highest-order importance to China. Our colleagues Jia Qingguo and Alan Romberg discuss the question in depth in Chapter 9. But in this century, there cannot be mutually exclusive core interests among nations. Those issues in which China has a core interest are also issues that the United States and other nations have a stake in, and vice versa.

Moreover, Taiwan's status simply does not have the same terrible implications for the globe as Iran's nuclear program, economic rebalancing, or climate change. If Iran succeeds in developing a nuclear weapons program in contravention of its UN obligations, that could well start a regional arms race, further destabilizing an already unstable region and calling into question the entire international non-proliferation regime. Rebalancing holds the key to prosperity for billions. Climate change could result in the death and displacement of millions.

In contrast, the issue of Taiwan's political status could well spark a confrontation between our countries, but it is the confrontation that would have global ripples, not Taiwan's status. Most people in the world care little about the question of Taiwan on the merits, but they are deeply concerned about economic growth, food security, climate change, and nuclear-armed terrorism. If China chooses not to cooperate on international challenges in order to protest America's policy on Taiwan, China itself and the whole globe will suffer.

Thus I would respectfully suggest that linking these policies is not the best approach for China. Curbing nuclear proliferation or fighting pirates is assisting the international community but it's also serving China's own interests. North Korea's nuclear program could cause a buildup of military assets in Northeast Asia that Beijing would not welcome. As for Iran, China is more affected than most by sharp, unpredictable rises in energy prices.

America certainly does not have a perfect record in upholding the international system. The United States has not ratified the Law of the Sea, and it should. But the fact is that the United States is abiding by all the provisions of the treaty anyway, because it reflects customary international law. The American interest in the South China Sea is not in any particular outcome, but to ensure a rules-based process for resolving disputes peacefully. That is not being a "selective stakeholder." On the contrary, it is entirely consistent with a desire to strengthen the international system, uphold the collective right to freedom of navigation, and preserve the peace. When nations cannot agree on how to interpret the rules, finding a fair process is critical. Wu Xinbo and Mike Green take up this issue in Chapter 10.

In any case, I'm glad to hear you say that China will contribute "based on the norms of international law, on its own strengths and capabilities, and on the expectations of the international community." China's own strengths and capabilities are significant and so are the expectations of the international community. I'd like to know more: How does China make judgments about when to contribute?

I sympathize with your point that China needs to psychologically adjust to its new station, especially given its domestic challenges. It is not easy to come of age as a pivotal power in this modern era. After all, for centuries, great powers had only to focus on being stronger militarily than the next power. In the early 20th century, as the United States became a global superpower, there weren't many institutions to join or rules to follow, nor a massive global economy nor multiple global threats.

Now we live in a different time, when global warming poses enormous risks, economies are hopelessly intertwined, and pandemics can travel as fast as an airplane. That is why the demands on China are different. These are the facts of life for a modern power. They are not obligations dreamed up by the West to constrain China's rise, as I've heard a number of Chinese experts suggest.

So what is the answer to a better U.S.–China relationship and a more secure, prosperous globe at the same time? We both come to the same conclusion—Beijing and Washington should exercise their joint responsibility as major powers to tackle challenges within a rules-based framework. Together the United States and China should work to reform and strengthen the system. If both nations operate within the rules, that will also help contain our rivalry, allow us to better predict how the other will act, and help our relationship remain peaceful and constructive.

Unfortunately, the fact that we need to cooperate does not mean that we will. America and China agree on many high-order goals, but not on how to get there, who bears the costs, and who has to change. How do we begin? I like your idea of "case by case" and "step by step." We can work on relatively small, but concrete, operational issues. Areas like coordinating disaster relief, pursuing drug traffickers, and conducting scientific research hold promise. The United States and China already do some of this, but we can do more.

I agree with you that we can build trust by working side by side. My understanding of China's position was that we should first establish a trusting relationship and only then could we collaborate closely on issues together. But your idea is sensible. Perhaps it is best to start by the United States and China working together closely on discrete challenges and in doing so develop "tactical trust." Perhaps this can evolve into strategic trust over time.

I look forward to your thoughts.

Best,
Nina

• • •

Dear Nina,

Thanks for the frank and comprehensive response to my argument. I agree with many of your comments and think you are among the most objective and rational American observers of U.S.–China relations. However, I still disagree with you on some issues.

When I say non-Western powers (including China) are emerging while Western countries (including the United States) are relatively declining, I have two frames of reference in mind. One is historical. America became the world's No. 1 economy in 1890. If China's GDP surpasses it sometime in the 2020s (as estimated by the IMF, World Bank, and many economists), it will be the first time in 120 years that the American economy is no longer the largest. It was also historic when China's GDP surpassed Japan's in 2010 to become No. 1 in Asia and the second-largest in the world. This marked the first time since the Sino–Japanese War of 1894 that another East Asian power surpassed Japan. Even if GDP means less than comprehensive national strength, relatively speaking, these are still major historic events that carry significant symbolic weight.

From a global perspective, we also see a shift. Today many middle powers are changing the landscape of the world. Countries such as South Korea, Turkey, Indonesia, Mexico, and Saudi Arabia are playing important roles in transforming international institutions. Non-Western and non-governmental powers are playing more important and visible roles than anytime in the past century. This is another reason why I suggested that Western powers are declining.

However, these observations cannot change two other basic realities. First, even if Western control of international affairs is decreasing, the United States will still continue to be the sole superpower for the next 20 to 30 years. Not only because its natural, military, intelligence, scientific, cultural, cyber, geopolitical, strategic, alliance, and thinking powers are still the strongest in the world, but because, after recent financial crises, the relative powers of both the European Union and Japan are decreasing, which in turn will force the European Union and Japan to rely more heavily on America rather than pursue strategic independence. This will be a decisive reason that America will maintain its superpower status. Second, even though non-Western countries' relative power is rising, many of them still face a series of challenges. For example, in the next 10 to 20 years, China will have to overcome the "middle-income trap," negotiate the upheavals of further urbanization, accomplish a "well-off society in an all-round way," protect the environment, ensure adequate natural resources, and more. Any single one of these problems could slow down or even reverse the course of China's rise. That is why China will still focus on its domestic and internal affairs for a long time to come. And that is why I describe China as a "reluctant No. 2." It's not to downplay or escape responsibility. It's because of the brutal reality of China's own problems.

Although China faces serious challenges in the future, that does not mean China will long be a free-rider of the existing international system.

I agree that China has benefited from the system, but I don't agree that China "is probably the No. 1 beneficiary of the existing international system," as you mentioned—not only because that statement is hard to quantify, but because the magic weapon of China's success in the past 30 years has been the hard work of the Chinese people, the right strategic choices by the Chinese leadership and the adjustments the Chinese Communist Party have made.

Actually, the United States benefits a lot by welcoming China into the international system and into institutions like the WTO. China's participation not only endorses the legitimacy of America's world leadership, but it also means America's own economy stays prosperous. This is obvious from the recent financial crisis. Without China's market, and its purchase of America's national debt, it's hard to imagine where the American economy would be. After Obama came into power, 48 of the 50 states increased their exports to China. China is also the key to President Obama's strategy to double U.S. exports. More than 20% of Apple's products are sold in China. So it is fairer to say that both the United States and China benefit from China's joining the existing international system.

It is our common duty to maintain and reform the system. But given the differences between our political and social systems, ideology and values, culture and histories, geopolitical conditions, economies, and most importantly, our levels of development, it is more difficult for the United States and China to cooperate than it is for the United States and its Western allies to do the same. What can we do to improve our effective and meaningful cooperation? I think mutual trust is the key. I don't want to link U.S. policies on Taiwan, the South China Sea, the Diaoyu Islands, and human rights to China's contribution to the international system, but if the United States keeps hurting our national interest in these areas, how can we shape a good environment for more significant cooperation?

China's major external concern remains sovereignty and territory disputes. Its interactions with its neighbors Japan and the Philippines are tense. But American policies are giving Chinese the strong impression that the United States is intentionally using the disputes to achieve its own strategic goals in the Asia-Pacific area. For example, America emphasizes its neutral stance in sovereignty disputes regarding the Diaoyu Islands, called the Senkakus by Japan, while at the same time declaring that the U.S.–Japan Security Treaty covers the Diaoyu Islands, conducting endless joint military exercises with Japan, and deploying advanced radar systems and weapons in Japan.

This self-contradictory policy may have a logic for Americans but it has triggered anti-American sentiment in China. Our colleagues are discussing regional issues in depth in Chapter 10, but these disputes are relevant for our discussion here because their unsatisfactory resolution undoubtedly hinders China and U.S. cooperation on other, more important issues affecting the whole world. If and how America will be truly neutral on territorial issues will be a test for the establishment of mutual trust between our two countries, which is a precondition for future cooperation on bigger issues, such as the Korean Penninsula nuclear issue, which is more consequential for security in Northeast Asia. Similarly, trade protectionism in the United States affects the relationship. The 2012 U.S. presidential election was like a "China show" with both candidates battling over who could compete more with China. Recent cases like Huawei and Zhongxin where the U.S. government stopped or protested Chinese investments have served to remind Chinese that even if China wants to invest in America to contribute to the American economy and employment, Americans will still view Chinese corporations as the "devil" due to an outdated Cold War, ideological mindset. Can we imagine the two countries cooperating well in the G-20, IMF, and WTO under these circumstances?

Chinese President Xi Jinping initiated the concept of a "new model of major power relations" to guide future Sino-American relations when, as vice president, he visited the United States in early 2012. I understand this to mean first, that China won't ruin the existing international system through wars; second, that China won't pursue a Cold War with the United States and won't challenge American world leadership and its Asian-Pacific presence; and, third, that China hopes to find a win-win or non-zero-sum way to cooperate with America in addressing world problems and shaping the future world. The essence of the initiative is to communicate, coordinate, and cooperate with the United States in the Asia-Pacific region and across the globe in general. I do hope this attracts more positive response from American officials and strategists.

The last question is how the United States and China can cooperate. I'll try to answer the question in this way. First, at the level of bilateral issues, both China and the United States should establish some basic mutual trust and also develop some new arrangements to deal with sensitive issues. I agree that mutual trust can only be established through concrete actions, but I also believe that agreements and statements matter. Mechanisms like the Strategic and Economic Dialogue annual meeting are still important. But we need a roadmap as soon as possible to guide our future interactions in the Asia-Pacific area. With America "back to Asia" in a comprehensive and strategic way with its "rebalance," while China is rising in the same region, it will be much easier for the two to end up in a conflict triggered by an accident or misunderstanding without a new roadmap. These questions should be addressed: How can we draw "redlines" in maritime conduct? How should we deal with the parallel arrangements of U.S.-led bilateral alliances and the Trans-Pacific Partnership on one side and the existing arrangements China has already been involved in in the region, such as ASEAN's "10+1" and "10+3," and the Shanghai Cooperation Organization, on the other? How can we find a win-win-win solution for the United States, China, and all the relevant "third countries" in the region? Would trilateral dialogues like the United States–China–Japan, the United States–China–Russia, the United States–China–India, or the United States–China–Australia help?

At the level of global issues, the United States and China need to find a new foundation for cooperation. During the Cold War, we had a common threat. After the Cold War, we had a common economic interest. But now, it seems we have lost the engine driving our bilateral relations. Henry Kissinger and others have suggested that dealing with "common problems" should be the foundation for cooperation in the future. I think this is wise and realistic. At least three areas are ripe for future cooperation. One is to jointly reshape and rebuild the international system with the other powers. The G-20 is a very good start. A second possibility is to jointly develop new rules and regulations for the "global commons," such as cyber, maritime, and space. Even though we may have differences, if we can agree on common rules, we can provide a huge space for cooperation. The last area of cooperation is to deal jointly with new problems such as climate change, energy and natural resources, food shortages, terrorism, and others. When it comes to traditional security issues like those concerning Iran, Syria, and North Korea, though we have different philosophies and opinions of the best methods to deal with those, we should remember that we are pursuing the same goal, peace and stability of the world.

You asked how China makes judgments about when to contribute. It's very easy to understand China's motivation to contribute to the international system. It is a "3 in 1" answer: when it benefits the peace and stability of the region and the world, when it benefits the countries suffering from various problems, and when it benefits China's national interest.

Both the United States and China are in a period of political transition and economic transformation. Over the next three to five years, both will inevitably focus more on domestic matters than on international ones, though the changing world needs big power cooperation to lead to a bright future. As the No. 1 and No. 2 world economies and two of the five permanent members of the United Nations Security Council, the United States and China should not shirk their responsibilities but instead should bond to cooperate.

Sincerely,

Yuan Peng

• • •

Dear Yuan Peng,

We agree on many points and, as always, your perspective is clear and informative. Power is indeed flowing to more countries and to more non-state actors. And, yes, of course the United States benefits by China joining the international system. I acknowledged that. Many countries do. We also agree that that system is worth preserving—our joint project on G-20 reform is a concrete demonstration of this belief.[5] Greater understanding between the United States and China on the questions you raise about the Asia-Pacific would be welcome and could help reduce tensions.

I continue to disagree on the linkage you make, however, between individual issues on which our countries disagree and their ability to cooperate on shared global problems. You describe a number of actions America is taking that deeply trouble China, including Washington's position on the Diaoyu/Senkaku Islands, and the tone of the China discourse during the last U.S. presidential election. I am not going to address these here, but suffice it to say I could describe a similar set of things that China is doing that deeply trouble America—massive stealing of commercial assets through cyber-espionage, the extremely costly failure to protect American intellectual property in China (which undermines China's desire to promote "technological innovation"), and blocking solutions to the Syria crisis in the UN Security Council, to name a few. In these cases, our two countries see the issues quite differently and have narratives to explain our positions that make sense to ourselves but not to the other. When it comes to these issues, suspicion of each other's motives is rife on both sides, with vocal minorities in each country assuming the worst about each other.

In your essay, referring to this "bad blood," if you will, you ask, "Can we imagine the two countries cooperating well in the G-20, IMF, and WTO under these circumstances?" My answer is an emphatic *yes*. We have to. And if we cannot imagine it, then we are stuck in the zero-sum thinking that you reject. America and China must be able to compartmentalize their differences and move forward where they do see eye to eye. That is the only way big powers in the modern era will be able to make any progress on global challenges because, for the foreseeable future, we will have profound differences. Disagreements will inevitably hinder cooperation to some degree—officials are humans, after all, and cannot build impenetrable walls in their minds around issues. Deep strategic trust would certainly facilitate cooperation, and we should continue to find creative ways to foster it. But if China and the United States wait for resolutions to their major differences to act, in the meantime, the international system will fall apart and global problems will spin out of control. Both peoples will be far worse off. China would end up needlessly sacrificing one set of interests for another.

Our publics may not always understand this approach. Some Chinese may ask: "How can Beijing cooperate with Washington on climate or North Korea when Washington is supporting Japan's territorial claims or preventing reunification with Taiwan or stirring up trouble in the South China Sea?" Some Americans will demand, "How can Washington cooperate with Beijing on clean energy or financial stability when Beijing is stealing our secrets or supporting the dangerous regime in Pyongyang or bullying our allies to assert its maritime claims?" It is our governments' job, and ours, to continue to explain why bilateral relations are so important and to make clear that disagreements, even fierce ones, are par for the course in a complex relationship between pivotal powers. Tension is normal. We have to be very careful, however, that nationalism does not raise the political cost of a peaceful path for China and the United States insurmountably high.

When it comes to global cooperation, I like your formulation for jointly reforming the international system with others, developing new rules for the global commons and addressing global problems like climate change. That is a useful menu, and we should work in all these areas.

In terms of reforming the system and addressing global problems, you describe China as a "reluctant No. 2" "not to downplay or to escape responsibility" but because of the "brutal reality of China's own problems." I appreciate that. It cannot be easy to be arriving on the global stage and still developing at the same time. But the global challenges are what they are. Problems like climate change or nuclear proliferation define the scope of contributions necessary. Someone needs to take the risks and bear the costs so humanity, including Chinese and American people, does not suffer terribly. What other country has more capacity and resources than China? The United States, Europe, and Japan, you might say. But though these nations are still wealthy, their growth is stubbornly slow or non-existent, whereas in China and other emerging economies it is going strong. In other words, capacity and resources are lacking everywhere, and there is plenty of blame to go around. All nations need to step up and offer the most they can. China's "most" is more than most other countries, and it has more at stake too.

You write that China decides when to contribute to the international system based on three factors: "when it benefits the peace and stability of the region and the world, when it benefits the countries suffering from various problems, and when it benefits China's national interest." This reminds me of a test for global responsibility that I once suggested. It evaluates a nation's actions according to three criteria:

- Will the action in question benefit the global community as well as the country?
- Does the action strengthen the international system or weaken it?
- Is the action enough, given the magnitude of the problem and the capacity of others to act?

While you and I would evaluate differently whether certain actions that China takes benefit the international community or just China, and whether they strengthen the international system, it's really the last question that we are debating here—one of sufficiency. That is why forums like the G-20 are so important: they provide a setting in which our leaders can try to assign responsibility to every major economy, in a fair way, so that progress can continue.

You mention the need to develop international rules, and I could not agree more. I want to build on your thoughts there, because they connect to another concept you raised of a "new model of major power relations." It's good that both Beijing and Washington are actively thinking about how to avoid the historical pattern of conflict between a rising and an established power. To do this, in my view, it is crucial to determine a plausible vision for the future relationship. On both sides, we lack imagination about what this relationship could become other than more and more confrontational.

Here is where rules come in. A peaceful future that I can imagine is based on the idea of China and the United States, along with other major and emerging powers, embedded in a matrix of international rules, norms, and institutions. This architecture would draw boundaries around the two nations' natural rivalry. When countries can be sure that the rules are fair and followed, competition need not be hostile. Forums for dispute resolution—such as the one in the WTO—can channel frictions. And collaboration will be easier when countries know that they are shouldering a fair share of the burden along with other nations.

So your idea about the United States and China, along with others, developing more international rules is important not only to address conflicts related to the global commons but also because it could become the very framework in which the bilateral relationship itself operates. Some analysts in both our countries might argue that rules can never trump power. Can rules prevent a powerful nation from taking an action it has firmly decided to take? No. But rules, norms, and institutions do shape what choices a state will see as in its best interest. International governance is evolving, because it must. Nations cannot solve 21st-century problems with 15th-century methods. As you describe in your opening essay, the world has transformed. Today's international system is flawed, but it is robust and like nothing that has come before. Resolutions in the United Nations carry real force—they influence what nations do. Countries, even ours, choose to take disputes to the WTO and are willing to be bound by its determinations. Agreements on human trafficking, pandemic disease, non-proliferation, marine protection, and hundreds of others have, without doubt, affected national laws and national actions in the real world.

It's critical that those who understand the value of the international system push back on the narrow nationalism in each of our countries that suggests great countries should not be bound by international rules. In a world that grows smaller by the day, in which no power alone can solve big problems, that kind of thinking will doom us to a dark future.

The three principles you suggest as elements of new major power relations—that China won't ruin the existing international system through wars, won't challenge American world leadership and its Asian-Pacific presence, and hopes to cooperate with America (and others no doubt) in addressing world problems—are very constructive. On the U.S. side, counterparts might be these: first, the United States welcomes and respects a prosperous, successful, rule-abiding China; second, the United States seeks to resolve all disagreements involving China peacefully, respectfully, through dialogue, and according to international rules and norms; and, third, the United States welcomes China's peaceful and constructive involvement and leadership in regional and world affairs.

I've enjoyed our exchange, Yuan Peng, and hope that these discussions play a part, however small, in creating a path for our countries to coexist in peace and solve common, global challenges together.

Best,

Nina

CLIMATE AND CLEAN ENERGY

KELLY SIMS GALLAGHER

Tufts University

QI YE

Tsinghua University

Framing questions: *What is the most likely trajectory of each country's greenhouse gas emissions? How does each country's actions or inactions on climate play into the politics of the issue in the other country? In what ways will each country likely contribute to—and hinder—international cooperation to address climate change? How do China and America see each other's global roles and responsibilities when it comes to climate? What is China's assessment of America's energy policies, and vice versa? What does the other country not understand well enough about local conditions that make action difficult? What are the ultimate solutions? How well are collaborations on clean energy working, and what promise do they hold?*

•   •   •

Dear Qi Ye,

I am sure you will agree that it is deeply disappointing that China and the United States are no closer to a formal treaty on climate change than they were in 1997 right after the Kyoto Protocol was adopted. On the bright side, the July 2013 agreement between President Xi Jinping and President Barack Obama demonstrates that climate change can be a fruitful area for U.S.-China cooperation. Domestically, the Chinese central government's recent domestic policies and initiatives related to climate change are exciting and encouraging. It appears that the central government in China has decided that climate change is an urgent threat that must be addressed. In the United States, there is little leadership from Congress, but many states and municipalities are enacting laws and regulations to regulate carbon emissions and support clean energy. On June 25, 2013, President Obama committed himself to implementing executive actions that would make good on his pledge to reduce U.S. emissions by 17% below 2005 levels by 2020. While there has been virtually no progress in the international negotiations, it is remarkable that both China and the United States have begun to make major investments in clean energy. Our two countries have been the top two investors in clean energy for the past few years.

As you know perfectly well, the Kyoto Protocol was the first international treaty containing binding commitments for industrialized countries to reduce their greenhouse gas emissions. Even though the United States actively participated in the negotiations, the U.S. Senate refused to ratify it on the grounds that it was unfair that other major emitters, especially China and India, did not have similar commitments. The reason that China did not have the same obligations as the United States was that it was, and still is, a developing country with tens of millions of people living on less than $1.25 per day, and negotiators had agreed that developing countries had "common but differentiated responsibilities" (CBDR). This term was included in the original climate change agreement in 1992 that was ratified by the U.S. Senate. Most people, myself included, believed at the time that after the industrialized countries had taken the first steps to reduce emissions, developing countries, including China, would follow their lead. It hasn't worked out that way. The Kyoto Protocol spurred some countries, mainly in Europe, to greatly reduce their emissions. The United States managed to prevent major growth in its emissions, while China's emissions tripled between 1997 and 2012.[1]

We are now in a situation where global emissions have grown faster than anyone expected, largely because of China's explosive economic growth (see Figure 6.1), and the threat of disastrous climatic change is very real. As the two largest overall emitters accounting for about 45% of global emissions, China (29%) and the United States (16%) must urgently reduce their emissions as soon as possible for the sake of future generations of the planet. Even though I'm sure you must believe that it simply isn't fair, China now must work just as hard as the United States to reduce emissions if we are to have a chance to prevent devastating climate change. We are already seeing the emerging consequences of global warming. High summer temperatures coupled with drought are causing the northern latitudes to experience devastating wildfires. In 2010, after enduring the hottest July ever recorded in Russian history, wildfires spread across Russia, leading to an estimated 56,000 dead and $15 billion in damages. These fires ignited again in the summer of 2012 with an even greater extent of wildfire damage. In the United States, Colorado experienced the most destructive wildfire in its history after experiencing the hottest and driest June since records began. The United States experienced one of the worst droughts in history in 2012, with more than half of the United States in moderate-to-severe

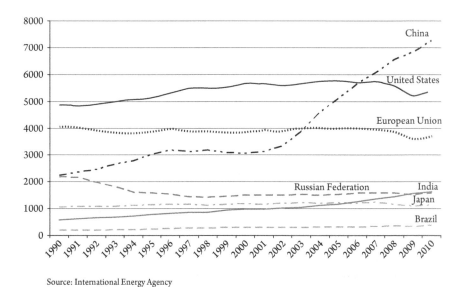

Source: International Energy Agency

FIGURE 6.1 Carbon Dioxide Emissions of Major Emitters, in Megatons

drought. This drought led to higher prices for corn, soy, and wheat, and the need to drastically shrink the U.S. cattle herd because ranchers could not graze them or afford to buy hay. In the Arctic, the area covered by sea ice shrank again to record lows in July 2012. Meanwhile, China experienced the worst flooding in 60 years during the summer of 2010, with Beijing receiving six months' worth of rain in a single day. These crises are consistent with the consequences of climate change, and they are expected to become much more severe and frequent in the absence of decisive steps to reduce global emissions of greenhouse gases.

To reduce the risks of climate change (such as loss of Arctic ice, sea-level rise, droughts, wildfires, extreme weather, heat waves), most scientists agree that it would be wise to limit global warming to 2°C. If we want to have a good chance of doing so, the world only has an emissions budget of 890 billion tons of CO_2. Between 2000 and 2006 alone, we used up 234 billion tons (25% of the budget), so at the current rate of emissions, which is faster than ever due to China's rapid growth, we will exhaust our global budget between 2024 and 2039, after which we would have to have zero emissions, which is pretty hard to imagine.[2] Given this hard time constraint, we really have very little time to reduce our emissions. Because of its historical emissions, I believe that the United States has an obligation to help China to accelerate its efforts in order to give the world a better chance to stay within the global emissions budget.

These two countries have a number of shared challenges, interests, advantages, and opportunities, but they also have some strikingly different challenges as well. The first shared challenge is the fact that China and the United States are the top overall emitters of greenhouse gases. China surpassed the United States in 2007 to become the biggest current emitter, but in terms of cumulative emissions since the beginning of the Industrial Revolution, and in per-capita terms (see Figure 6.2), the United States is still a far larger emitter. Nevertheless, pressure is rising on both countries to act responsibly given the awful consequences for the rest of the world if climate change is not slowed down and managed.

Second, both countries still rely heavily on the most carbon-intensive of fuels: coal. China is the world's largest producer, consumer, and importer of coal, and the United States has the largest coal reserves in the world. It is natural and reasonable from an energy security point of view for our countries to want to use their coal, but a true disaster from an environmental point of

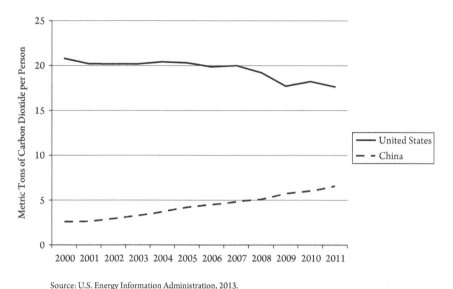

Source: U.S. Energy Information Administration, 2013.

FIGURE 6.2 Per Capita Carbon Dioxide Emissions, in Metric Tons

view unless both countries aggressively pursue carbon capture and storage (which neither is doing).

As the two largest economies in the world, the third shared challenge is how to pursue economic development, competitiveness, and rising prosperity without wrecking the climate. When it comes to implementation, this challenge is totally different for China and the United States given the structures of their economies—China still relies on an export-led, heavy manufacturing model, whereas the U.S. economy is based more on services. But the shared challenge is how to achieve more sustainable prosperity. Both economies are relatively energy-inefficient compared with Japan and Europe, although China's economy is much less energy efficient even than the United States' economy. Improving energy efficiency would be good for their economies (less resource-intensive), the environment (less pollution), and national security (less need to import fuels).

I recognize that tackling the climate challenge is exceptionally difficult for China. China's reliance on coal is much greater than in the United States, with coal accounting for 71% of the primary energy supply there compared with just 20% in the United States. China has many more very poor people than the United States, and thus the government needs to be highly focused on poverty alleviation and economic development. You are the expert on central-local relations, but it seems to me that although the central government is very committed to addressing climate change, it still has a difficult time enforcing environmental regulations and convincing local governments to improve energy efficiency or to reduce emissions.

In the United States, the problem is mainly a political one. Highly conservative Republicans are ideologically anti-science and anti-environmental protection, and have no sense of global responsibility for the climate change problem. They likewise have an absolute aversion to the use of a tax or any other policy instrument that might increase government revenue (even if it were recycled to the public in the form of income tax reductions). The Senate structure in which two Senators are elected from each state gives an outsized influence to these conservative Republicans, who are joined by conservative Democrats from coal-producing states to block climate change legislation. Even as an American, it's hard for me to understand why the Republicans are so violently opposed to climate mitigation, especially since the Republican Party used to champion environmental conservation. It is particularly puzzling when one realizes that at the state level, there is plenty of Republican support for clean energy because 39 states have adopted either a renewable portfolio standard or a goal. Texas, for example, while a majority Republican state, has one of the nation's most aggressive renewable portfolio standards, which were enacted when former President George W. Bush was governor. Colorado, an independent-to-conservative state, was the first to pass a law requiring the production of renewable energy, and as of 2012, it was producing more than 15% of its energy from wind. Despite the perceived economic benefits of cleaner energy at the state level, many Republicans in Congress are aligned with fossil fuel interests, some are genuinely fearful about the consequences of clean energy in terms of changes to their way of life, and some are willfully ignorant about the science.

In addition to these formidable challenges, shared and different, China and the United States also have shared interests. As the two biggest energy-consuming countries, they are both vulnerable to supply disruptions and could cooperate more to diminish the threat of them. Energy imports account for large fractions of their total import bills. Both countries are projected to suffer greatly from the impacts of climate change, whether it is the loss of freshwater supplies from glacial retreat on the Tibetan plateau in China or wildfires and droughts in the American heartland such as those we've seen in Colorado, where I grew up. Finally, both countries have shared interest in economic prosperity in the other country given the integration of their economies.

My American colleague, Bill Chandler, has called the current situation between China and the United States a "suicide pact."[3] It's true that if both countries wait for the other to lead, then there is virtually no chance of success. I have come to believe, however, that the Chinese leadership has already decided it cannot wait for the United States any longer. I am grateful and relieved to see that with China's Renewable Energy Law, its Golden Sun and solar feed-in tariff policies, its wind concession programs, its energy efficiency targets and programs like the Top 1000 enterprise program, and its recent decision to set a target for reducing carbon intensity, China's leaders are beginning to take decisive action. Still, it must be hard for the leaders to justify these actions in the face of recalcitrance from the United States. Meanwhile, the legacy of the Byrd–Hagel resolution that prevented Senate ratification of the Kyoto Protocol in 1997 (based on the argument that China was not sufficiently obligated to take action against global warming) still has a chilling effect on U.S. climate legislation even though I think it could be convincingly argued that China's effort to date has been larger than the U.S. effort. On the other hand, China and the United States have taken some important steps forward during the Obama administration by establishing a joint U.S.–China Clean Energy Research Center (CERC) for joint research, development, and demonstration (RD&D) on buildings, transportation, and advanced coal. This center allows the countries to pool their research dollars to accomplish more, to experiment in novel contexts, and to introduce firms and researchers to each other. While the funding for the center is very small, it is an initiative in the right direction.

I believe there is a path that could lead to a more fundamental solution. A major impediment has been the lack of linkage to other issues that are important to each country. What does China want from the United States? In terms of climate change, China wants the United States to make a serious commitment to reduce emissions, and also reasonable access to low-carbon technology. China is also committed to negotiating an international agreement under the auspices of United Nations Framework Convention on Climate Change (UNFCCC) (which the U.S. Senate *did* ratify). China believes that the principles enshrined in the UNFCCC are important and should guide any international agreement. Beyond climate change, China would like its investments to be welcomed in the United States. The United States only receives 2% of Chinese foreign direct investment, in part because some previous Chinese investment efforts have been firmly rebuffed.[4] As U.S. business executive David Marchick has argued, Chinese investment in the United States would expose Chinese companies to Western standards of corporate governance, reporting, and accounting, boost U.S. exports to China (as Chinese companies look to their U.S. operations to export back home), and create jobs in the United States as Chinese investors generate economic activity in the United States.[5] My guess is that China's leadership would also welcome greater consideration as a global power.

Turning to the United States and what it wants from China, in the climate domain, U.S. firms want equal access to China's clean technology market, which is now the largest in the world. Most U.S. firms do not feel that they have the same access as Chinese firms. U.S. firms would also appreciate greater access to Chinese capital given that finance in the United States continues to be a big constraint for U.S. firms. Beyond the climate change issue, U.S. leaders, and especially the Senate Republicans, would welcome specific mechanisms to reduce the U.S. trade deficit with China. A commitment to continued RMB appreciation would be applauded too, as would reduced cyber-espionage by Chinese actors.

I have a specific idea in mind that I will share with you in my next letter, but the key point is that the United States and China need to negotiate directly. Given the aversion that the current Senate Republicans have to ratifying UN-sponsored treaties, China needs to be practical and relax its insistence on negotiating only under the auspices of the UNFCCC. Once the two countries reach an agreement, it could be brought back under the UN umbrella if and when the timing is more auspicious. As the two largest emitters, the United States and China must lead the way together, as equal partners, in the quest to protect the planet for future generations.

I look forward hearing from you.

With warm regards,
Kelly Sims Gallagher

• • •

Dear Kelly,

Thank you for your letter regarding U.S.–China collaboration on climate change and green development. I found your analysis of the critical importance for our two countries to take more proactive measures toward alleviation of global climate challenges fascinating. I believe you and I are in fundamental agreement on these issues. I even joked with Hairan, our mutual friend, that it would be hard for you and me to find something to debate about in this particular discussion! Nevertheless, I will take this opportunity to clarify some of my views. I assume that you and I agree that neither of us represents an official, national position or intends to defend or criticize a national position. We are trying to provide helpful analyses in our role as scholars.

I am in complete agreement with you that the case is clear and strong for nations the world over, and of course, for the United States and China, to take action. The course of international negotiations has not met the expectations of concerned citizens and has lagged behind the rapid change in global climate and human development. It is understandable that some people feel pessimistic about the future of this "top-down" approach. But it is important to make progress down every avenue to tackle the unprecedented challenge of our age. Humanity should not underestimate the challenges the world faces right now. We badly need optimism and a "jubilant spirit" to continue our hard work on a global agreement.

In 2012, the world celebrated the 20th Anniversary of the United Nations Conference on Environment and Development held in Rio de Janeiro in 1992. Personally, I think that the Rio Conference was quite an amazing achievement. It produced agreements on major global environmental challenges such as climate change, biodiversity, and desertification. What was so impressive was the level of political will and leadership shown by nations and their leaders. As people get ready for further negotiations today, they really should look back at the commitment their predecessors made 20 years ago and ponder what their foresight means to us today.

Indeed, the world was very different 20 years ago. When the world leaders met in Rio de Janeiro in 1992, the West was still in the thrall of winning the Cold War, the collapse of the Berlin Wall, and the decisive victory of Desert Storm. Back then, there was no such thing as "emerging economies" the way we refer to them today. And in 1992, the United States' carbon emissions alone were more than 20% of the world total. From that point of view, the West was largely responsible for the global warming problem, as 20% of the world population had emitted 80% of greenhouse gases historically. Developing countries had to bear a disproportionate share of the consequences. Therefore, it seemed quite reasonable for the Rio framework to require countries to take action under the principle of common but differentiated responsibilities, under which it is understood that while all countries have a responsibility to act, developed countries have to take the lead and do more to address their emissions. It is this very principle that served as a cornerstone for the global agreement on UNFCCC in 1992 and the Kyoto Protocol in 1997. Because of its critical importance, this principle was reiterated in the declaration at the Rio+20 in June 2012.

However, in practice, the principle of CBDR is threatened in international climate negotiations. The Durban Platform of 2011 effectively neglected the principle. And in his commencement speech at Dartmouth's 2012 graduation ceremony, Mr. Todd Stern, U.S. Special Envoy on Climate Change, emphasized common (not differentiated) responsibility. He remarked that "[d]ifferentiation among parties is an accepted premise of climate diplomacy. But in the world of the Durban Platform, it can no longer be the differentiation of two distinct categories of countries; rather, it will have to be the differentiation of a continuum, with each country expected to act vigorously in accordance with its evolving circumstances, capabilities and responsibilities."[6]

While I understand the criticisms of the principle of CBDR, it is not obsolete. It was and still is critically important because it provides a foundation for social fairness and environmental justice, something that you and I emphasize when we teach our respective students. With this principle, all countries can rally together toward a common goal to tackle the global environmental challenges as they did in 1992. As a result of some parties attempting to abandon this principle, we have seen more divisions among countries than agreement. This is the big lesson we must learn from the Rio Conference and from the bumpy course of international negotiations in the last decade. Because of the importance of this principle, I think the United States and China should consider reaffirming their support of it in the negotiations ahead.

Some argue that China and emerging economies have been trying to hide behind the CBDR principle to avoid making binding commitments to control greenhouse gas emissions. Yet, this argument is not supported by the facts. A major difference between the world today and that of 20 years ago is the emergence of a few fast-growing economies in the developing world. These economies are big largely because of their large populations. While they have not become rich enough to be considered members of the developed world, their influence has been growing in political and economic arenas worldwide. Their environmental footprints have also grown considerably over the last two decades. Therefore, these large emerging economies will have to take on responsibilities appropriate for their environmental impact as well as their economic and technological capabilities. In other words, the principle of CBDR applies just as much to these countries as it does to developed countries. Because it is fundamental, the principle should apply to every party of the Convention. No country can hide behind the principle.

With the principle reaffirmed, all parties will have the political will to move forward rather than constantly looking back. For example, you mentioned in your letter that many have criticized the U.S. withdrawal from the Kyoto Protocol as a step backward for the global effort on climate change. In particular, many attribute this failure to former President George W. Bush. While there may be some degree of truth in this charge,[7] it is not useful now to blame anyone. We have to move forward.

Even President Obama has had huge difficulty in rallying enough support for any kind of national legislation on climate change. He simply could not get enough votes to deliver on the promise he made in his 2008 presidential campaign. However, he did not give up. With his executive order, the EPA is now able to regulate carbon dioxide emissions just like it does other pollutants. Leadership matters.

You also pointed out there have been numerous state and local initiatives that have been flourishing all over your country. These represent exciting progress. Thus, despite the slow progress on a global agreement, the world is moving forward in addressing climate change, however incrementally. National, state, and local initiatives have been critical in taking the lead. This is true in the United States, and it is also true in China.

It took a while for the Chinese leadership to finally prioritize the issue of climate change on the national political and policy agenda. In my view, China's 11th Five-Year Plan (FYP) for economic growth promulgated in 2006 was a turning point. Because the top leaders in the nation reached a political consensus, the central government could formulate policies and act quickly and decisively. In June 2007, it established the National Leading Group on Climate Change with Premier Wen Jiabao as the head. Three months later, President Hu Jintao announced at the Asia-Pacific Leaders Summit that China would develop toward a low-carbon economy.

Then in November 2007, the State Council published a regulatory scheme developed by the National Development and Reform Commission (NDRC) on data collection, monitoring, and performance evaluation of energy-saving actions of governments and enterprises. This landmark regulation established the so-called energy-saving target responsibility system, a scheme for implementing energy-saving policies in China. I compare it to the European Union's Emissions Trading System and the legal system in the United States. With more stringent policies and mechanisms of policy implementation, China was able to reduce its energy intensity (measured by energy use per unit of the GDP) by nearly 20% from 2005 to 2010, a mandatory national target set for the 11th FYP period. With such a cut in energy intensity, as much as 1.55 billion tons of carbon dioxide was eliminated compared to the status quo.

As you are well aware, however, these savings came at a very high cost. For instance, within the five years from 2006 to 2010, China closed 73 Gigawatts of smaller, low-efficiency power plants and coal-fired generators. To give you a sense of scale, this closure represented an amount 20% more than the total capacity of the United Kingdom. As a result, China's power generation efficiency is among the best in the world now, but at great cost to the economy and ordinary people.

The government also made large investments for a better environment. My team's analysis showed that $30 billion was spent on energy efficiency in China during the 11th Five-Year Plan. In the same period, an annual $50 billion was invested in the renewable energy industry and power generation. These investments are showing results. The Bloomberg New Energy Report found that China has been leading the world in renewable energy development in recent years. China's wind power generation has been increasing capacity by almost one and half times each year. China also produces more than half of the world's solar photovoltaic panels each year. These panels are installed in Europe and the United States, helping produce clean energy in these countries, and indeed helping the importing countries meet their targets for greenhouse gas emissions. Unfortunately, the solar panel industry is currently fighting for its very survival due, in part, to trade disputes with the United States and Europe.

Just as in the United States, local actions are also impressive. In a rough survey, my team found more than a hundred cities and provinces have set goals for low-carbon development. In 2010, the NDRC selected five provinces and eight cities to take part in the first round of a national pilot program that set a target higher than the national one for reducing carbon intensity. These places have been trying to come up with innovative measures for addressing climate change while developing their economies. Half of them joined the national attempt to develop a cap-and-trade program for carbon emissions. Recently, the NDRC reviewed applications for the second round of low-carbon pilots. The local enthusiasm for joining the pilot program was overwhelming.

Bottom-up efforts in the United States and China are instructive for the international negotiations. First, many localities now see actions on climate change as an opportunity rather than a burden for the economy in part because their leaders realize that the current economic development model is not sustainable. An economy built on massive resource input, fossil fuel energy, and pollutant emissions no longer works for China itself and even less for the world. I think this was why former President Hu Jintao told his colleagues in the Politburo that China should take climate change actions as an opportunity to transform its economic development model in February 2010.

What this means for international negotiations is that the focus should now shift from determining the specific global and national targets to the actions and resources needed for reaching targets. The world should and can work together to come up with the resources and means for tackling our common challenges. National and local initiatives have developed many useful mechanisms that could be applied to the international agreement. For example, a domestic measurement, reporting, and verification (MRV) system was already established in China for energy saving and it could be considered at the International Consultation and Analysis process and procedures.

Following this line of thinking, I think that China and the United States should build upon what we have now, such as the joint Clean Energy Research Center you mentioned, and significantly broaden and deepen the existing cooperation on research and development and industrial deployment of low-carbon technologies. While I look forward to your ideas for cooperation, I would like to offer one here. Now that China owns so many U.S. Treasury bonds, it is perhaps possible to use some of these resources to establish a fund for technology cooperation for common use by the two countries. This would help to address some concerns about intellectual property protection on the U.S. side as well as the devaluation of the bonds resulting from the Federal Reserve's bold monetary policy to stimulate the national economy.

I know this proposal is by no means easy. It may even sound naïve. But courage and leadership are really critical at this moment. I watched on television the Republican Presidential candidate attacking President Obama's $90 billion package for renewable energy. I wish the president could have taken the opportunity to affirm to the American people, and indeed the people of the world, that he did the right thing. From the Chinese perspective, President Obama's blocking of a Chinese-related wind power generation project in 2012 over concerns about national security is discouraging for bilateral cooperation on clean energy development.

This leads me back to the point you raised about the two countries negotiating directly and then bringing their negotiated results to the global deal. While I understand the merit of this approach, I doubt the practicality of it in the current setting of the international negotiations. For example, the European Union, which has been an ardent driver of the global process, will continue to push hard for an all-party-involved process. Just as few countries were enthusiastic about Niall Ferguson's idea of "Chimerica" or a G-2 proposed a couple of years ago, I am afraid probably even fewer would feel comfortable seeing the two biggest emitters strike a deal and try to install it in the global agreement.

However, if China and the United States work directly on low-carbon technologies, rather than on negotiations on climate change, especially if the results of the collaboration could be shared by the rest of the world, they could form the core of a coalition. The coalition of low-carbon development could grow and benefit all. We have seen the momentum of, for example, the C-40, a coalition of major cities of the world that collaborate on addressing climate challenges. We could imagine the power of such a partnership built between the two biggest carbon emitters who are willing to work together for the future of their countries and the future of the world.

I look forward to hearing from you.

Best regards,
Qi Ye

• • •

Dear Qi Ye,

It seems as though we are approaching a common viewpoint about how to resolve the differences between our countries on climate change.

A pragmatic approach is the only one that will move us beyond the political posturing and ideological rhetoric that has prevailed for the past decade. Let me first respond to your comments about the principle of common but differentiated responsibility, and then return to possible future pathways to an agreement.

CBDR actually embodies two principles for which I have great sympathy and that should resonate strongly with Americans. First, those who create a problem have a responsibility to help solve it. Second, those with the capacity to help should, especially when others do not have the means to do so, even if the latter contributed to the problem. Everyone would agree that if a company releases hazardous waste into a river, it has the responsibility to clean it up. And, if a person does not have enough food to eat, the person fortunate to have extra food should share it with the one in need. There is an old adage that "to whom much is given, much is expected," and of course it applies in the case of climate change.[8]

Applying these two principles to climate change, it is clear that the largest emitters have the greatest responsibility to address the problem and to prevent it from getting worse, as well as to help the most vulnerable adapt to a changing climate. It follows that the wealthier should help the less wealthy with both of these tasks. More wealthy countries should help less wealthy countries, and even within countries, the wealthier citizens should help the less wealthy, more vulnerable citizens. You are correct that the United States not only agreed to the principle of CBDR when it ratified the UN Framework Convention on Climate Change, but it has not lived up to the spirit of the idea by taking a leadership role in tackling the climate change problem. I fully understand that many around the world believe that the United States has abandoned the principle, and I agree that it could and should be reaffirmed.

That being said, the far more difficult question is how to operationalize this principle, and here I think there is some truth to the possibility you raised that some countries are "hiding" behind CBDR because it has become a convenient excuse for inaction.

So, yes, let's reaffirm the principles behind this concept, but perhaps use new language so that ordinary citizens can understand the concepts and why they matter. CBDR has become a toxic acronym in the international negotiations, insinuating guilt and bad behavior on the part of the industrialized countries and an avoidance of responsibility on the part of developing countries. As you said, the time for blame has passed unproductively and the climate threat has become even more urgent to address. Global concentrations of greenhouse gases in the atmosphere have now surpassed 400 parts per million, well past the point of dangerous human interference in the climate system. As you know, all countries agreed in the original climate convention to avoid such interference.

I see two possible pathways to agreement. First, I agree that the U.S.–China Clean Energy Research Center has been a success. It is funded equally from both sides, and brings together U.S. and Chinese researchers and firms to do collaborative research and development on low-carbon technologies. An intellectual property agreement was negotiated and has been applied to all of the collaborative R&D being done under this initiative. We could certainly build upon this excellent foundation in several ways. First, we could add to the current areas of cooperation, which are in building energy efficiency, advanced coal, and clean vehicles. We could work on other energy efficient or low-carbon energy technologies, and also on adaptation approaches. We could also expand the types of collaborative innovation, as you suggest, and do joint demonstrations of low-carbon and energy efficiency technologies. I've recommended this step in the past, and I believe that there is much wisdom in experimenting together. Through joint demonstrations, we can share costs, enhance global learning networks, and provide platforms for U.S. and Chinese firms to work together in order to achieve more rapid progress on low-carbon innovation. Joint deployment programs would also be a wise step forward. We could work on harmonizing performance standards and developing a common market for low-carbon technologies, which would improve market access for firms in both countries. Such an agreement could be negotiated under the auspices of the Science and Technology Cooperation Agreement of 1979.

The other approach is more comprehensive in nature, which could prove to be either a major advantage or distinct disadvantage. Here, the United States and China could squarely face the fact that their relationship is multifaceted and complex, and that climate change is just one of many important issues facing the two countries. A broader compact could be negotiated at the presidential level that would result in a package of agreements where the issues are linked. Trade, foreign direct investment, national security, and climate change are inextricably connected as challenges and opportunities, and perhaps we would achieve greater mutual gains by taking a more integrated approach.

Neither of the above options prevents a parallel process from continuing under the auspices of the UN Framework Convention on Climate Change, but they greatly enhance the likelihood that an agreement will ever be reached in this context. I could not agree more that a partnership between the United States and China would be an incredibly powerful force to tackle climate change. They are the two largest economies, emitters of greenhouse gases, and energy consumers in the world. Without question, our shared interests in economic well-being, energy security, and a stable global climate are greater than the issues that divide us. I hope to have the opportunity to work together with you and others in China to realize the dream of joint leadership to stabilize the global climate for the sake of future generations.

Warm regards,
Kelly

• • •

Dear Kelly,

You and I both agree that there is an urgent need for cooperation between China and the United States on energy and climate change. The good news is that the political environment seems to be changing in that direction. The reelection of President Obama and the election of Mr. Xi Jinping as the General Secretary of the Chinese Communist Party (CCP) in November 2012 may create new opportunities for China–U.S. cooperation, particularly in energy, environment, and climate change. As President Obama indicated in his inspiring inauguration speech for the second term, climate change will once again become a priority in his policy agenda. China, in my view, is an indispensable partner for the success of this endeavor.

On the Chinese side, I am sure that you noticed that "ecological civilization" is a key theme of the policy agenda of the new administration, highlighted at the 18th Party Congress. Some might think this term is too vague. But the three pillars that support the concept include low-carbon development, green development, and circular development (meaning a recycling-based economy). Skeptics may suspect some of this is green-washing propaganda. But one only needs to spend a day in Beijing, soaked in heavy smog, to realize how serious the situation is and how real and urgent the need is to take immediate and radical measures to curb coal use and carbon emissions. Unfortunately, China is trapped in a corner and now has to act quickly and forcefully on the environment.

The recent 12th Five-Year Plan on Energy puts a cap on China's total energy consumption at 4 billion tons of coal equivalent by 2015. If this target is achieved, energy-related carbon emissions would be limited also. This cap marks a major shift in China's national policy from a relative intensity target—that aims to slow emissions growth relative to GDP growth—to an absolute limit on emissions. This change, in turn, could affect China's position in international climate negotiation.

This shift to a hard ceiling on energy consumption also implies that officials can make climate change policy based on the idea of a recognized "peak" of the nation's carbon emissions, after which they would be set to decline in absolute terms. I would expect that some of the more economically advanced cities in the coastal areas will be asked to limit their overall annual emissions as soon as in the 13th Five-Year Plan period. Further, two lines of legislative work are underway: a new climate change law and a low-carbon development promotion law. Both of them are likely to become national laws (as opposed to regional or local directives), indicating that the central government and legislature take this issue very seriously. In his remarks at the China Council of International Cooperation on Environment and Development in November 2012, Premier Li Keqiang reemphasized the concept of ecological progress.

But China faces formidable challenges, and its road toward ecological progress will be long and bumpy to say the least. Because of the complementarity of the two economies, the United States could become China's most important partner in helping it overcome the challenges on its path to ecological progress. The two countries bear global and historical responsibilities to lead the world toward a new form of civilization built on a harmonious relationship between Man and Nature, and among all nations and all people. The two countries should and could work together to move beyond the age of fossil fuel.

You have noted the existing China–U.S. cooperation on advanced coal technology. That is not the only promising area. The greatest success in the U.S. energy sector in recent years is the development of shale gas, which has not only made the United States less dependent on oil imports, but has also helped reduce U.S. carbon emissions. Ironically, it seems that the road toward a non-fossil future travels through a different form of fossil fuel. Respected energy organizations have reported that China has the world's largest reserve of shale gas. Can China achieve a similar level of success as the United States did with shale gas? Cooperation in this area could have significant implications for greenhouse gas emissions worldwide.

Another area of collaboration that has been particularly productive is between America's EPA and China's Ministry of Environmental Protection. During Obama's first term, the two governments continued their work under the Ten-Year Framework of cooperation on environment, energy, and climate signed during the Bush Administration. It makes great sense to find policies that address climate change and combat severe environmental pollution at the same time. After all, a huge share of the smog that in early 2013 covered 1.4 million square kilometers of northwestern China—an area the size of Texas, California, and New Mexico combined—was from the burning of fossil fuels, particularly coal.

The United States is considered the world's most successful nation in curbing pollutants from coal burning due to its sulfur dioxide emissions trading program. Many have attempted to transfer this system to China, with little to show so far. But new developments may help. In October 2011, China launched a pilot program on carbon market, in two provinces and five cities that cover about 20% of the population. To advocates of market instruments, this is an exciting development. Pessimists, however, note the weak performance of the European Union's Emissions Trading System and the difficulty of establishing a similar system in the United States, and predict either failure or low efficiency of such a system in China. Can the two countries work together to develop viable mechanisms for emissions reduction, building upon the success of the U.S. sulfur dioxide cap-and-trade system?

I am intrigued by your idea about harmonizing performance standards and developing a common market for low-carbon technologies. While I would very much like to learn more about the details, I do feel this would help promote collaborations involving both the research and business communities. Perhaps business leaders, think tanks and other policy researchers from the two sides could form a special taskforce to identify certain areas of technology, say in the wind and solar sectors, and offer recommendations to government agencies on how to set performance standards and develop common markets.

I agree with you that a larger framework for Sino-American collaboration would be ideal. On the Chinese side, that would require a greater degree of mutual trust between the two governments and their leaders than we currently have. Effective implementation of existing programs such as the Clean Energy Research Centers or development of new collaborative programs would help promote mutual trust. Of course, cooperation could also cover a broader area, encompassing economics and security policies.

The current leaders and administrations of the two countries have a lot in common when it comes to clean energy, climate change, and the environment. The two governments should seize opportunities before this window closes. You and I as part of the policy research community should do our best to help enhance the much-needed cooperation. I certainly look forward to working with you and other colleagues in the community on the challenges of climate and the environment.

Best wishes,
Qi Ye

GLOBAL DEVELOPMENT AND INVESTMENT

ELIZABETH ECONOMY
Council on Foreign Relations

ZHA DAOJIONG
Peking University

Framing questions: *In what ways do the U.S. and Chinese approaches to development and foreign investment differ? Are they evolving, and how? What are the benefits and drawbacks of each approach both to the investing country and the recipient? In what ways are China and the United States competing in third countries? In what ways are their efforts complementary? Would closer coordination be helpful? Is it possible? What role does "soft power" play? How real is "resource competition?" Is there a "China model" of development? What is the American perspective on China's relationships with human rights-abusing regimes that provide energy and raw materials? What is the Chinese perspective on America's investments in the developing world?*

• • •

Dear Daojiong,

As you know, the United States and China are constantly in search of common ground—areas where the two countries can cooperate rather than condemn or conflict with each other. Certainly they share broad objectives, for instance, peace and stability in the Asia-Pacific region and free trade. However, they differ often on how best to achieve their common aims.

You and I may have the solution in our hands. As China joins the United States as one of the world's largest sources of foreign direct investment, the two countries have a unique opportunity to help shape the development environment throughout much of the rest of the world. By adopting best practices and learning from each other, Washington and Beijing can contribute to both the economic and social health of the countries in which they invest. This is particularly important in many of the world's resource-rich countries where hard and soft infrastructure—both buildings and institutional capacity building—still lag behind much of the rest of the international community.

Given the size of both the U.S. and Chinese economies and their considerable demands for resources, the two countries bear a special burden to lead. The statistics are staggering. In 2011, China consumed 48% of global zinc supplies, 50% of lead, 50% of copper, and 45% of aluminum.[1] All told, mineral imports made up 30% of China's foreign trade.[2] In 2013, China also surpassed the United States as the world's largest importer of oil. In agricultural products, as well, China is shaping the global market. In 2010, China consumed almost half of all pork, one-third of global rice supplies, and one-quarter of the world's soybeans. Not surprisingly, as the U.S. economy has moved away from manufacturing toward services and has developed a mature infrastructure, American investment in extractive industries has declined. Still, while the U.S. claim on most resources lags far behind—ranging anywhere from 20 to 25% of Chinese global demand—it is, nonetheless, a top consumer and a significant player in broader issues of global corporate governance, foreign aid, and international security.

The threat of global resource competition looms large in the future—particularly as other populous developing countries such as Indonesia and India also seek to develop their economies. However, I am optimistic that innovation, as well as market forces, will meet the world's future demands. My concern for now is how the United States and China can ensure that their global footprints via their foreign aid and investment practices are positive for the rest of the world.

For both countries, getting their investment and aid strategies on track means striking an appropriate balance on two fronts: first, a balance between their economic interests and the development interests of the resource-rich countries in which they invest; and second, a balance between their economic interests and their broader political and strategic aims. Finding this balance is a tall order, and while I don't think that either the United States or China has yet achieved such an objective, I do think that China will need to travel a greater distance to achieve such a balance. With few exceptions, its multinationals have yet to institutionalize world-class levels of corporate social responsibility and thus can inflict serious damage on the well-being of the communities in which they operate. In addition, Beijing's willingness to invest without question in countries where the regimes brutally repress their people only deepens and prolongs the suffering of the people in those countries. This is not a sustainable policy for a country with global reach and influence.

Of course, China's extraordinary economic growth and demand for resources have redounded with benefits to the developing world, rejuvenating industries and economies that had been moribund for decades. And its particular mix of state-owned enterprises (SOEs) and government-targeted investment, coupled with private enterprise, makes its model unique. Beijing combines trade, aid, and investment in attractive packages for developing countries. With government political and financial support, for example, Chinese companies often undertake projects that other multinationals consider too risky: investing in, for example, conflict-ridden Sudan, in Zambian copper mines that have not been operational for more than a decade, or in a nickel mine in Papua New Guinea that other multinationals regarded as unprofitable.

Beijing also listens to the leaders of the countries in which it does business. It earns diplomatic points for extensive support for infrastructure development, which not only facilitates the ability of Chinese companies to transport their resources but also serves as a critical component of the long-term development of a country. Leaders from Venezuela, Cambodia, and the Democratic Republic of Congo have welcomed Chinese investment and infrastructure as the type of practical assistance they need most. In Ghana, China has provided assistance through grants, interest-free loans, and preferential government loans in a wide range of areas, including hospital buildings, hydropower, telecommunications, irrigation construction, the military, and police barracks. In addition, Chinese experts have offered agricultural, health, and management training. The economic benefit of this broad engagement to Chinese companies is clear: Sino-hydro, for example, is now the world's largest developer of dams, commanding roughly 70% of all current construction.

As an issue of broader strategic engagement, China's policy has been defined largely as "we don't mix business with politics." Some officials in developing countries applaud this strategy. Bheki Langa, South African Ambassador to Beijing, noted in a 2011 interview in *People's Daily* that Chinese investment is a "far cry from the Western colonial exploitation that undermined the development of Africa.... China is a reliable partner that meets the development needs of Africa."[3] His Sierra Leonean counterpart, former Ambassador to Beijing Sahr Johnny was somewhat more cautious but still supportive of Beijing's approach, noting "If a G-8 country had wanted to rebuild the stadium, for example, we'd still be holding meetings! The Chinese just come and do it. They don't start to hold meetings about environmental impact assessment, human rights, bad governance and good governance. I'm not saying that's right. I'm just saying Chinese investment is succeeding because they don't set high benchmarks."[4]

Yet my sense is that Beijing's business-at-any-cost strategy will not be viable much longer. It is a short-sighted policy that is detrimental to the long-term health and stability of the countries in which China invests. Increasingly, communities in a number of different countries—including Peru, Papua New Guinea, Vietnam, and Australia, among others—have begun to voice opposition to Chinese investment in their natural resource sectors. Poor environmental, labor, and safety practices have caused intense conflicts with local residents, as has China's predilection for importing Chinese labor for its massive infrastructure and mining projects. In Peru, for example, the Chinese SOE Shougang Hierro has faced more than five years of protests as a result of a series of measures it adopted: lowering wages, reneging on a plan for local infrastructure and housing, and contaminating local water supplies by pumping waste illegally into the San Nicholas Bay. Evidence of weak corporate social responsibility among Chinese companies is widespread, despite the fact that a number of Chinese government agencies, including China EXIM Bank, the Shanghai Stock Exchange, and the State-Owned Assets Supervision and Administration Commission, have clear guidelines regarding environmental protection, worker safety, and product quality standards.

The reliance of Chinese actors on striking deals with central government players while ignoring broader popular concerns and potential corruption is also deeply troubling. Beijing, for example, has been criticized by NGOs and Western governments for failing to provide clarity and transparency on the loans it provides to many developing countries. And Chinese companies have encountered trouble as a result of their willingness to skirt the rules—even if in collusion with domestic actors. In Zambia, for example, the Zhonghui Mining Group—reportedly the largest privately owned company operating in sub-Saharan Africa—was able to begin its mining efforts without an environmental impact assessment. The Zambian Minister of Mines and Natural Resources, Maxwell Mwale, was later arrested for possessing over 200 campaign bicycles paid for by Zhonghui. When the new government came into power in 2011, it halted Zhonghui's license on the grounds that there had been no environmental impact assessment. As you have written in the context of China's engagement in Burma/Myanmar, "Worldwide, pursuit of development has changed from accepting growth as the key rationale to a greater focus on rights, human and environmental.... China's state-owned companies see their action as implementing government-to-government agreements and little else. They badly need investment risk management 101 lessons."[5]

The United States brings a different set of opportunities and challenges to the foreign investment table. There are no state-owned firms, and the U.S. government does not offer the type of comprehensive package of trade, aid, and investment that China does. Certainly, there are mechanisms for supporting U.S. firms through the Overseas Private Investment Corporation (OPIC) or private organizations that promote U.S. trade and investment such as the U.S. Chamber of Commerce, but the U.S. government does not have the capacity to integrate corporations into a broader package of development assistance. Unlike in China, there are few ways in which business objectives are reinforced by a vast array of other investment and assistance tools, and vice versa.

Indeed, there are numerous instances in which broader U.S. strategic interests on issues, such as human rights or proliferation, work in opposition to the interests of U.S. firms. Government sanctions on doing business in countries such as Burma/Myanmar, Iran, Sudan, and North Korea have left natural resource and oil companies at a significant disadvantage with their competitors in countries that have not levied such sanctions, including China.

On the plus side, schooled in the United States—with an investigative media, strong rule of law, and comparatively more watchdog NGOs—U.S. firms generally bring a reputation for strong corporate governance practices. Most, although certainly not all, American companies have integrated corporate social responsibility guidelines into the fabric of their operations, viewing doing business "the right way" as making reputational sense and essential to profitable business over the long term. In addition, the United States has on its books a Foreign Corrupt Practices Act that promises to penalize any company engaging in extralegal activities abroad, such as bribery.

The importance of good governance also commands significant attention in U.S. foreign assistance—both public and private. The United States Agency for International Development (USAID), the chief aid body, states "U.S. foreign assistance has always had the twofold purpose of furthering America's foreign policy interests in expanding democracy and free markets while improving the lives of citizens in the developing world."[6] Generally, the U.S. government pushes countries to adopt better practices in areas that will also provide a better investment environment for American companies, such as market access, services, and intellectual property rights. In addition, USAID's priorities include broader issues of governance, such as citizen safety and effective governance, focusing on the links between security, economic prosperity, and strong democratic institutions. The U.S. government's initiatives on good governance get further support from NGOs such as the Revenue Watch Institute, which focuses explicitly on developing transparency and accountability in the minerals sector. The Institute works with governments to draft mining and oil laws and to improve revenue management, including revenue sharing arrangements among various levels of government. A wealth of NGOs, such as the Gates Foundation, also support soft infrastructure, such as developing and deploying hygienic toilets to help curb the spread of disease or the provision of ant-imalaria bed nets. What is largely missing from the U.S. equation is the type of massive infrastructure assistance that China provides as part of its engagement in the developing world.

Despite significant rhetorical commitment and boots on the ground, both U.S. companies and U.S. agencies have encountered significant criticism for the nature of their engagement in the developing world. There have been a number of cases of local communities in countries such as Indonesia and Ghana protesting against U.S. companies on environmental grounds. Moreover, many developing countries have accused the United States of tying its aid to particular political allies or using aid as a reward or punishment for governments that do or do not support U.S. interests. Even within the United States, there are accusations that foreign investment contracts— particularly reconstruction contracts—are awarded to firms with political ties to the current party in power.

There are lessons for both China and the United States in their foreign investment and assistance efforts. Alongside its traditional preference for supporting governance reforms, the United States should think more about the need for infrastructure assistance to resource-rich developing countries. China, in turn, should place greater emphasis on supporting good governance in the countries in which it does business, along with the strong support it provides for infrastructure and other economic development needs. As Beijing has discovered in Burma/Myanmar and Zambia, working in partnership with poorly governed states can have very negative consequences for Chinese companies when these governments transition. Good governance and strong infrastructure support and sustain each other but suffer without the other. China should also consider developing a foreign corrupt practices act and a more proactive approach to educating its SOEs on corporate social responsibility. Some Chinese firms are already pushing forward on this front, particularly as they seek to access markets in the advanced industrialized countries.

Despite the size of their collective footprint, it's clear that neither the United States nor China has perfected its role as responsible investor and shaper of development in resource-rich developing countries. Each has different strengths and weaknesses. Yet in those differences exists the opportunity to learn each from the other, and we should encourage both countries to do so.

Best,

Liz

• • •

Dear Liz,

Indeed, China and the United States are two important actors in addressing a long list of issues beyond the realm of bilateral interactions. Foreign investment and development aid stand out as issue areas in which collaboration is *theoretically* feasible. However to translate the ideas that you and I, together with many others in the community of experts on Sino-American relations, believe are worthwhile into concrete action, it is necessary to sort out some of our differences, both factual and perceptual.

Let me begin by putting into perspective the role natural resource acquisition plays in China's foreign investment strategy. Here I limit my discussion to physical extraction operations. Before I begin, I want to remind readers that the international financial market plays a big, but not very visible, role in making new investments in extraction as well as trade of commodities possible. Many of China's large energy companies, including the well-known China National Petroleum Company (CNPC) and China National Offshore Oil Corporation (CNOOC), are listed in the stock markets beyond China's own borders. As such, part of their mission is to satisfy demands from a worldwide network of investors, not just China.

Many Chinese in government and business circles find it hard to understand the level of Western interest in China's acquisition of natural resources from developing countries. This trade is a common phase in many countries' development paths. Until the mid-1990s, China itself earned over half of its foreign currency income through exports of raw materials such as coal, oil, mineral ores, grain, and the like. In particular, from the early 1970s to the late 1990s, China entered into long-term trade agreements with Japan to sell raw materials in exchange for a supply of equipment and machinery. In the 1970s, China also exported oil to the United States. The lesson from China's history is this: if exporting natural resources is what a country has to rely on for income at a particular stage of development, so be it. Those countries that are supplying China with resources today have the chance to climb the ladder of industrialization in the world economy just as China did.

Furthermore, China is a latecomer in the global search for natural resources beyond its borders. Companies from Europe, North America, and Japan have the advantage of having won global access to oil, minerals, and other commodities for their domestic consumption much earlier. They dominate world trade in commodities and have established rules and norms for new entrants to follow. When China entered the global competition, alas, only "leftover" assets remained in difficult geological and geographical terrains and in politically unstable countries. Because of the time when it entered the global history of natural resource extraction, China has had little choice but to pursue relationships with resource-rich but politically unsavory countries in Africa and Latin America, and among its Asian neighbors.

Over the years, numerous studies and news reports in the West have documented societal dissatisfaction with the behavior of Chinese companies operating in countries like Zambia, Sudan, Venezuela, Papua New Guinea, and Myanmar, to name just a few. Complaints about substandard corporate practices have been numerous and, in many instances, well justified. For example, a pervasive charge levied in the international media is that Chinese resource companies bring workers from China and by so doing compete with the local communities for jobs. That complaint is valid, because it would be inconceivable if foreign investors operating in China did not contribute to job creation in Chinese society! However, as Dambisa Moyo, a native of Zambia, wrote in *The New York Times* in 2012, this fear is overblown. In her home country "the ratio of African to Chinese workers has exceeded 13:1."[7]

My point here is not about any one case. In fact, part of the problem is confusion about the entire spectrum of Chinese and other international investments in one particular developing country. Many developing countries do not have reliable mechanisms for collecting basic data about Chinese and other foreign companies operating in their societies. This leaves room for accounts by advocacy groups that highlight a particular company or a particular case to stand in for the complete picture. Advocacy groups, regardless of their focus on human rights or the environment, do have a role to play. They keep all companies, Chinese and Western, on their toes. At the same time, they tend to dramatize singular failures. When Chinese companies fail to sufficiently engage international NGOs or Western media when controversies arise, they are doing themselves no favors. This leads further to individual cases becoming generalized, which is not conducive to meaningful dialogue.

Do Chinese companies willfully disregard norms of corporate social responsibility? The barest minimum indicator of that responsibility is specified in the contracts a foreign company signs upon entry. As you would agree, it takes effective legal and judicial agencies in a recipient country to enforce those contracts. Many Chinese companies err by assuming that the general procedures and attitudes toward foreign direct investment of any developing country are the same as in China. For example, in China, governments at various levels are responsible for dealing with such tasks as resettlement of human inhabitants, when construction of a factory or a mine so requires. Many of the countries Chinese companies operate in do not have even the most rudimentary but essential legal structures like land title in place. Thus, companies may end up trampling on people's rights without meaning to because they assume the local government will look after the interests of their own citizens. Though certainly not a point of pride, even within China, there have been numerous incidents of resident protests against mining and other industrial operations. Cost cutting is a powerful instinct for a company. The acceptable amount of compensation for resettlement is often a moving target. As such, genuine dialogue about performance in corporate responsibility has to consider a large spectrum of actors and interactions between them.

Right here I see an opportunity for cooperation between China and the United States. As you noted, a number of Chinese government agencies have issued guidelines regarding environmental protection, worker safety, and product quality standards for companies to observe, both at home and abroad. But these guidelines are not enough, as reports of troubling incidents (however isolated they are) remind us. Interested parties in the United States can be more productive by joining hands with Chinese companies to agree to abide by developing country specific and industry-specific codes of conduct. Such Sino-American cooperation would also involve the host government of an investment project. With the host government being on board from the start, we stand a better chance of avoiding a situation of a company claiming that whatever it is doing is in line with unspecified "best practice" norms.

Last but not least, it would help win more hearts and minds among Chinese skeptical about American and other Western criticism if those critics could show more understanding of the role China's foreign energy and mineral acquisition plays in the global process of production. China imports raw materials such as mineral ores, does the preliminary processing in China (and keeps the environmental side effects there, too), exports semifinished products to countries with more sophisticated manufacturing facilities and know-how, and reimports the finished products.[8] Indeed, Chinese energy policymakers often note that 28% of China's energy goes into making products for export, while the country is 85% self-reliant in terms of total energy supply. That makes China a net energy exporting country, in actuality.

I can easily imagine that such Chinese sentiments may not easily win sympathy from the West. Western as well as Chinese academics and policy makers have repeatedly warned China against the practice of putting fast growth ahead of adopting the most energy-efficient equipment and industrial methods available in the world. There is a legitimate point that China has put itself in the position of having to rely on ever-increasing amounts of energy from abroad due to the failure of faster and more energy-efficient industrial innovation at home. Yet, there is no meaningful competition for a high moral ground here. We are all part of the global chain of industrial production. Products have to be made somewhere in order to meet daily needs around the world. There is not that much we can do other than working to make each stage of the process more resource efficient.

Speaking about efficiency in energy and natural resource use, China and the United States have a record of cooperation worth celebrating. Beginning with the Carter administration, the United States has made energy and, more broadly, industrial efficiency a prominent area for cooperation with China. Chinese scientists work with their American peers to propose concrete projects, endorsed by their respective host institutions, and eventually have their governments provide the policy support. In the area of energy alone, over the past 30 years, more than 30 government-to-government agreements were signed, resulting in over 30,000 collaborations. Such cooperation not only benefits the two sides involved, but Chinese companies are able to practice more efficient production in third countries with the better equipment and enhanced know-how gained from interactions with Americans.

Now let me turn to the issue of development aid. This is a contentious topic between China and the United States. Since the Kissinger-Nixon détente with China in 1971, the United States has not made development aid an underpinning instrument for U.S. companies to enter the Chinese market. For the past three decades, the main supplier of bilateral aid to China was Japan, followed by European countries. Of course, the United States did help indirectly. The United States is one of the largest contributors to the World Bank, which has been the single most important multilateral agency to assist in the transformation of the Chinese market, in both policy making and project development. The point here is that there is little history of collaboration between Chinese and American aid policy makers and practitioners through which to develop a common sense of acceptable behaviors, or norms.

It is far-fetched to conclude that China uses aid as an instrument to promote a "China model" of development in recipient countries or to enhance China's "soft power" influence vis-à-vis the United States. China's aid provision is rooted in its experience in receiving aid from donor states. In the 1950s, the Soviet Union was the single most important provider of development aid to China. As a matter of fact, China's first five-year economic plan, especially the industrial component therein, was almost entirely based on provision of monetary, equipment, and human-resource aid from the Soviet Union. In exchange, the Soviet Union demanded that China adhere to its preferences in every aspect of domestic and international policy. The political burden of relying on Soviet aid was so heavy that China opted to allow a break-up of its alliance with the Soviet Union in 1960, including offering to repay Soviet aid ahead of schedule. As such, China chose to relate to countries that receive its aid by doing the opposite of what the Soviet model mandated. Today China de-links its aid provision from such political issues as a recipient country's human rights reputation, to try to prevent a similar backlash to what the Soviets experienced with China. Furthermore, tying aid to foreign company entry is a feature of development aid that China has itself experienced since the early 1970s. The unspoken logic is that if the approach worked out well with China, it should also work when the time comes for China to be a donor.

China's development aid has generated controversy on the domestic front as well. For example, in late 2011, when the domestic media reported that China had donated three dozen school buses to Macedonia, a public uproar erupted over the lack of safe school buses provided to Chinese children. The National People's Congress jumped on the bandwagon of public dissent by holding a public hearing on school bus safety.

China's development aid, understandably, is partly designed to foster political goodwill in developing countries when it comes to such matters as UN deliberations regarding human rights in China, and long-running contentious issues like Taiwan, Tibet, and Xinjiang. The area where Chinese and American approaches do differ is whether or not aid dispersal must be preconditioned upon regime change or improvements in human rights certified by the outside world. Those differences are unlikely to narrow in the foreseeable future.

Meanwhile, there is no reason to despair. In countries from Myanmar to Zambia to Venezuela, the American approach contributes to improving soft (political) infrastructure, while the Chinese approach contributes to improving hard (economic) infrastructure. These two approaches reinforce one another. A more transparent and stable host government in the developing world is conducive to protecting China's investment interests. The other side of the coin is that with a vibrant economy, which foreign investments from countries like China help create, democratic change has a better chance to sustain its momentum. At the end of the day, however, positive change has to come from within.

When I bring my observations together, there is clearly a rationale for consultation and collaboration between China and the United States when it comes to development assistance. Mechanisms like the U.S.–China consultation on the Asia-Pacific region, held at the assistant ministerial level between the U.S. State Department and the Chinese Foreign Ministry, are a step in the right direction. Collaboration is important because the nature of the interaction between China and the United States is increasingly consequential for those countries under discussion. When experts like you and me help to socialize larger communities of stakeholders in development and aid in both of our countries to better appreciate each other's positions, our two countries also stand a greater chance of making third-country issues less contentious in our bilateral ties.

Regards,
Daojiong

• • •

Dear Daojiong,

Your thoughtful commentary has prompted me to look anew at some of the issues surrounding China's resource acquisition strategy and its broader implications. In some ways, we occupy common ground; in others, our differences now seem more pronounced. In either case, I hope you agree that greater communication and clarity only open the door to more fruitful cooperation down the line.

One question your essay raises is how China's behavior compares to that of other countries. You express surprise on behalf of many in China that the rest of the world is so interested in China's resource acquisition strategy. You note that China is simply moving up the economic value chain from resource exporter to resource importer, as many countries have done previously; and, you argue China's willingness to do business in politically unsavory countries is a function of its latecomer status.

I think, however, that the world's interest in China's global investment and aid strategy is easily understood. First, in terms of the sheer level of consumption of global resources, as I mentioned in our first exchange, China today matters more than any other country. While I don't believe that the scale of Chinese resource consumption, itself, poses a problem, it certainly reinforces the importance of China: either through direct investment in mines, land, or oil and gas fields or through trading on the global market, China has a profound impact on the global investment in and supply of commodities.

Moreover, while it is true that in the late 1990s-early 2000s in the initial stage of China's going out strategy, in which the Chinese government formally encouraged its enterprises to seek investment opportunities overseas, the country's opportunities were overwhelmingly in places where no one else wanted to (or legally could) do business, that is no longer the case. Chinese companies are very actively and often successfully bidding top dollar to secure access to resources in places such as Brazil, Australia, and Canada. It is no longer the case that China has "no choice" but to do business with "politically unsavory countries." It can increasingly afford to relax its prohibition against "mixing business with politics" and think through the broader political ramifications of its investment deals in places such as Iran or Sudan.

Second, your discussion of the large Chinese oil and gas companies, such as CNPC and CNOOC, reminded me that not all resource sectors and resource companies are created equal. Different resource sectors are characterized by very different types of actors and market orientations. There are, for example, only a handful of significant players in China's oil and gas industry, the most important of which are both state-owned and publicly listed. In contrast, there are thousands of actors in China's mining industry, some of which are state-owned, others that are owned by provincial or local governments, and still others that are privately held with far less government oversight. While there have been some corporate social responsibility problems reported with China's oil and gas companies (in Gabon, for example), there are many more in the mining sector from all over the world. From the Shougang-owned Marcona mine in Peru to several Chinese-owned mines in Zambia, to the China Metallurgical Group's Ramu nickel mine in Papua New Guinea, reports of serious violations are commonplace. The decentralized nature of China's mining industry, as well as the often weak state capacity in the recipient country, provides fertile ground for lax corporate social responsibility. Individual Chinese miners have even struck out on their own: in 2012, Ghana arrested 41 Chinese miners for illegal mining activities, and reportedly there are hundreds more miners operating illegally.[9] Thus, when we talk about where the challenges and needs for cooperation are greatest, it is worth thinking through systematically which actors in which sectors are most in need of attention.

Third, you explain that some of the difficulties Chinese companies have encountered abroad stem from weak state capacity in the recipient country and from a misunderstanding on the part of the Chinese companies concerning the role of the state in protecting its own people. Most notably, you suggest that Chinese companies believe that it is the job of local governments to protect their people from poor labor and safety practices and to ensure meaningful compensation in cases of relocation. Given the practices of Chinese resource companies at home in terms of labor, safety, and environmental practices—not to mention the problems with mass relocations—it is hard to believe that Chinese companies have learned that the state's role is to protect the people. In fact, I would suggest that at least with regard to the mining sector, the number of popular protests in China over environmental pollution and health problems, as well as labor and safety violations, suggests that Chinese companies have learned precisely the opposite lesson: they can behave with relative impunity, exporting their practices from home, as long as they are dealing with a weak government. It is easy to place responsibility on the victim in the case of a multinational's poor corporate social responsibility—particularly when a deal may involve corruption on the part of officials in the recipient country—but over the longer term, as many other countries' multinationals continue to learn, both the company and host country will pay a steep reputational price.

Finally, I would agree with you that China is not seeking to export a China model of development. By virtue of its size, its dynamic and wealthy overseas community, and its political system, the Chinese model is unique and really can't be exported wholesale. On the other hand, I don't believe it is "far-fetched" to argue that through its development assistance and its investment decisions, Beijing is in fact seeking to enhance its soft power. In her article, "More Soft Power Needed in Africa," Chinese Academy of Social Sciences scholar He Wenping noted, "China has long maintained its comparative advantages [with the United States] in its relations with Africa by expanding its investment in the continent and aiding African countries with hard projects such as infrastructure building. As a result, China's presence on the continent is widely welcomed by the African people. In comparison, western countries such as the U.S. have concentrated their input in soft projects that have produced intangible results.... "[10] Again, I don't think that there is anything untoward about China using all the tools at its disposal—from Confucius Institutes to building the African Union headquarters—to enhance its reputation and influence, particularly in countries in which it would like to do business. However, it is somewhat disingenuous to argue that China's overall development assistance program is not designed at least in part to accomplish precisely this end.

So where does this leave us? I don't think it leaves us far from where we started, which is to say that both China and the United States need to do more and can do some of it together. First, I appreciate the point that I think underpins much of your argument: we shouldn't oversell the negative in the case of China, because, as you point out, real data are scarce. For example, you cite a fact provided by Dr. Moyo—that there is one Chinese worker in Zambia for every thirteen Zambians—as evidence that there is no need to be concerned about China importing labor in significant numbers. In fact, when I reviewed her source for that fact, it appeared that the statistic derived from a single case in which there were 62 Chinese managers and 853 Zambian miners at a particular Zambian mine.[11] Dr. Moyo's generalization from this one case seems misguided. I have not found any comprehensive statistics regarding the ratio of Chinese to Zambian workers in the mines, but I would be interested if you have. My sense is that investigating whether—as I think—there is a pattern of poor corporate social responsibility on the part of Chinese mining companies that exceeds that of other multinational mining companies or whether—as you think—these are one-off cases given too much prominence by NGOs, would lead to a determination that both of us are less right than we think we are. A data-gathering exercise would seem a useful collaborative project among the United States, China, and the resource-rich developing countries, perhaps conducted by local NGOs and think tanks.

Second, I would reiterate the point I raised in my first letter about the importance of Chinese and all multinationals signing on to international agreements that ensure transparency in resource sector investments, such as the Extractive Industries Transparency Initiative, and donor countries such as

China agreeing to lend under IMF terms. You may be right that differences between the United States and China won't be solved quickly, but until they are, I am afraid that I don't share your optimism that we can rely on the United States to improve the soft infrastructure while China improves the hard infrastructure. In too many instances, China improving the hard infrastructure in places such as Sudan, Zimbabwe, or Angola may well help leaders in those countries avoid efforts by the United States or others to improve the soft infrastructure. Even more troubling is the possibility that Chinese infrastructure investment is not even achieving its development goals in these countries. As Angolan anti-corruption activist Rafael Marques de Morais has argued, ".... the Chinese-built roads, hospitals and schools began to crack as fast as they were being built. Luanda's General Hospital had to be shut down in June 2010, when bricks started to fall from the walls, threatening it with imminent collapse. Newly tarred roads were washed away after one rainy season.... The Chinese are not investing to develop the country. They have brought more corruption and, consequently, more poverty."[12]

It seems clear that both the United States and China need to be on the same page, assisting in both the physical and political development of the countries from which they derive so much of their resources and their wealth.

Sincerely,

Liz

• • •

Dear Liz,

I hope our exchange is a useful start to more rigorous communication between Chinese and American observers about our respective country's performance and goals in the areas of resource security and development aid. In the space below, I'd like to offer a couple of clarifications and additional thoughts.

My overall conclusion is that Chinese and American resource companies need to collaborate more with each other to enhance corporate social responsibility in developing countries. In the area of development aid, one way to narrow our differences is not to treat aid as an instrument of "soft power" but instead continue to explore ways and means to foster stability though a gradual process of socio-economic transitions of poor developing countries.

On resource security, let me just say that the trigger for attention on China, and indeed any major consumer of natural resources ranging from food, to oil, to minerals, is usually an unexpected change in the price of these commodities. When viewed as a market phenomenon, as economists remind us, the law of supply and demand is at work. Chinese resource companies are part of the changing dynamics of a global resource market. They operate overseas, amid controversies, but they enlarge total world supply.[13] The resource extractive industry operating in the developing world has been controversial for many decades. Now it's Chinese companies' turn to get their share of international attention. The real question is how to make such operations more acceptable to the multitude of stakeholders, rather than focusing most attention on the nationality of company ownership.

When it comes to corporate social responsibility in the resource extraction industry, let me emphatically say that my earlier comments should not be read to imply a desire "to place responsibility on the victim" when a dispute arises over a Chinese operation in a developing country. My point is simply to say that improved corporate social responsibility performance must involve a host government that works more rigorously to protect the environment and its own people's welfare. The same logic applies to China itself. As you are aware, a debate has been going on in China about whether or not the Chinese government—at the national and local levels—has been too lenient with environmental protection standards in its own bid to attract foreign investors.[14]

Few Chinese officials or scholars (including myself) condone substandard practices of social responsibility. Even here in China, we've seen more and more public and even violent protests against companies, be they Chinese or foreign. The triggers are the same as those in Africa—water and air pollution, the treatment of workers and residents, to name just a few.[15]

Outbreaks of disputes in Africa that involve Chinese companies, some of which you rightly mention, not only carry monetary and reputational costs for the companies in question but also run counter to efforts to enhance the image of China and the Chinese people abroad. Events like the evacuation of roughly 40,000 Chinese industrial workers out of Libya in 2011 certainly reinforced a broad awareness in China of political risks that can come from involvement overseas. In that incident, the Chinese government was a loser on the domestic front as well, as many questioned why their compatriots were put in a precarious foreign location in the first place. Managing those risks on the ground is a process of continuous learning, with its predictable pattern of trial and error. Out of self-interest, the Chinese government and Chinese companies take these incidents seriously. So there is no reason to despair over developments thus far.

During this process, the community of Chinese and American foreign policy academics can play a role. Though we do not live in the corporate world, we can advocate two agendas that can help bring positive change to performance on the ground. One task is to help publicize practices of corporate social responsibility by American companies in China and Chinese companies in the United States. By so doing, we can help convince Chinese companies—when they go to any third country—to adopt the same standards as American and other foreign companies do in China and they themselves do in the United States. A second agenda is to advocate for collaboration between Chinese and American companies that are investing in the same third country to establish common minimum standards.

As a foreign policy matter, China and the United States do differ over whether or not to invest in certain third countries. China has, by and large, adopted a policy of investing in any country that cares to receive an offer, just as China itself has encouraged direct investment from all other countries. The United States is more active in stipulating preconditions for American companies when they seek to invest abroad. Both China and the United States use government agencies such as export and import banks to promote or discourage specific investment proposals from their respective business communities. However, since both countries are member states of the Multilateral Investment Guarantee Agency, which offers political risk insurance to promote investment in underserved markets, as well as similar mechanisms, what China and America can do together is increase their compliance with established international rules and norms.

Arguably, the strength of the Chinese approach is that Chinese companies are afforded as wide a range of investment options as possible. Among the drawbacks is that companies can take up projects in societies where they are ill prepared to handle the cultural, legal, and political complexities. Also, those Chinese companies that engage in labor-intensive operations on the ground are by nature prone to local protests when unemployment in a destination country is high and Chinese laborers are brought in—from the companies' standpoint—to expedite construction. The American approach, on the other hand, can shield American companies from volatile societies and can, the United States hopes, positively influence the evolution of those governments. But the downside can be a diminution in market share, though often temporary.

Competition between China and the United States in development need not be destructive nor inevitable. We should remember that a third country will have its own political and economic agendas to pursue. Competition between Beijing and Washington can help enlarge that third country's set of choices. At the project level, cost-and-benefit considerations of technology and finance are just as decisive as the nationality of a particular company. A Chinese company is competing with an American one only when they are engaged in bidding over the same project. In a broad sense, Chinese companies' comparative advantage still comes from lower labor costs. Do Chinese and American companies make investment decisions in a particular third country with a focused motivation to compete with each other? It seems unlikely, as each has its own niche.

The bilateral issue in question is that the United States disapproves of Chinese companies going into certain countries, and it so happens that many of these countries still rely heavily on the resource sector. China does not heed unilateral sanctions the United States has imposed on countries such as Iran, Sudan, and Myanmar, though it does partake in UN-imposed sanctions at times. But in each of these and other cases, China's overall approach is to work with international forums and institutions that attempt to induce gradual change in those countries. In a nutshell, the difference between the Chinese and American approaches is over the pace of change, rather than its overall direction.

On the utility of sanctions in affecting positive change in a developing country, in no small part because China was on the receiving end of Western sanctions in the 1950s to early 1970s, we have to admit that conceptual gaps between China and the United States on this issue will remain wide for some time to come.

In looking at the impact of third and developing countries on relations between China and the United States, we need to be mindful of the narrowness of such notions as "soft power"—investment and aid for the sake of promoting an image—when both countries stand to benefit from stability and prosperity in every country and region. Development is a long process and truly sustainable forces of change are endogenous in those complex societies. Some third countries are quite adept at exercising asymmetric power in relating to big powers, but in the end, there is no such thing in our modern era as one big power "losing" a small country to another.

In September 2012, China and New Zealand entered into a partnership to improve water quality in Rarotonga, Cook Islands. The partnership has both Beijing and Wellington contributing funds and focused on delivering tangible benefits to the local community, which in turn will help the Cook Islands' tourism industry.[16] Similar joint efforts between China and the United States would be welcome.

At the end of the day, we do agree about the room for improvement in foreign direct investment operations. As I suggested earlier on, in order to make our discussions matter in the real world, we must think of ways to motivate Chinese and American corporations to work with each other on specific projects. International development institutions like the IMF and the World Bank are useful in moving forward the agenda of inclusive growth, but in the end we need to have demonstration projects on the ground. I hope you and I will see some of those soon.

Sincerely,
Daojiong

MILITARY DEVELOPMENTS

CHRISTOPHER P. TWOMEY
U.S. Naval Postgraduate School

XU HUI
National Defense University, China

Framing questions: *Why is China modernizing its military? What are its draw-backs and benefits from the point of view of America and its regional allies? What changes to its military is the United States making, and how do they affect China and others? How does China view America's military basing and activities, especially near its borders? What are its benefits and drawbacks? What are both countries' concerns about cyber-security and conflict in space? To what degree are the United States and China caught in the dynamics of the "security dilemma"? How do each side's decisions about the development of military capabilities influence the other side's decisions? What are the key security concepts of each country that the other does not adequately understand? To what degree do differing national interests drive China and the United States toward military confrontation? Could a misunderstanding or misperception trigger an armed conflict? What are ways in which China and the United States can seek to avoid military conflict?*

• • •

Dear Xu Hui,

Since we met at a conference some 15 years ago, there have been great changes in military relations between our two countries. I worry about many of these changes, as I am sure you do.

China is rapidly modernizing its military. Yes, it remains much less powerful than the United States, and it is not increasing its capacities in order to challenge Washington for global leadership. Still, the reasons for China's military modernization pose challenges to the bilateral relationship. First, there are two central conflicts of interest involving other actors: Taiwan and the competing claims for sovereignty over regional waters and reefs among China and other countries. Second, some spending increases, even if they are not driven by arms race dynamics, may still be worrisome. If they serve as a sop to the military, to ensure its loyalty to the party in a system with weak civilian control over the military, this suggests grounds for concern. Worse than these two specific points, there is a gradual development of a downward spiral in military dynamics that will be hard to escape because it will increasingly become self-perpetuating. Let me lay out these points in the hopes that we might find ways to avoid this dangerous future.

Over the period we've known each other, China has modernized its military rather substantially, albeit from a low base (as we see in Figure 8.1). Even after adjusting for inflation, official Chinese military spending has risen by about 11% per year for the last two decades.[1] I believe, as do most analysts outside of China, that the official budget figures are incomplete. Detailed non-governmental analysis suggests that true spending is 40 to 70% higher than China's official figures.[2] Based on that assessment, Chinese spending in 2012 was in the range of $148 billion to $180 billion, with comparable U.S. spending at $846 billion.[3]

Increased funding for the Chinese military is going, in part, to develop a range of new specific capabilities for the People's Liberation Army (PLA) that worry many in my country, and indeed, observers throughout Asia. While the PLA has stopped adding to its large arsenal of short-range ballistic missiles, it continues to build long-range cruise missiles, medium- and intermediate-range ballistic missiles, and intercontinental ballistic missiles with a mix of conventional and nuclear warheads. China fields multiple variants of quiet diesel submarines and a large number of small missile boats. Its new anti-ship ballistic missile is nearing a usable capability—at least

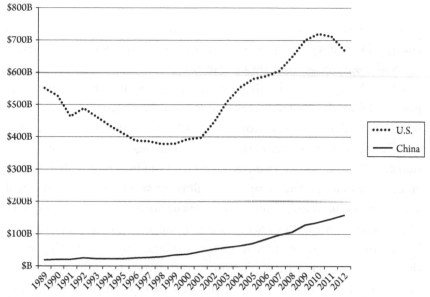

Source: Stockholm International Peace Research Institute's (SIPRI) Military Expenditure Database, available at http://www.sipri.org.[4]

FIGURE 8.1 Military Expenditure by Country, in Constant (2011) US$ Billions.

in theory. China also fields a small "blue water" naval force, such as fleet air-defense destroyers, nuclear-powered attack submarines, heavy attack cruisers, and a small carrier (the latter two both imported from Russia). Many of these are equipped with advanced Russian anti-air or anti-ship missiles. China's "informationalization" of its military aspires to apply technology to command and control (C2) and intelligence, surveillance, and reconnaissance (ISR) networks that have shown their value in American military campaigns. Trading a large quantity of soldiers for increased quality in soldier training, experience, and education is also enhancing China's capabilities beyond these hardware developments.

Not all of the PLA changes are equally destabilizing, of course. China has also developed a nuclear arsenal that is less vulnerable to preemption; this secure second-strike nuclear capability should reduce dangerous fears in Beijing of a "closing window" in which to strike, were military conflict imminent. This will reduce instability in some crisis scenarios (although it may also embolden China's leadership to take provocative actions that could prompt a crisis in the first place). China's ability to deploy substantial military force to distant seas remains modest and, in fact, through anti-piracy patrols, has been used to promote freedom of navigation.

Chinese conduct in "new" areas such as cyber and space, however, does raise deep questions about Chinese intentions for many Americans and China's neighbors. Both private American actors and government officials face constant threats from Chinese network penetrations. Much of this activity is limited to espionage, but that exacerbates the tendency to view China as an enemy.[5] Chinese government-sponsored cyber-theft of commercial intellectual property is particularly egregious[6] and is related to broader Chinese laxity with regard to intellectual property rights (IPR) protections as discussed in Chapter 2 on the economic relationship. Beyond that, some Chinese intrusions have been aimed at penetrating the defenses of critical infrastructure.[7] The information these ventures gather could, in theory, facilitate Chinese attacks against the U.S. homeland.

While this new domain poses new challenges for the two sides, attribution is not the primary one. The official PRC canard that it is impossible to trace the source of such activity has been rebutted convincingly by private sector investigative efforts by Mandiant, McAfee, and Google, among others. Certainly, U.S. government intelligence agencies, with budgets in the scores of billions of dollars (and more legal leeway), have even better information.

There are two aspects of cyber-activity that are especially problematic. First, in the cyber-world it is difficult to differentiate acts aimed at gathering intelligence and those paving the way for subsequent sabotage: both tend to require surreptitiously obtaining "root user" level access to key systems. Intelligence gathering regarding military affairs is, to a degree, acknowledged as a "normal" activity in peacetime; sabotage is an act of war. Second, attacking civilian targets such as critical infrastructure, even with non-kinetic cyber-attacks, would likely be viewed in the United States as a dangerous, unprecedented escalation. The absence of a shared understanding about how provocative such a possible attack would be is disturbing. Reducing these potential challenges is difficult in the face of blithe Chinese denials of its cyber-activities.

In space, Chinese activities such as the anti-satellite missile test in 2007 and a satellite that shifted orbits (as a weapon might) in 2010,[8] suggest an active and offensive military space program that is profoundly at odds with Chinese diplomatic rhetoric. New pieces of PLA hardware such as the aircraft carrier, nuclear missile–launching submarines, and a stealth fighter also create new dynamics. Where does China plan to project power with its aircraft carrier? How will China control its nuclear missiles on the submarines? Does China view the messy destruction of satellites as an effective military tactic? Is China engaged in an arms race with the U.S. Air Force? Because each of these are new capabilities for China and China has not discussed them, they raise questions for Americans and China's neighbors.

Of course, as I have heard you note, it is a natural development for China's military spending to rise with its economy. That said, Chinese military spending has grown somewhat faster than the economy as a whole. A country might do this if it felt less secure over time. But over the past two decades, China has resolved nearly all of its land border disputes. The intense superpower rivalry between the United States and Soviet Union that drew in China in various ways is over. The United States has supported China's economic growth by welcoming it to the world trading community. Political relations across the Taiwan Strait are showing the first signs of improvement in 60 years. All of these developments should lead China to feel much more secure today. So it is hard to understand China's motives for this rate of military spending growth.

The centrality of the Taiwan issue to China's military modernization is well understood in the United States, as you and I have often heard discussed. As part of its broader national strategy of "countering intervention" (反介入) by the United States in a Taiwan conflict, China hopes to deter U.S. intervention if it can, and defeat U.S. forces if they do intervene. The military aspect of China's national strategy is "near-sea active defense" (近海积极防御). You and I both know that China doesn't refer to this basket of capabilities as "anti-access and area denial" forces (A2/AD), still, that is a useful description of what they can do, is it not? They can threaten vessels trying to access coastal waters, and actively deny the use of them. China could use many of the capabilities described above to deter and potentially defeat U.S. intervention in any conflict over Taiwan. Related capabilities, the short-range missiles in particular, are aimed to deter Taiwan from any moves toward de jure independence.

Until recently, it was clear that preventing Taiwan's independence was the primary motivation for China's military modernization. But that is less clear now. Domestic politics certainly plays a role: Chinese Communist Party (CCP) rule depends on the military's support. China's leaders learned the importance of the military's loyalty during Tiananmen in 1989, and

President Jiang Zemin's order to the PLA to cease commercial activity created resentments in the military, which felt its livelihood threatened. Increasing the military budget is one way of ensuring fealty of the PLA to the Party. But this also raises questions about civilian control of the military, because if the military needs to be bribed to follow orders, it probably is not the most obedient of actors.

Another narrow, less positive element in Chinese regional interests likely plays a role in shaping China's military policy. American (and other) reconnaissance missions and freedom of navigation patrols near China's borders are long-standing expressions of Western interpretations of proper and legal use of the seas, and the United States conducts them to gain information on opaque Chinese activities. China, however, has claimed expansive and unjustified rights in exclusive economic zones (EEZs) extending 200 nautical miles from its coastline. It is possible that Beijing views its military buildup to protect its rights in the EEZs as defensive. But given that many maritime territorial claims are contested and that Beijing's views of EEZ rights deviate substantially from widely held international views, that "defensive" desire looks quite offensive to others. Coupled with Chinese military capabilities in these areas (including dedicated coastal patrol organizations who exert these claims with armed patrol craft), this raises questions about China's views on freedom of navigation for many.

Beyond Taiwan and disputes related to maritime rights, other factors seem unlikely to be motivating China's military modernization in a major way. Countries might increase military spending if their interests were expanding, and President Xi Jinping seems intent to continue former President Hu Jintao's advocacy for "new historic missions" for the PLA. This, and President Xi's references to a "Chinese dream," suggests to some observers precisely that expansion of interests. However, many of these are not conflictual interests, and they generally do not drive significant budgetary increases. Indeed, some are well aligned with U.S. interests, such as non-traditional security. Others refer to emerging Chinese global interests, such as securing global (energy and other) supply routes in the long term. I think a nuanced reading of Chinese writings on this topic, as well as the underlying geostrategic realities, suggest that unilateral military activity is not the solution.

While a vocal minority in Washington does think these missions, and hidden aspirations to dominate Asia, are important drivers for Beijing's military modernization, when I look at China's policy making in any arena, I am struck by the multiplicity of views pushed by an expansive range of actors that shape policy. The range of voices expressed on foreign policy is similarly wide.[9] The most notable priority for the CCP over the past 35 years has been economic development, and the reforms in this area are often described, as you know, in former paramount leader Deng Xiaoping's phrase "crossing the river by feeling for stones." This same process of Chinese decision makers gradually developing policy as the situation emerges is likely to characterize Chinese security policy making, precluding any "long-term" plan for global leadership (or anything else, for that matter).

The U.S. military has not been static over the past few decades either. It has wound down two wars in the Middle East that sapped the ground forces in particular, although all services were strained. Military spending soared during these wars, primarily to cover their operational costs, but some also went to military-related research and development and broader procurement. This investment and the ending of those two wars have allowed an increased attention to ensuring the military balance in East Asia remains strongly in favor of the United States. This is formally referred to as "rebalancing" toward Asia and emphasizes renewed attention on the existing alliances in the region, and to some extent, situating the U.S. military strategy for the region within a broader political and economic context.

China's provocative behavior in 2009 and 2010 accelerated the demand from the region for exactly this "pivot" in U.S. attentions. Not only Singapore, but also the Philippines, Vietnam, and Australia are encouraging a greater U.S. role in Southeast Asia. Beijing's tacit, and at times overt, support for North Korea's provocations in 2010 pushed South Korea to slow any warming of its relations with China and to strengthen relations with the United States. Japan, too, has responded to Chinese and North Korean actions by pushing for a tightening of its alliance with the United States.

A second, distinct element in American policy is a set of military operating concepts known as Air-Sea Battle (ASB). ASB aims to maintain the United States' ability to defend its interest in a changing technologic and military environment, and the most challenging of these is in East Asia. As the heads of the Air Force and Navy describe it:

Our future investment, doctrine development and innovation will be guided by employing tightly integrated, cross-domain operations to defeat anti-access and area-denial threats and restore our freedom of action. This central idea is embodied in the construct of "Networked, Integrated Attack-in-Depth." This construct is used to pursue three lines of effort to disrupt, destroy and defeat adversary anti-access and area-denial capabilities.[10]

It is tactically offensive, explicitly aimed at anti-access technologies (of which China is the leading purveyor), and requires early attacks on the full range of military infrastructure of an adversary. ASB will be centered on deep strikes at an adversary's command and control and intelligence, surveillance, and reconnaissance assets. Stealthy long-range bombers, long-range precision munitions, advanced jamming, cyber-attacks, and submarines are all likely to receive added attention. To some, Air-Sea Battle is "a concept in search of a budget;" others argue that it is simply a way to repackage ongoing programs. Certainly, it would be wrong to view ASB as fully developed in concept, or as solely aimed at China: it will evolve in response to the threat environment and bureaucratic pressures in Washington. Still, declaring a unified, public strategy will help decision makers set priorities. Congress will understand the importance of programs serving to enhance ASB.

These ASB operational concepts would not be viable without tighter relations with an increased number of allies and partners. Thus, the "pivot" has the potential to provide the geostrategic basis that will make Air-Sea Battle more effective. This will be a tricky issue for U.S. decision makers to balance, however. ASB is intended to help the United States to maintain its significant operational advantages against a modernizing China, allowing the United States to reassure its allies about its capabilities. Yet some partners in the region view the tactically offensive nature of it as excessively provocative.

All of this greatly worries me, not because there is a direct, bilateral threat to the United States from China, but rather because these dynamics (spirals, misperceptions, third-party actors, contested norms) can lead to inadvertent conflict. Scholars and analysts tend to shy away from stating that the United States and China are in an arms race. But at the very least, I have to conclude that our two countries are locked in a very interactive pattern of military modernization where each side takes the other as its most likely "demanding security threat" and develops its own responses with the other in mind. So if China's anti-access, area-denial capabilities were a response to the U.S. deployment of a U.S. aircraft carrier to the Taiwan Strait in the 1995–1996 missile crisis, then the U.S. Air-Sea Battle concept is a reaction to that response. And certainly China will react to ASB. That is a classic spiral. (Perhaps as Chinese naval and air assets have increased their ranges, they have had more frequent encounters with pre-existing and long standing U.S. reconnaissance. If these drove, in part, China's anti-access and area denial response, then it would be yet another inadvertent spiral.) In other areas, U.S. missile defense—in large part aimed at smaller threats like North Korea—sparks concerns in China, leading to a range of strategic modernization programs that threaten America. Space might be viewed similarly, with (messy) Chinese anti-satellite missile tests being followed by a (cleaner) American shot with a missile defense system and experiments with the advanced X-37B space drone. In these cases, there is a tendency for both sides to assume a continuity of purpose that further solidifies assessments of malign intent. This tightens the hold of such spirals.

Were our two countries' military relations solely characterized by these "spirals," one might hope that confidence-building measures and transparency would be sufficient. However, several factors will complicate such efforts. First, some of the spirals are occurring in areas that are new and poorly understood, like cyber-warfare and the militarization of space. These are prone to worst-case analysis, with few sober-minded counterarguments from comparable experience. Further, both these areas are highly "offense-dominant;" defenses can do little to stop attacks. Worse, in space in particular, the use of such offensive weapons by China would destructively pollute that "commons" to the detriment of *all* actors. Moreover, several interactions involve a third party's interests as well; in the largest of these cases, Taiwan's own nationalist identity will complicate the long-term prognosis, despite recent positive political dialogues between Taiwan and the mainland. Our colleagues address Taiwan in Chapter 9.

Finally, while spirals are increasingly playing a role in our countries' relations, even worse is what I see as fundamental, if narrow, conflicts of interest. Regarding Taiwan and on China's expansive claims of rights in equally expansive EEZs, I think the two sides have very different interests that are likely to drive conflict even in the absence of misperceptions. These would exist in the absence of any such narrowly military dynamic, but give life to the spirals mentioned above and deepen the sense of inevitable, global rivalry.

I hope you can give me grounds for more optimism.

Regards,

cpt

• • •

Dear Chris,

I feel honored that you shared your worries about the changes in military relations between our two countries. I do appreciate the views U.S. scholars commonly express about the Chinese military. However, these opinions also trouble me because they are largely negative and founded on the faulty assumption that China and the U.S. are adversaries.

I believe this is very dangerous. As constructivists argue, international relations are, in large part, mentally constructed. Therefore, if one defines Sino-American relations as adversarial from the outset, one will tend to interpret the other nation's actions in a negative light and make it out to be an enemy, thereby creating a self-fulfilling prophecy. For this reason, we urgently need China and the United States to view each other as objectively as possible.

You mentioned Taiwan and divergent views of China's rights in its offshore regions as two central conflicts of interest that are likely to breed Sino-American security spirals and escalate into global rivalry. I would like to take this opportunity to put various events in their correct historical perspective.

First, as commonly acknowledged by the international community, the issue of Taiwan's separation from the Chinese mainland was mainly created and still persists due to U.S. support of Taiwan, and could easily be resolved if the United States were to take the initiative. As Jia Qingguo points out in Chapter 9, the Taiwan issue would not have existed if the U.S. government had not interfered in China's domestic affairs by sending the its Navy's Seventh Fleet to the Taiwan Strait in 1950 during the Korean War. In December 1978, the U.S. government agreed to sever its diplomatic relations with Taiwan, withdraw its military forces, and establish diplomatic relations with China. However, to China's despair, after only three months, the U.S. Congress passed the Taiwan Relations Act and vowed to continue arms sales to Taiwan. To resolve the issue of U.S. arms sales to Taiwan, the Chinese and U.S. governments held negotiations for nearly ten months and reached an agreement on August 17, 1982. In a joint communiqué issued at the conclusion of these talks, the U.S. government stated that it

> does not seek to carry out a long-term policy of arms sales to Taiwan, that its arms sales to Taiwan will not exceed, either in qualitative or in quantitative terms, the level of those supplied in recent years since the establishment of diplomatic relations between the United States and China, and

that it intends gradually to reduce its sale of arms to Taiwan, leading, over a period of time, to a final resolution.[11]

However, the United States backtracked shortly afterwards, and instead of decreasing arms sales, it substantially increased military cooperation with Taiwan and even interfered militarily in the Taiwan Strait crisis in 1996 arousing many suspicions about U.S. intentions toward China.

Going by simple logic, there should not be a fundamental conflict of interest between the United States and China, as there is no territorial dispute between the two nations nor do they feel national hatred toward each other. In fact, many Chinese even show some degree of admiration for Americans. However, U.S. policies toward Taiwan have been and are the fundamental cause of some anti-American sentiment among the Chinese public. It may be prudent for the United States to carry out a cost-benefit analysis of the Taiwan issue in the context of its overall national interests. I assure you that a posture change of the U.S. policy on Taiwan will remove the major obstacle for our military-to-military relations and also strengthen Sino-American cooperation by winning the hearts and minds of 1.3 billion Chinese people.

Second, you mentioned that the U.S. reconnaissance missions and patrols near China's borders are legal based on American interpretations of maritime law and freedom of navigation. However, a majority of countries have a different interpretation. From a Chinese perspective, these actions may indicate unfriendly, even hostile, intentions and increase the possibility of crises and clashes. Even from a legal point of view, these actions violate the United Nations Convention on the Law of the Sea. This treaty provides for the right of freedom of navigation and overflights in EEZs (exclusive economic zones) to all countries, but the right is not without conditions. As Article 58 reads, "In exercising their rights and performing their duties under the Convention in the EEZs, states shall have due regard to the rights and duties of the coastal state and shall comply with the laws and regulations adopted by the coastal state."[12] U.S. reconnaissance and patrols near China's borders certainly go against established diplomatic norms between friendly nations and pose a threat to China's security by going well beyond the right of free navigation and overflights.

Third, you mentioned your concerns over China's military spending. You argue that official Chinese military spending has increased by about 11% per year for the last two decades, but it wouldn't be fair to object to the *increase* while ignoring the *decrease*. You may have forgotten that Chinese military spending went through a *period of tolerance* for almost 20 years, when former Chairman Deng Xiaoping made economic development the absolute priority in national development. During that period, national defense received a very low share of the budget and could barely sustain itself. According to China's National Statistics Bureau, from 1979 to 1989, defense expenditures decreased over 6% annually after adjusting for inflation. Although defense expenditures increased during later years, it was to a limited degree. For example, from 1990 to 1997, it increased only by 6.1% annually after inflation adjustments.[13] Given this background, it is quite easy to understand why the Chinese government has increased its military spending. You have admitted yourself that China's defense budget is still much lower than that of the United States.

In fact, the Chinese have learned a very bitter lesson from history: that economic development alone cannot guarantee national security. Britain defeated China in the Opium War of 1840 even though China was a prominent economic power and accounted for about 33% of the world's GDP at the time.[14] It did not end there. China continued to suffer from foreign invasions in the 19th and early 20th centuries primarily due to the weakness and backwardness of its military.

Even now, compared to other major countries, China's defense expenditures are relatively low. In 2011, China's total defense expenditures were almost one-eighth of those of the United States, while its per-capita defense expenditures were only 4.5% of those of the United States. In 2010, China's military spending as a percentage of GDP was 1.3%, which is lower than many countries including the United States (4.7%), the United Kingdom (2.5%), Russia (2.8%), India (2.5%), and Brazil (1.7%).[15]

What confuses Chinese is why China can't modernize its military when all countries are seeking to modernize their militaries? Why does the U.S. Department of Defense annually publish a Report of Military Development targeting China, a practice once used by the United States to monitor the Soviet Union, a peer enemy during the Cold War?

I remember you once told me that it was not necessary for China to modernize its military since its security environment was improving significantly. If this logic stands, then I am afraid to say that the United States should have given up its military transformation a long time ago. After all, America has continued to enjoy superior military power for decades while having an advantageous geographic position with no strong neighboring countries to threaten it. If China's motives for military modernization are to be questioned, then what explains America's motivation to seek absolute military superiority?

China's security environment has truly been improving, but it remains the only country among the five permanent members of the UN Security Council that has not been territorially united. It faces numerous non-traditional security threats such as terrorism, separatism, and extremism. It also needs to secure its shipments of energy and resources. Besides, a strong military is a prerequisite for China to shoulder increasing international responsibilities. You would appreciate that by December 2010, China had dispatched 17,390 military personnel to 19 UN peacekeeping missions, far exceeding America's contributions to these missions.[16] China has also actively participated in anti-piracy patrols in the Gulf of Aden as a responsible member of the world community.

You have also expressed your worries over China's development of some offensive platforms like aircraft carriers, nuclear missile-launching submarines, and a stealth fighter, among others. These concerns arise mainly when people misunderstand China's active defense policy. Self-defense is at the core of the policy, based on the principle of not firing the first shot while maintaining the capability to strike back in a fitting manner. Therefore, development of these weapon systems is essential for national defense. At the same time, China does not envisage any preemptive strikes on other countries and has declared a policy of *no first use* of nuclear weapons as a responsible state.

Foreign countries have invaded China many times throughout history. As Confucius said more than 2,000 years ago, *do not do to others what you don't want to be done to you.* Deng Xiaoping declared in the 1970s that China neither pursues hegemony now nor will it pursue hegemony even when it becomes stronger. In the new century, China's leaders have also repeatedly declared that China is taking a route of peaceful development, which is different from historical models. But some observers still tend to interpret China's development based on their own country's development experiences, holding that a country will inevitably pursue hegemony when it is strong enough. Contrary to American ambitions of global leadership, China's fundamental purpose for military modernization is to safeguard national sovereignty and territorial integrity.

To be frank, China's peaceful development model is an unprecedented experiment in the world, which does not only require China's own efforts but also requires other countries' understanding and support. New thinking patterns are needed in the new century. As the only superpower in the world, the United States needs to take a fresh look at China's military modernization and accommodate it as a partner rather than a rival.

You also mentioned that private American actors and government officials "face constant threats from Chinese network penetrations." I am afraid this accusation needs to be reconsidered for the simple reason that it is technologically not yet possible to locate the real source of attacks. In this context, it would not be responsible to attribute cyber-attacks to China's government without actual evidence. China is also the victim of cyber-attacks, but China has never accused any other country subjectively. In fact, cyber-space and space are both public domains in which cooperation is the only solution to safeguarding security rather than making accusations.

You mentioned that China's military development worries the international community and Asia, but that is not so. Rather, based on our unpublished interviews at China's National Defense University with senior-ranking officers from more than 100 countries, most countries, except a few that have disputes with China, believe China's military modernization is a natural outcome of its economic development. They expressed their appreciation for China's long-enduring peaceful foreign policy, describing it to be a cornerstone for stability and development of the Asia-Pacific region over the last 30 years.

I believe the main obstacle in constructive development of Sino-American military relations is not so-called "spirals" but American security conceptions and strategic intentions toward China. After all, the Chinese and U.S. militaries experienced successful cooperation in the 1980s when their relationship attained the level of quasi-alliance. But American strategic intentions toward China seem to have changed after the end of the Cold War. The DeLay amendment to the National Defense Authorization Act of FY 2000, which placed limits on military to military contacts and limited high-tech transfers to China, as well as U.S. efforts to prevent the European Union from lifting its arms embargo to China, were viewed by the Chinese as expressions of hostile U.S. intentions.

President Obama's strategic pivot to the Asia-Pacific region, especially during the financial crisis of 2008 and political riots in Northern

Africa, makes China even more suspicious of U.S. strategic intentions. Although you opined that the pivot was aimed at strategic rebalancing and not focused on China, many analysts believe that it was intended to contain China's rise.

To make matters worse, some countries that have disputes with China have exploited the strategic pivot. Recent provocative acts by Japan and the Philippines are examples of ramifications of the U.S. strategic shift toward China. The U.S. media utilized these events to malign China rather than highlighting the truly destabilizing acts of Japan and the Philippines.

Some scholarly works do provide a rationale for the U.S. hostile attitude toward China. A well-known American scholar, Charles Krauthammer, stated in the 1980s that "A country needs an enemy; when one enemy disappears, it will find another one,"[17] whereas Samuel Huntington believed that the ideal enemy should be a country that is ideologically, racially, and culturally different and militarily strong enough to pose threats.[18] If these scholars are right, America will make the U.S.–China rivalry a self-fulfilling prophecy.

All in all, I appreciate that you expressed your views rather bluntly in your letter. And I don't anticipate your total agreement with my views. Anyway, it's not the end of our discussion. I am looking forward to your reply.

Regards,
Xu Hui

• • •

Xu Hui,

Thank you for the thoughtful reply. You raise many issues, and unfortunately we don't have the space to address each of them. Thankfully, our colleagues are addressing a few in more detail.

Still, let me say a word here about your views on Taiwan. I agree this is an important source of contention between our two countries and recognize that the United States' involvement goes back to the waning days of your civil war when the Soviet Union armed and supported the CCP's Red Army. But rather than debate the merits of the Cold War antagonists' involvement on opposite sides of that war, I will turn to the contemporary issue of arms sales to Taiwan.

I think it is important for our Chinese friends to recognize that the United States reads the 1982 Joint Communiqué in its entirety and does not isolate the passage you highlight from its broader context. Specifically, the American intention to reduce arms sales was explicitly predicated on "the Chinese policy of striving for a peaceful resolution of the Taiwan question."[19] As Chinese military capabilities optimized for attack have grown dramatically over time, the aspiration for a peaceful resolution increasingly carries a coercive edge. China has repeatedly reserved the right to use "non-peaceful means" in pursuit of reunification. Given that reality, and deep American ties to Taiwan, I suspect arms sales will continue through our lifetimes.[20] However, because of China's extensive military buildup, such sales will not be able to achieve "balance" across the Straits, nor effectively defend Taiwan from attack by the PLA Air Force and China's missile force in the Second Artillery.

As you agree, the issue of the legality of naval activities in China's EEZ is another important subject. While the definition of what constitutes "marine scientific research" is really an issue for lawyers to address,[21] I will align my views with the 176 nations who agree with the United States' position rather than the 15 that side with China's.[22] Indeed, I will side with the Chinese Navy, which uses the same justifications as the United States when patrolling uncontested Japanese EEZs outside of territorial waters.

Reconnaissance and espionage are facts of life between our two countries. Let's not pretend that China does not spy on the United States. Today, China does not do so with naval vessels; that may change. But cyber-espionage is unambiguously an important technique—again, for both sides.

I have to take issue with your assertion that it is "technologically not yet possible to locate the real source of cyber-attacks." There is plenty of evidence of Chinese involvement in many cyber-activities. U.S. commercial actors, government offices, and several European entities have all come to this conclusion. Large commercial Internet security firms have uncovered major operations.[23] Google pulled out of China because the situation got so bad, and the Politburo is said to have approved those operations.[24] The U.S. Office of the Director of National Intelligence labeled China a "persistent collector" in its annual report on industrial espionage.[25] European Union officials and the German Chancellor have had their systems hacked by groups based in Shanghai and affiliated with the PLA.[26] The evidence of PRC state-sponsored cyber-activity is pervasive.

Of course, the United States also engages in espionage over the Internet, and, in some cases, even more disruptive cyber-activities.[27] In contrast to China, however, the U.S. government does not engage in commercial espionage. My larger concern here is that hacking, cyber-espionage, cyber-sabotage, and cyber-attacks are all new areas where red lines are unclear. This raises the prospect that misperceptions may occur and, as you noted in your letter, constructivists would state that such activities enhance perceptions of rivalry. I, like many Americans who work on China policy or travel to China, have to spend an inordinate amount of time reducing my exposure to your government's endeavors in this regard.[28] Undoubtedly, this has had an effect on my views of China. Hopefully, unofficial dialogues as well as initial government-to-government conversations on this topic can expand into serious discussions in official channels.

You make some good points on the issue of China's military budget. Indeed, China has started modernizing its military from a modest capacity, and China's history does paint vividly the dangers of military weakness. That said, China's low "defense spending per capita" neither reassures nor enhances analytic clarity. What matters is how large militaries are relative to each other since military power is relative power (i.e., total budgets) and how much effort countries are putting into defense relative to other priorities (i.e., budgets as a percent of GDP).

Part of what is problematic about the PRC's military growth is China's lack of transparency. Again, this is not just an American concern. It is no longer a legitimate defense (if it ever was) to claim that China, as the weaker side, should be permitted a degree of opacity about its military modernization plans. That rings hollow to countries like the Philippines, Japan, and South Korea, all of whom are much more transparent about their militaries, and all of whom spend less.

There is some truth to the claim that China is not acting "hegemonic," at least not yet. However, there are some concerning signs. Chinese claims to islands in the South and East Chinese Seas are increasingly being made in strident terms and at times defended with paramilitary or military forces. This is different from prior Chinese behavior in the first decade of this century when such claims were advocated more gently, and "peaceful development" remained at the fore. Chinese diplomacy toward its South China Sea seems increasingly bellicose, causing southern neighbors to increase their ties with the United States. Your foreign minister's public scolding of Singapore in 2010 is one such (un)diplomatic example: "China is a big country and other countries are small countries, and that's just a fact."[29]

China's seizure of Scarborough Shoal with the involvement of paramilitary forces—consistent with its long-standing claims, I understand, but in violation of the 2002 Declaration of Conduct agreed to with the Association of Southeast Asian Nations (ASEAN)—is another example. Further, Xi Jinping's call for a "new model of major power relations" presumes an accommodation of Chinese interests and pushes the United States to view its regional relationships through the lens of bilateral Sino-American relations.

Perhaps you are right, "people misunderstand China's active defense policy." I would be interested in reading your "interviews ... with senior-ranking officers ... from more than 100 countries." My reading of international perceptions comes from the Pew Foundation's president who summarized the 2011 *Global Attitudes Survey:* "Outside the Muslim countries, however, there is a general consensus that it would be bad if China were to rival the U.S. militarily."[30] In any event, I would certainly welcome a more detailed discussion of China's active defense policy.

For many, both history and current force capabilities raise questions about the sincerity of China's rhetoric.[31] One source of doubt comes from the PLA deploying weapons that seem optimized for first strikes:

- Short-range missiles arrayed against Taiwan to seize air superiority;
- High speed "Sunburn" and "Sizzler" cruise missiles to sink U.S. carriers (launched from ships that are vulnerable to air strike, so they must be used at the outset of any conflict); and
- The DF-21D, the anti-ship ballistic missiles (whose command and control systems would be targeted in a conflict, and thus are most potent in the opening hours of a conflict).

Similarly, increased discussion of distant seas (远海) operations suggests that the PLA Navy has other interests beyond its traditional focus on "local wars under informationalized conditions." Aircraft carriers, blue water naval squadrons, air-to-air refueling capabilities, and nuclear-powered attack submarines are all assets being developed to project China's power. These are reasons for some skepticism about Chinese "defensive" policy. More discussion about how these weapons combat the "three evils" of "terrorism, separatism and religious extremism" or counter-interference in a Taiwan scenario would be welcome.

You also state that "China does not envisage any preemptive strikes on other countries." That is a welcome assertion, but the last 60 years of PRC security policy can be interpreted to show such strikes are common, and there is a large amount of Chinese literature emphasizing the value of "seizing the initiative."[32] Vietnam has suffered at least two "first strikes" from China (and South Vietnam suffered a third). Taiwan did not brandish military force first in 1995; China did. The United States did not cross China's border in 1950. Perhaps those past cases of the PRC military attacking first are no longer relevant under the current CCP leadership and in the current international environment. I hope that to be true.

Well, as you noted, we disagree about much. I do find some grounds for optimism in some areas. On issues of EEZ rights, I sense the beginnings of a shift in the Chinese party line. Elsewhere, I agree China has played a constructive role in its participation in anti-piracy patrols. I am pleased that a long-postponed joint humanitarian assistance and disaster relief exercise between our two countries is back on track. These "non-traditional" security areas will be important for China as it becomes more of a global player, and in many of these our national interests are actually quite compatible.[33] As China's role in the global security environment grows, perhaps certain Chinese and U.S. interests will converge more. It is my hope that cooperation in these non-traditional areas might mitigate the pressures for conflict that stem from the points raised above.

I hope you, too, can find some grounds for optimism. Otherwise, we make for a very depressing pair.

Best,

cpt

•   •   •

Dear Chris,

I really appreciate the concerns expressed in your letter about the People's Liberation Army. For the past 15 years, you have remained consistent in your suspicions and doubts about the PLA. For me, this is of great concern. After all, as an influential scholar, your opinions will surely exert a certain influence on the U.S. government and populace. I feel obligated to clarify some of the points you raised in order to provide a less-biased impression of the PLA.

To begin with, your letter contains a great deal of research and numerous citations and references. But we should review the data you have cited, since some of the sources may be very misleading. Given the limits of this short paper, I will clarify just some of them. For example, you refer to the Pew Research Center's poll when discussing international society's responses to the PLA. This poll was conducted in only 22 countries, and most of those countries are U.S. allies. How can we expect this poll to reflect the general attitude of the international community, which has more than 200 member countries?

Additionally, when talking about the legality of naval activities in EEZs (exclusive economic zones), you refer to data suggesting that 176 countries side with the United States, while only 15 countries side with China. But when, at an international conference, my colleague, Ms. Zhang Haiwen,[34] questioned Mr. Dutton, the editor of the book in which this data is included, he failed to prove the validity of the data. Actually, contrary to that essay's conclusion, most countries actually do take China's side on this issue, according to my rich experience participating in international seminars with foreign officers. My views on this topic are also quite logical if you consider that most countries have neither the capability nor the intention to send military surveillance or reconnaissance ships to patrol other countries' EEZs.

As to cyber-space, I have to let you know that the assertion I made that "it is technologically not yet possible to locate the real source of cyber-attacks" is not a Chinese notion, but rather the view of Professor Gil Duvall of your National Defense University, a responsible leading expert on cyber-security.[35] As to the "evidence" you cited from secondary sources, they were refuted by Sr. Col. Geng Yansheng, the spokesman for China's Ministry of Defense, as groundless. He said, as is known to all, that it is common for hacking attacks on the Internet to take place by masking the actual originating IP addresses. Allegations of cyber-espionage that only catalogue some routine cyber-activities lack a legal basis, since cyber-attacks are transnational, anonymous, and deceptive; their source is often extremely difficult to identify.[36] Mr. Hong Lei, Spokesman of the Ministry of Foreign Affairs, said, in 2012, about 73,000 overseas IP addresses controlled more than 14 million computers in China and 32,000 foreign IP addresses remotely controlled 38,000 Chinese websites.

Statistics show that attacks originating from the United States rank first among foreign hackings of Chinese targets, and the Chinese military in particular. But we do not point fingers at the United States based on the above-mentioned findings.[37] Why does the United States? *The People's Daily*, a leading publication in China, said that American allegations about cyber-attacks serve as an excuse for Washington to expand its cyber-security forces and levy more technology restrictions on China as a containing measure.[38] Professor Jin Canrong, an American studies expert with Renmin University, said the real motive behind the U.S. hacking accusations is to seek an upper hand in Sino-American relations against the backdrop of the U.S. fiscal constraints.[39]

Given this, I am afraid that lodging one-sided media accusations will not help solve problems, but only jeopardize existing cooperation. Cooperation rather than confrontation is the only right approach in dealing with this new transnational security issue. For this purpose, China not only bans all cyber-sabotage activities, including hackings, and in fact always resolutely fights them,[40] but has established bilateral law enforcement cooperation with over 30 nations and regions, including the United States, the United Kingdom, Germany, and Russia.

You mentioned that the PLA's Navy also patrolled uncontested Japanese EEZs beyond their territorial waters, but this is not the case. The PLA Navy patrolled high seas, not EEZs as suggested by Japan. According to the UN Convention on the Law of the Sea, the Chong zhi niao jiao/Okinotorishima reef is a reef rather than an island, and thus Japan is not in the legal position to claim EEZs in this area. I suggest our U.S. friends take a fairer position consistent with international norms and rules even when dealing with issues involving their allies.

The United States has declared that the U.S.–Japan Security Treaty covers the jurisdiction of the Diaoyu Islands (the Japanese call them Senkakus). This declaration is contrary to international norms and rules, has escalated tensions, and has shifted the status quo of Sino-American relations. Many Chinese, including myself, are wondering what the United States' intentions are in this case. The Diaoyu Islands were first discovered, named, and used by the Chinese and have long been part of Chinese territory. Only in 1894 did Japan take them, during a war. On December 1, 1943, the Cairo Declaration jointly issued by China, the United States, and the United Kingdom stipulated that "All the territories Japan has stolen from the Chinese shall be restored to the Republic of China." This point was further confirmed in the Potsdam Proclamation in 1945. However, the United States soon violated international law by transferring the jurisdiction of the Diaoyu Islands to Japan, declaring that their administration was covered by the U.S.–Japan

Security Treaty. Not only did these acts initiate conflict between China and Japan, but they also helped Japan challenge and even overthrow the international order established by the United States after the Second World War.

You also questioned my statement that China will not act in a hegemonic manner or launch preemptive strikes, citing several examples from history. Again, both your position and examples need to be "rebalanced," to use a term from U.S. policy. I would like to share the other side of the story that readers deserve to know. China did not enter the Korean War until after the U.S. Air Force bombed its borders and many Chinese civilians had been killed. The Sino-India border clash in 1962 was caused by India's "nibbling" of China's territory through its "Forward-Policy."[41] Similarly, it was Vietnam's invasion of Cambodia and systematic persecution of Chinese residents in Vietnam that inflamed the Sino-Vietnam border clash in 1979.[42] This is why China justifies her actions as *counterattacks in self-defense*, rather than *invasions*, as the Western media inevitably describe them. The important but often ignored fact is that China did not seize even an inch of the other countries' territories in these operations. Moreover, while China did not initiate war with these countries, it did initiate ceasefires, and its soldiers retreated to their original places even though they had absolute military advantages. I do not think you can find any parallel in world military history.

Similarly, I believe you need to reexamine the facts before concluding that China has become more aggressive and assertive in the South and East China Seas in recent years. The tensions in these two regions have been caused by other countries' provocative acts, along with a shift in U.S. policy, namely the "pivot" to Asia. If you followed the development of the Sino-Philippine clash on Huangyan Island and the Sino-Japan clash on Diaoyu Island in 2012, you know that China did not provoke the clashes. The former clash was triggered by the Philippines using military ships to arrest Chinese fishermen, while the latter by the Japanese government's illegal purchase of the Diaoyu Islands. Thus, it is not China that destroyed the consensus nor attempted to change the status quo of the region.

Rather than say China lacks military transparency, it is better to say that China lacks the luxury to pursue transparency in the manner demanded by the United States. As a developing country, China has made genuine efforts to increase military transparency at a suitable pace. China issues defense white papers on a regular basis, established the position of "spokesman" for the Ministry of Defense, and developed a military program on China's

Central Television channel. According to American scholars Michael Kiselycznyk and Phillip C. Saunders, China is at the same level of transparency as other Southeast Asian countries.[43] It is widely accepted that military transparency has been used as a tool by the United States to maintain military dominance and primacy.[44] Surely, American's unclear intentions and some unfriendly behavior toward China have negatively influenced China's willingness to be more transparent about its military.

It is easy to understand the strong suspicions about China's active defense policy you expressed in your letter, because this policy is closely linked to Chinese culture and ways of thinking, which happen to be different from American policy and culture. It takes time to fully understand this concept, so I will elaborate.

The first point to note is that China's defense policy is defensive in nature and is characterized by China's strategic restraint. The security concepts proposed by China, such as non-interference in others' internal affairs, shelving territorial disputes and pursuing joint development, and the pursuit of mutual security illustrate well China's doctrinal restraint in the use of force. Second, China's restraint is exemplified by the limits of China's strategic aims. China aims to defend her sovereignty, territorial integrity, and economic development rather than pursue expansion and aggression. China also wants to guard and reform the current international order rather than revolutionize or topple it.[45] Third, it is common sense that an active defense policy does not exclude the necessity for developing offensive weapons. There is ample evidence in world military history to prove that defensive actions cannot be realized without having offensive weapons for deterrence. It is not wise to jump to the conclusion that China's defense policy has changed simply because of the development of a few offensive capabilities. This conclusion would be comparable to adopting the view that the U.S. government is encouraging people to kill rather than pursue self-defense by allowing them the right to bear arms. I am afraid to say that the United States would be perceived as the most dangerous country in the world if you simply conclude that a country is aggressive because it has offensive weapons. The key to understanding China's active defense policy is to put it into the framework of China's history and culture, and the focus should be on the ends rather than means.

Misperceptions abound in your interpretations of China's policy statements. For example, you refer to Mr. Yang Jiechi's statement as a public scolding of Singapore, although what he means is that a big country should not bully the small ones, but the small countries should not bully the big one either. Your understanding of Xi Jinping's call for a "new model of major power relations" also needs to be clarified. What he is really asking is for people to stop looking at Sino-American relations through the traditional lens of power politics. He wants to promote a new type of major power relationship that is different from the geopolitical rivalries of history, given the uniqueness and complexity of this relationship and the changing nature of the time.

With these views clarified, I suggest that our colleagues who care about Sino-American relations and military relations move away from the assumption that a clash is inevitable, and instead focus on working toward the development of a new Sino-American military relationship. In order to build a new type of relationship, we will need to follow some general guidelines. The first is mutual respect. Each side needs to respect the other's core and legal interests. The Pacific and the world are large enough for both countries to grow and develop. The second is to promote cooperation. The Chinese and U.S. militaries have already cooperated in non-traditional security areas, which will gradually facilitate cooperation in traditional security areas, such as jointly maintaining regional stability. The third is managing our differences for mutual gain. We need to establish new and different channels of communication between our two governments and militaries to manage differences and crises, preventing them from escalating and hampering our cooperation on common interests. Last but not least, it is important to build mutual trust. As both sides understand each other better and cooperate more, it will be possible to build the mutual trust that is needed right now. I believe we can still expect the smooth development of Sino-American military relations in the future if these guidelines are implemented fully.

All in all, our exchange clearly illustrates that differences and misunderstandings between our two countries still exist. This is precisely the reason why exchanges and dialogues for promoting mutual understanding and mutual trust should be continued into the future.

Best,
Xu Hui

TAIWAN AND TIBET

JIA QINGGUO
Peking University

ALAN D. ROMBERG
Stimson Center

Framing questions: *Why is the status of Taiwan important to the People's Republic of China (PRC)? To the United States? What are Chinese and American interests and goals with respect to Taiwan? What are views of the people in Taiwan as to its status? What is China's strategy with respect to the status of Taiwan? America's? Taiwan's? What do the Chinese think motivates America's position on Taiwan? And vice versa? What are the obstacles to a lasting peaceful solution to Taiwan's status? What does China want from the United States on its Taiwan policy? And vice versa? Why are those demands possible or impossible to meet? What are the political pressures on each government? Under what conditions would China use military force against Taiwan? When would the United States intervene militarily? How are the Tibet challenge and the Dalai Lama viewed in the United States and China? How do developments in the exile community factor in? Why are each side's ideas for lasting peace and stability in Tibet seen as inadequate or counterproductive by the other?*

• • •

Dear Alan,

In China, the Taiwan problem is considered the most important and most sensitive issue between China and the United States. Most people agree that if it is not handled well, it could spark a war.

The Chinese believe that despite Taiwan's political separation, it remains part of China in terms of territory and sovereignty. Taiwan was part of China long before anybody else laid claim to it. Although it was ceded to Japan after China's defeat in the Sino-Japanese War in 1895, it was officially returned to China in 1945 after Japan's defeat in the Second World War. The current separation between the Chinese mainland and Taiwan is a result of the civil war between the Communists and the Kuomintang (KMT) that began in the late 1940s.

Most Chinese believe that U.S. military intervention in the wake of the Korean War in 1950, which prevented China from liberating Taiwan, created the whole problem. At that time, the authoritarian and corrupt KMT government, which had fled to Taiwan when it lost to Communist forces, was on the verge of collapse. U.S. intervention and large-scale military and economic assistance rescued the KMT.

The Chinese government believes that the best way to resolve the Taiwan problem is through peaceful dialogue, consultation, and negotiation. However, it has repeatedly announced that it is ready to fight a war to defend China's territorial integrity if Taiwan moves toward independence either on its own, by declaring independence or organizing a plebiscite, or through

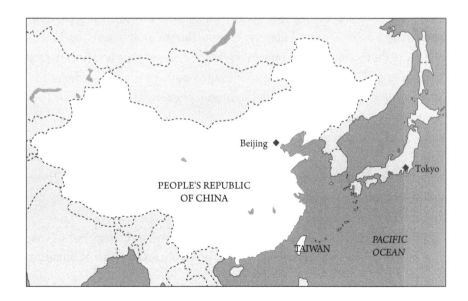

international intervention. The Anti-Secession Law passed by the Chinese National People's Congress, the Chinese legislature, in 2005, codifies this policy.

China wants peace, and it wants unification with Taiwan. Unification would fulfill a desire of the Chinese people and conform with China's history. China has remained a unified country for the better part of more than the 2,000 years since its first unification in 221 BC because the Chinese people repeatedly fought for it. At the same time, peace is both a means and an end in China's development strategy. Peace is not only desirable, but also necessary for China's economic development. China's Taiwan policy reflects a balance between these two fundamental objectives and interests.

The United States, on the other hand, believes that Taiwan has already attained *de facto* independence. But it also believes that Taiwan should not seek de jure, or legal, independence, at least for now, because that would almost certainly invite war with the Chinese mainland. Moreover, given China's growing power and determination to oppose Taiwan independence, the United States realizes that the international community may not even formally recognize Taiwan's independence.

As for the residents of Taiwan, after many years of anti-communist indoctrination under KMT "presidents" Chiang Kai-shek and Chiang Ching-kuo and more than a decade of anti-China indoctrination under "presidents" Lee Teng-hui and Chen Shui-bian, they generally do not trust the Chinese government. Political reforms created space for activists to fan anti-China sentiment and promote Taiwan independence. Decades of physical separation have created a new political identity among Taiwanese residents, and more and more they identify with Taiwan as an independent state under the name "Republic of China." According to various popular surveys conducted in Taiwan, about 30% of those polled want independence now. Less than 10% want immediate unification with China, and the rest prefer to maintain the status quo. It is conceivable that the number supporting Taiwan independence would be much larger if that shift did not promise war. Confronted with reality, though, most people in Taiwan support the policy of "Three no's"—no independence, no unification, and no war—as advocated by the current Taiwanese leader Ma Ying-jeou.

Why is the political status of Taiwan so important to China? For China, the Taiwan problem is first a matter of sovereignty and territorial integrity.

That itself is important for any country. Second, it is also a matter of national dignity and respect. For over a hundred years after the Opium War in 1840, imperialist powers repeatedly invaded China and carved up its territories into spheres of influence. Restoring national independence and reunifying the country therefore has become a most cherished aspiration of the Chinese people. After the founding of the People's Republic of China in 1949, China did become independent and regained most of its territories. However, Taiwan has remained separate—an enduring symbol of China's weakness and humiliation.

Third, the Taiwan problem implicates national unity. China suffers from separatist movements, especially in the minority areas of Xinjiang and Tibet, and Taiwan independence may encourage separatism in those regions. Fourth, the Chinese Communist Party (CCP) promised national reunification to the Chinese people, and its political legitimacy would be undermined if it did not stop Taiwan's independence. Finally, to many people in China, Taiwan has great strategic value. It is located off the Chinese coast and, if independent, could block much of China's access to the outside world and become a platform for foreign invaders.

The political pressures on the Chinese government when it comes to Taiwan are tremendous and growing. In the past, Chinese people knew that China was weak and could not stop the United States from selling weapons to Taiwan. Now, many believe that China should no longer tolerate such insulting behavior. Confronted with this mounting domestic pressure, the CCP is finding it increasingly difficult to justify its "weak" responses, such as verbal protests, to U.S. weapons sales and believes it needs to demonstrate its courage with concrete acts of retaliation. Because national unification is an important source of political legitimacy, the CCP could face a serious domestic political crisis if it does not handle the Taiwan issue deftly.

The United States also considers the Taiwan problem important. The United States wants Taiwan to remain separate from China, at least in the foreseeable future, for ideological, political, economic, and strategic reasons. Proclaimed as a champion of democracy, the United States could never let the "authoritarian" Chinese mainland take over "democratic" Taiwan. Politically, strong pro-Taiwan groups pressure the U.S. government to adhere to the 1979 Taiwan Relations Act, which, among other things, requires the United States to take measures to help Taiwan defend itself. Taiwan is also a significant trading partner of the United States and an investment destination for U.S. businesses.

Strategically, in case of a China–U.S. military confrontation, some in the United States believe that the United States can use Taiwan as an "unsinkable aircraft carrier." Separation also helps reduce the perceived China threat because a united China would be much stronger and pose a greater threat to U.S. security than a divided one. Finally, if the United States gives up Taiwan, it believes that it would lose credibility in the eyes of its other allies and undermine American leadership in the world.

Although less than for China, the political pressures on the U.S. government are significant, and any mistake could be very costly in elections. If Washington makes any concessions on Taiwan, it will be severely criticized. It is believed to be politically suicidal to allow the Chinese mainland to take over Taiwan, and as China's rise continues, it only becomes more important for any U.S. administration not to show weakness in its dealings with China. Only when an administration is so comfortable with power that it does not care about public reactions could it make a significant concession on Taiwan. Given the political configuration of the United States, that is highly unlikely.

However, there are also a variety of considerations that prevent the United States from supporting Taiwan independence. To begin with, some Americans believe that Taiwan has been very successful in adopting a democratic system and that if Taiwan remains part of China, it will have a greater positive political influence on China. Second, the United States fully appreciates how much the Chinese treasure their country's territorial integrity. Supporting Taiwan independence would amount to a direct affront to China, and this could jeopardize America's economic interests and even lead to war. A war in the Taiwan Strait would pose a grave strategic dilemma to the United States: if it were to intervene, it would have to fight a costly, perhaps even a nuclear war with China; if it did not intervene, its international credibility would be damaged. And even a conventional war between China and the United States would destroy the existing regional arrangements that the United States has painstakingly built since the end of the Second World War. Thus, the U.S. government wants to maintain the status quo and preserve the peace.

China wants the United States to stay out of Taiwan affairs, or at the very least, honor the commitment it made in the 1982 China–U.S. Joint

Communiqué to reduce and phase out arms sales to Taiwan. While the United States says it does not oppose peaceful unification, China hopes that the United States will respect the wishes of the majority of the Chinese people and support peaceful unification instead.

How are the three parties seeking to achieve their goals? While preparing to fight if Taiwan declares independence, the Chinese government's strategy is to try to win the hearts and minds of the people in Taiwan in pursuit of national unification. It has set up Taiwan affairs offices throughout the mainland to provide various investment services and advice (about how to locate lost relatives, for example) to Taiwan residents. It has also encouraged Taiwanese investment and introduced policies to enable Taiwan residents to receive education and accommodation in Chinese universities as if they were residents of the mainland.

Beijing has also adhered to its offer of a "one country, two systems" formula for reunification. The formula promises that, in the case of peaceful unification, the mainland and Taiwan may maintain their separate political systems, judicial systems, and ways of life, as in the case of Hong Kong and Macau. Moreover, the Taiwan side could even maintain its military. The Chinese government believes that Taiwan residents will ultimately see the light and realize that unification is in their own interests.

America's long-standing strategy to address the Taiwan problem has three components: the "one China" policy, the principle of peaceful resolution, and arms sales to Taiwan. The "one China" policy derives from the three communiqués signed between the two countries in 1972, 1979 and 1982 and means that the United States acknowledges that both sides of the Taiwan Strait believe there is only one China, and the United States does not challenge that. However, the United States has deliberately avoided clarifying what that "one China" means, that is, whether it means the Chinese mainland plus Taiwan or only the Chinese mainland. Some in the United States argue that now it only means the Chinese mainland because Taiwan residents no longer want unification.

The second component of U.S. policy is "peaceful resolution." The United States claims that it does not have any preference in terms of Taiwan's future—whether it remains part of China or becomes a separate state—as long as both sides reach an agreement through peaceful negotiations.

Finally, the United States maintains the right to sell needed defensive weapons to Taiwan to ensure that Taiwan residents cannot be pressured into an agreement with the Chinese mainland against their will.

The United States has not spelled out when it would intervene in Taiwan militarily. It has deliberately maintained "strategic ambiguity" because it does not wish to send the wrong signals either to the Chinese mainland or Taiwan. Here is the logic: if the United States says it will intervene if war breaks out in the Taiwan Strait, this would encourage the Taiwan separatists to be more provocative toward the Chinese mainland. And if the United States says that it will not intervene, this would encourage the Chinese mainland to take over Taiwan. Nevertheless, it is generally assumed that the United States would intervene if the Chinese mainland attempted to take over Taiwan by force.

The U.S. believes that its strategy has served its interests and enjoys broad domestic political support. It finds the current "no war, no unification and no independence" quite acceptable. It hopes that China will give up the use of force as a means either to unify the country or to deter Taiwan independence, arguing that it would inflict serious damage not only to Taiwan but also the Chinese mainland. Despite China's demands, America is not inclined to change its Taiwan policy.

For its part, Taiwan's strategy has been changing over time. Before current leader Ma Ying-jeou came to power in 2008, his predecessor Chen Shui-bian sought legal, *de jure,* independence. Among other things, he tried to persuade developing countries to grant diplomatic recognition to Taiwan in exchange for aid, attempted to upgrade relations with developed countries (especially the United States) to more official levels, sought Taiwan's membership in the United Nations and other international organizations, and tried to revise the Republic of China (ROC) Constitution through a plebiscite in Taiwan. Chen's maneuvers led to significant tension across the Taiwan Strait. Washington and Beijing both voiced concern and opposition.

After Ma Ying-jeou came to power, he replaced Chen's policy of confrontation with one of pragmatic accommodation. He acknowledged a 1992 agreement between Beijing and Taipei according to which both agree that there is only one China, but they reserve the right to define what that means. He suspended efforts to seek diplomatic recognition by foreign governments and membership in intergovernmental organizations. Finally, he has successfully worked with the Chinese mainland to encourage trade and economic relations across the Taiwan Strait.

These are the current strategies of the three parties. At the moment, the United States can make China accept its weapons sales to Taiwan because China is weak. However, this policy carries significant costs. First, it hurts China–U.S. relations. Every time the United States approves a weapons sale to Taiwan, China–U.S. relations suffer and often China curtails or suspends military contacts. Weapons sales encourage the Chinese government to spend more money developing military capabilities to try to thwart U.S. military intervention. In addition, such sales reinforce Chinese suspicions that the United States has an evil intention of splitting Taiwan from China forever. This strategic distrust hampers China–U.S. cooperation on many other issues, including the North Korea and Iran nuclear problems.

In the long run, if the current rise of China continues, China will have more capacity to influence the final outcome of the Taiwan issue. It can persuade Taiwan residents to accept unification either by making itself more attractive through domestic reforms or through the threat of economic sanctions or military pressures, or both. In the meantime, China will increasingly push the United States to give up weapons sales to Taiwan. In the past, China has tried unsuccessfully to impose sanctions against individual U.S. companies involved in these sales, but it will be in a better position to do so in the future. By that time, whatever the United States has in mind for Taiwan will not matter that much.

Let me turn now to address briefly the question of Tibet. China views the Tibet challenge as a serious domestic problem that is complicated by international anti-China forces. But the sovereignty issue is different from that of Taiwan because Tibet is under the full authority of the government in Beijing.

The Chinese government believes that the Dalai Lama has used his spiritual position to promote Tibetan independence and is responsible for the unrest in Tibet. In August 2011, the Dalai Lama officially retired as a political leader of the Tibetan exile community in India. The new leader vowed to seek "genuine autonomy" for Tibet. But the Chinese government believes that despite this political change, the Dalai Lama remains the leader of the exile community and still promotes Tibetan independence.

Despite its tremendous efforts to improve the living standards of the Tibetan people over the past decades, China is still confronted with serious problems of Tibetan separatism and instability, as the riot in Tibet in

2008 and the more recent run of self-immolations show. Accordingly, it has stepped up investments in the Tibetan economy, education, public health, and welfare as well as making greater efforts to combat separatism and international intervention.

China believes that the United States has no right to interfere with China's efforts to deal with the Tibet question. Despite this, in a serious political affront to China, almost every U.S. president in recent years has met the Dalai Lama on the grounds that he is a spiritual leader. The United States also makes clear that it is concerned with human rights and religious freedom in Tibet and has urged the Chinese government to improve them. Specifically, the United States has suggested that China open a dialogue with the Dalai Lama and the new leader of the Tibetan exile community to reach a peaceful resolution. China recognizes there are human rights problems in Tibet just as in other parts of China and other countries but also calls people's attention to the fact that the human rights situation in Tibet has improved tremendously over the years. The Chinese government regards these U.S. demands as an unwelcome attempt to intervene in China's domestic affairs and does not believe that the true intent of the U.S. government is to promote human rights and religious freedom in Tibet. Rather, it suspects that the U.S. government wishes to use this issue to weaken and undermine the Chinese government. China hopes that the United States will leave China alone in managing the Tibetan question.

China and the United States do not see eye to eye on the Tibet issue on several fronts. We cannot agree on the U.S. right to intervene, the assessment of the situation of human rights and religious freedom in Tibet, and the appropriate approach to dealing with the issue. I'm afraid that is not very encouraging, but I look forward to reading your analysis of the Tibet situation and, of course, your point of view on Taiwan.

Best regards,
Qingguo

· · ·

Dear Qingguo,

You lay out in systematic and comprehensive fashion a very accurate account of China's perspectives on Taiwan and Tibet. I agree with much of what you have said, but I don't think you will be surprised that I don't totally share your perspectives, especially with regard to American policy.

Let me start by agreeing that Beijing views the "Taiwan question" as the most important and sensitive issue in U.S.–PRC relations. Although you did not use the term, the Chinese government often calls Taiwan a "core interest," which means it would take whatever steps are necessary should there be a risk of Taiwan's permanent separation from the mainland.

Whether or not Americans fully understand why this is (or should be) the case—and frankly many do not—the fact that your government sees it that way makes it a reality that my government must, and does, take seriously. I agree with you that, should the situation deteriorate, and should Washington and Beijing not handle it well, this could spark a war. I have long believed it is the only issue that could lead the United States and the PRC to conflict. And despite periodic tensions in the East and South China Seas, I still think that is the case.

Fortunately, the chances of a clash over Taiwan are far lower today with Ma Ying-jeou in Taiwan's presidency than they were a few years ago, when Beijing saw the Chen Shui-bian administration in Taipei striving for de jure independence. Frankly, much as he might have wanted it, I never thought Chen felt Taiwan independence was a realistic goal. He knew Beijing would use force to prevent independence, and he saw that the United States was willing to step in if things seemed to be spiraling out of hand. In 2007 and 2008, Washington helped defeat Chen's highly provocative referendum about joining the United Nations under the name "Taiwan," just as it had dispatched aircraft carriers to the area in 1996 when Beijing seemed to be threatening use of force. Moreover, because of the obvious risks involved, the people in Taiwan would never go along with a government initiative that could provoke PRC military intervention.

On this last point, you note that public opinion polls in Taiwan have shown over many years that more than 80% of people on the island want to maintain the "status quo" but that this could change if independence were a realistic option. I agree. However, if people on Taiwan are anything, they are pragmatic. And as long as independence is not a realistic option, they will not push for it, or allow it.

You note that people in Taiwan do not trust the mainland. Again I agree. You ascribe this to anti-communist and then "anti-China" indoctrination by Taiwan's leaders for six decades after the Second World War. While I'm sure those efforts were a factor for an older generation, they have very little to do with attitudes today. The sharp differences between present-day Taiwan's open, democratic society and far more constrained PRC politics and society, even after decades of economic reform, are the decisive factors now. Moreover, the PRC approach to Taiwan is perceived on the island as ranging from somewhere between demanding and unfriendly to paternalistic, none of which is attractive. Economic draw, yes, but political appeal, no.

The fact that Taiwan has never really been integrated into China—it only was formally incorporated at the end of the 19th century, and then quickly was ceded to Japan—is also relevant. Clearly Taiwan's is a very "Chinese" society in many senses. However, for the vast majority who have no personal history with the mainland but a great deal of historical awareness and local pride regarding Taiwan, it is not surprising that unification is unattractive. No one should be shocked that 70% of people in Taiwan reject unification. It's not that they are neutral about it. They reject it.

I agree with you that the PRC wants both peace *and* unification with Taiwan. As you note, peace, including peaceful development of cross-Strait relations, is crucial for the mainland's own peaceful development strategy at home. But when "peaceful reunification" is defined as "one country, two systems" this fails to take account of the deep and wide antipathy of Taiwan's residents toward unification. Hence, although that formulation was originally designed for Taiwan, and despite its application in Hong Kong and Macau, in my judgment it has no prospect of success in Taiwan.

You cite the importance of sovereignty, territorial integrity, national dignity, and respect as crucial reasons why Taiwan's political status is so important to the PRC. I agree. But I would ask you to consider those same factors for people in Taiwan who have no sense of political affinity with the mainland and who value their dignity and believe they have earned their own place and role in the world.

As the mainland seeks to win hearts and minds in Taiwan, it often acts as though nothing matters to people on the island but their pocketbooks. Economic well-being does matter, of course, as we saw in the outcome of the January 2012 presidential election. Then, Ma Ying-jeou, whose "one China, respective interpretations" policy has facilitated vigorous cross-Strait relations, was reelected by a larger than expected margin in important part because of voters' concerns that victory by the opposition Democratic Progressive Party would lead to disruption of the many beneficial—I would stress "mutually beneficial"—ties created since Ma was first elected in 2008.

But progress has not been robust in other areas. Beijing's failure so far to act vigorously on former president Hu Jintao's December 31, 2008, prescription regarding Taiwan's "international space" is among the most discouraging examples. You will recall Hu saying that fair and reasonable arrangements could be made regarding Taiwan's participation in the activities of international organizations, as long as those arrangements did not give rise to considerations of "one China, one Taiwan" or "two Chinas." To date the only notable advance has been the annual invitation to Taipei to send an observer to the World Health Assembly meeting each May under the name "Chinese Taipei."

As we correspond, there are hints that more international space for Taiwan could open up; I hope so. But as things stand, not only is the PRC missing an opportunity to win favor on the island, but it is actively alienating opinion there. This is not only due to Beijing's approach to Taiwan's participation in intergovernmental organizations, but perhaps especially to its rigid attitude toward participation by private organizations in the international NGO community (not allowing them to use "Taiwan" in their titles), where, by definition, sovereignty is not at stake.

As for the United States, I appreciate your recognition that the United States wants peace. Indeed, maintenance of peace and stability is at the heart of American policy; you might say that is our "core interest."

However when you state that, for ideological, political, economic, and strategic reasons, the United States wants to ensure that Taiwan remains separate from the mainland, to be very blunt, Qingguo, you seriously mischaracterize American policy.

It is true that Americans believe that, were the United States to stand by in the face of PRC use of force or coercion against Taiwan, it would directly impinge on the vital national interests of the United States and many other countries in the region. As you note, doing so would undermine American credibility with allies and others, which is an essential underpinning of the U.S. ability to contribute effectively to regional peace and stability. This is not a matter of the United States seeking hegemony or others wanting it. Neither is true. But abandoning the American sense of responsibility to ensure that Taiwan's future is decided willingly and peacefully, and simply allowing Beijing to use military means to attain its goals, would fundamentally upset the sense of confidence regional actors have in their own security and well-being. This would inevitably disrupt regional equilibrium and set the stage for greater tension and even conflict. Neither the United States nor others could afford to allow that to happen. So the likelihood of U.S. involvement in such circumstances is not small.

However, that is quite different from seeking to perpetuate separation, which is not an American goal. (You raise the impact of the Korean War on America's role in Taiwan. Chinese colleagues might want to ask whether the United States would have intervened in the Strait had Mao Zedong not supported Kim Il-Sung's plan to invade the South in 1950.)

You seem to believe that U.S. policy on Taiwan stems from the vulnerability of any administration to showing weakness in its dealings with China. Again, I think this misses the mark. It is true that, if a U.S. administration tried simply to abandon the 23 million people of Taiwan to the presumed "goodwill" of the mainland, this would be strongly criticized and probably rejected by the Congress and the public. But except for a few isolated academics, I don't know of anyone who thinks in those terms. No one seriously involved in policy making in either party is considering changing the "one China" policy that has been in effect for over 30 years.

As you say, the United States believes that policy has served its interests and enjoys broad domestic support. But rather than promoting "no unification, no independence, no use of force," U.S. policy is best summed up as seeking to promote peace and stability and to ensure that neither side engages in provocation—political, military, or economic—or tries to unilaterally change the status quo.

Just for the record, let me note that, although the United States has "acknowledged" the Chinese position that there is "one China" of which Taiwan is a part, it has never accepted that view. Still, U.S. policy is not aimed at determining the ultimate relationship between Taiwan and the mainland; that's up to them. The United States will not support independence, but neither will it support unification. It will support whatever outcome the two sides comes to peacefully, non-coercively and willingly.

Nonetheless, while the United States has not sought to force the pace of cross-Strait developments, Washington has encouraged cross-Strait dialogue and reconciliation, sometimes more energetically than Taipei has found comfortable, especially in the political and security arena.

Regarding the sensitive issue of American arms sales to the island, I would not deny that they are designed to provide at least a modicum of deterrence so that Beijing is not tempted to view use of force as a cost-free option. But the rapidly growing imbalance in the Strait is not going to be reversed, and no one thinks that arms sales will change that. In criticizing American performance under the 1982 Joint Communiqué, you overlook the critical linkage in that document between the U.S. position on arms sales and China's own pledges about peaceful reunification. While non-military aspects of PRC policy have accorded with those pledges, the substantial buildup of the People's Liberation Army (PLA), much of which has been directed against Taiwan, has not. It has instead eroded those essential understandings.

Another motivation for arms sales, however, is to provide president Ma Ying-jeou the wherewithal to demonstrate to his people that his robust relationship across the Strait is not at the expense of their security and is not the first step down a slippery slope to a unification that they don't want. If people in Taiwan felt they were being given no options, and that they were being forced to accept unification, not only would Ma be unable to do any of the multitude of things he has been doing to weave a web of mutually beneficial relationships across the Strait, but there would be pressure in Taiwan to assert an even more independent identity, regardless of its de jure status. In this way, while not limiting options for future peaceful resolution, U.S. arms sales contribute to the maintenance of stable cross-Strait relations rather than detracting from them.

I also think you misconstrue or overlook another important element of the U.S. policy. The United States does not seek to block China's peaceful rise either by "using" Taiwan or in any other way. If it did, it would have behaved very differently over the past several decades. Instead of working to integrate China into the international system, it would have worked to exclude it. Instead of opening American markets to Chinese products and allowing China to become such an important market for ours, the United States would have worked to thwart such developments, even at the expense of some of our own economic interests. But the United States hasn't done those things; quite the opposite.

What the United States does seek to do is work with China to ensure that, through cooperative efforts, the PRC's emergence as a powerful regional and global player is supportive of a stable world order, not disruptive. That doesn't mean China is expected to accept all existing norms and procedures without registering its own views. But it does mean that China's active participation is sought, including in rule setting, to promote peace, prosperity, and stability rather than to throw its weight around. My own sense is that, with some exceptions, China agrees that this is the appropriate course for it to follow.

You suggest that at some point, as China becomes even more powerful, PRC leaders could decide to threaten economic sanctions or employ military pressure to force unification on Taiwan. I cannot imagine a more self-defeating policy. Even if Beijing succeeded—and the risk of direct confrontation not only with the United States but also with others would be very high, so success would be far from assured—the lingering resentments in Taiwan and disrupted relations with the rest of the world would hobble the PRC's own peaceful development efforts for a very long time.

My sense is that American ties with Taiwan, especially security ties, are sensitive in the PRC not so much for their bearing on cross-Strait relations, per se, but because they are seen by many in the mainland as a manifestation of comprehensive American efforts to constrain China's rise and to limit its power and influence. This relates to the larger issue of Sino-American mutual strategic suspicion that goes far beyond Taiwan issues, and which merits the concentrated and urgent attention of leaders in both countries in a much broader context.

On Tibet, let me simply say that U.S. policy has consistently accepted that Tibet is part of China. Notions that the U.S. support for greater respect for the religious and cultural traditions of Tibet or dialogue with the Dalai Lama is a disguise for support for Tibetan independence are simply misplaced. But what has made the United States a leader in world affairs is not only its economic and military power; it is also its values, including forthright support for human dignity and human rights.

Our own record is, of course, hardly perfect. And so our best leaders approach the subject with a degree of humility. But the very fact of our own struggles with discrimination in the United States makes us painfully aware of the costs of degradation of minority populations.

Rather than weakening or undermining the Chinese government, respect for human rights of Tibetans would strengthen the relationship between the center and the Tibetan minorities and enhance the acceptance by Tibetans of the legitimacy of Beijing's authority there.

We all know that there are radical elements within the Tibetan community, especially in the Tibetan diaspora. My own hope is that Beijing will seize the opportunity presented by the unique qualities of the current Dalai

Lama to work with him to find a mutually acceptable way forward that will respect Tibetan values and aspirations within China.

Alan

• • •

Dear Alan,

Congratulations on your excellent representation of the U.S. perspective on Taiwan and Tibet! It is very comprehensive and nuanced, and I agree with many of the points you make. If you do not mind, for the sake of space, I will focus on just a few items on which we do not quite agree.

To begin with, you state that Taiwan has never been "really" integrated into China despite your acknowledgment that Taiwan is a very "Chinese society." I am a bit confused as to what you mean by "real" integration. Except for the aborigines who constitute roughly 3% of the Taiwanese population, the ancestors of Taiwan's residents came from China at different times over the past three to four hundred years. Despite all the changes that have occurred across the Taiwan Strait during these years, people in Taiwan still speak and write in Chinese and observe Chinese cultural traditions in their daily life. If that does not meet the criteria of real integration, then very few countries, including the United States, can be said to be really integrated. It is true that because of China's weakness and backwardness, Taiwan was occupied by European and Japanese invaders at different times and has been separated from the Chinese mainland because of the civil war and U.S. military intervention since 1949. However, that has not changed the fact that Taiwanese are Chinese, and Taiwan is part of China.

Second, you write that the most important reason that Taiwan residents at the moment do not want unification is political, that is, Taiwan residents do not want to live under the Chinese mainland's political system. This is true. However, to some extent that is a result of long-term political demonization of the Chinese mainland on the part of successive Taiwan authorities and alienation between people on either side of the Taiwan Strait as a result of prolonged physical separation.

And, despite the fact that most Taiwan residents are suspicious of any proposal on unification coming from the Chinese mainland, they do not reject unification in the long run. Various polls in Taiwan suggest that most Taiwan residents remain open-minded as to the ultimate settlement across the Taiwan Strait. Many Americans say that this is because the Chinese mainland insists on the right to use force to stop Taiwan independence. In contrast, many Chinese believe that the reason Taiwan residents do not favor unification now is because the United States encourages Taiwan to remain independent through arms sales and public and private support. Both explanations may contain some elements of truth. However, the fact remains that most Taiwan residents do not reject unification as a future option, as you put it. Personally, I believe that, in the long run, whether Taiwan residents will favor unification depends on the Chinese mainland, and whether the Chinese mainland will be able to improve itself enough for Taiwan residents to want unification.

Third, I agree with you that there is a lot of resistance among Taiwan residents to the Chinese mainland's proposal for unification, namely, "one country, two systems." However, that does not mean that the proposal is not a worthy one. In Hong Kong and Macau, this arrangement has been quite successful so far despite some problems with it. The two islands went through the reunification process smoothly and have thrived since their return to China. The arrangement works because it effectively addresses both the Chinese desire for unification and the particular interests and concerns of various groups of people in Hong Kong and Macau. From a mainland perspective, if the arrangement can be applied successfully to Hong Kong and Macau, it should also be applied to Taiwan.

There are many reasons for Taiwan residents' rejection of "one country, two systems." Among them are Taiwan's internal politics, Taiwan residents' distrust of the Chinese government, and U.S. support of Taiwan. Ironically, whether one likes it or not, the current situation across the Taiwan Strait is one of *de facto* "one country, two systems." That is, Taiwan is not an independent sovereign state, and it practices a different system from the Chinese mainland. It differs from Hong Kong and Macau only in that the two sides do not have a formal agreement on the matter.

Next, I agree with you that the Chinese government has been hesitant to give more international space to Taiwan. However, Taiwan enjoys considerable international space now. Taiwan has representative offices in most of the important countries in the world. A Taiwan representative has been participating in the Asia-Pacific Economic Cooperation meeting. Taiwan is a member of the World Trade Organization. Taiwan now enjoys observer status in the World Health Assembly, the decision-making arm of the World Health Organization. Taiwan's voice is heard on many global issues. Taiwan residents can also travel to many countries, most recently the United States, without a visa. Given the fact that Taiwan is part of China, it already has an unusual amount of international space. Imagine any other country giving part of its territory so much international space! And if Taiwan is willing to give up its claim on independent sovereignty, I believe that the Chinese government will make more room to accommodate Taiwan's desire for more international space. The Chinese government has a principle on the question of international space for Taiwan: whatever international space Taiwan gains should not come at the expense of China's sovereignty and territorial integrity. No country in the world is willing to compromise its sovereignty and territorial integrity over questions of international representation. China is no exception.

On the policy intent of the United States, you argue that the United States does not seek perpetuation of separation between the Chinese mainland and Taiwan. That may be true rhetorically, but the reality is quite different. The United States does maintain a one-China policy. However, as you point out, it also refuses to recognize that the Chinese mainland and Taiwan belong to China. The United States supports peaceful settlement between the two sides, but it also insists on the right to sell weapons and to provide security assurance to Taiwan. Ostensibly, the United States wants to make sure that Taiwan does not have to negotiate at a disadvantage. The United States claims it is ready to accept whatever settlement the two sides of the Taiwan Strait can reach peacefully. The real thrust of the U.S. policy, though, is to strengthen the hand of Taiwan to a degree that makes a negotiated unification very difficult if not completely impossible.

Finally, you mention that the United States cannot "simply abandon the 23 million people of Taiwan to the presumed 'goodwill' of the mainland." This is a standard line used by the U.S. government. It assumes that the United States has a responsibility to protect the people in Taiwan. That is an incredible assumption! Taiwan belongs to China, not to the United States! Following the logic of this claim, the United States should also have the right to sell weapons and give security assurances to China's Guangdong and Sichuan provinces wherein each over 100 million people reside, so as not to "abandon" them to the presumed "goodwill" of the Chinese government! Imagine how Americans would feel if the Chinese government made a similar claim about Texas and Hawaii! The assertion is incredible because it assumes that it is up to the United States to decide how the Chinese on both sides of the Taiwan Strait should deal with their problems.

Having said this, I am not suggesting that the United States has evil intent with regard to Taiwan. What I am saying is that the U.S. policy on Taiwan is not as benign and altruistic as it is portrayed. It was a policy designed to serve the U.S. interests when, in the past, China was weak, and the two countries were enemies with few shared interests. At that time, the United States could ignore what most Chinese people felt about its policy on Taiwan in order to make sure that Taiwan did not fall into the hands of its enemy. The policy appeared to have served the U.S. interests well at the time.

However, times have changed. China is no longer weak, and our two countries are no longer enemies. Instead, they have acquired an increasing stake not only in the success of their bilateral relationship but also in together maintaining global order and addressing global issues. The United States can no longer afford to ignore how Chinese feel about its policy on Taiwan because doing so harms the bilateral relationship at the expense of both countries and the world. The Chinese often say one should keep up with the times when facing a changing world. The United States may need to do so on the Taiwan question, if only to serve its own interests.

Best regards,

Qingguo

• • •

Dear Qingguo,

Thanks for your powerful and clear statement about where differences lie between us—and between our countries—on Taiwan. I very much respect the openness of your comments on these difficult issues. I will try to respond in kind.

To be honest, it is not simply that we do "not quite agree" but that we disagree in important ways.

When I say Taiwan was only briefly integrated into "China," I mean as part of the national political entity. I fully agree that, even though it has distinct characteristics, Taiwanese culture is very much a "Chinese" culture. But whatever the reasons, authorities on the mainland did not incorporate Taiwan formally into their system of governance until late in the 19th century, only to cede it to Japan a few years later. So while most people in Taiwan readily acknowledge that they are part of the "Chinese nation" or "people" (*zhonghua minzu*), they are quite divided over whether their homeland is part of "China" in a political sense. The Ma Ying-jeou government, of course, adheres to a "one China" approach and would not argue with you on this point. But for President Ma and those who agree with him, the nation they refer to when they say "one China" is the "Republic of China (ROC)." Even though in theory (and according to the ROC constitution) this includes both Taiwan and the mainland, in practice today it includes only Taiwan. (It is certainly not the People's Republic of China [PRC].) This distinction is not merely a matter of nomenclature but reveals a fundamental sense of sovereignty and citizenship.

So Taiwan people's opposition to unification is only partly related to their desire not to live under the PRC's political system. Many simply want to be left alone, feeling no affinity or affiliation with the mainland, considering Taiwan their home.

For those who do object to unifying with the PRC on political grounds, I repeat my point that the main reason is not the "demonization" of the mainland, but rather the stark difference between what they enjoy now in terms of freedom and democracy versus what the reality still is on the mainland despite all of the remarkable changes that have taken place there.

On attitudes toward ultimate reunification, it is true that most people favor maintaining the status quo. In fact, as I noted in my first letter, according to one highly respected polling organization, the number of people favoring maintenance of the status quo, at least for now, is well over 80%.[1] But a deeper look at those statistics leads one to a different conclusion from the one you come to, that "most Taiwan residents remain open-minded as to the ultimate settlement across the Taiwan Strait."

Those who actually favor unification now or at some later time amount to less than 10% of the total. While it is true that a third of the people want to maintain the status quo now and "decide later"—a figure that hasn't changed dramatically over the past 15 years—those who want either to maintain the status quo indefinitely or move to formal independence now or at a later time comes close to 50%. Within this group, the number of those who apparently fear the consequences of declaring formal independence and who want to maintain the status quo indefinitely is growing, from only 15% ten years ago and only a bit over 18% five years ago, to almost 30% today. Moreover, there is another figure from a different poll that I cited in my first response, that is, that 70% of people in Taiwan actively do not want unification. Beijing needs to take all of these points seriously.

Much of your argument rests on the idea that Taiwan is not an independent sovereign state. That is certainly the view of the United States and most other governments around the world, not just the view of the PRC. But it is not a view shared by people in Taiwan. Whether they call it "Taiwan" or the "Republic of China," they do not embrace the notion of "one country, two systems." While you can argue that "one country, two systems" is the reality "whether one likes it or not," it makes all the difference in the world for future cross-Strait relations whether the people in Taiwan like it. As we both know, they do not. So it seems to me diverting and even irrelevant to try to argue in favor of a concept that won't fly as a basis of a future resolution. How well it works in Macau and especially Hong Kong is a subject we could discuss at another point. But in any event those populations had no choice. The people of Taiwan do.

Don't misunderstand what I am saying. I think unification at some future point is possible, but only if both sides come to a common understanding on the definitions of "one China," "unification," and "sovereignty" that differ from the meanings given to them by either side today. That will, in my view, take decades to achieve. In any case, setting that aside, I fully agree with you that, in the long run, whether Taiwan residents will favor unification also depends heavily on whether the mainland is able to change—"improve itself," in your words—enough for Taiwan people to want some form of unification.

On international space, most of the examples you cite of Taiwan gaining ground were achieved in the past in situations where Beijing could not prevent it. But the achievements in recent years have been few and far between, except in cases where the PRC has not been represented and hence has not had a way to intervene.

What is critical is that the mainland now has a partner in Taipei that, while unwilling to give up its claim to independent sovereignty, is prepared to set that issue aside in its pursuit of international space and to accept solutions that do not give rise to questions of "one China, one Taiwan" or "two Chinas." In other words, it is willing to act on a basis that, while not yielding to the PRC's position on sovereignty, does not challenge it, either. This is where Beijing has failed to live up to its own principles as articulated by Hu Jintao and has not only missed opportunities to win hearts and minds in Taiwan—indeed, it has alienated people—but has also failed to treat people in Taiwan with appropriate dignity by giving them the chance to meaningfully participate at the international table, allowing them both to serve their own practical interests and to help serve the practical interests of others.

As I said in my first letter to you, I really do think you misconstrue American interests and policies. You challenge the bases of U.S. policy, arguing that the United States wants to block unification because it is in American strategic interests to do so. I'm sure there are some Americans who believe that. But that is not, and in my view will not be, what policy toward Taiwan is all about. As I said before, U.S. policy is about maintaining peace and stability. And that includes ensuring that no nation, including China but not only China, simply can push its way around because it is big and powerful. I know that that is precisely what many Chinese feel the United States does. But it is striking to me—and should be to Chinese friends, as well—that so many other countries in the world, including in Asia, want the United States to "be there" as a reassurance that they have the opportunity to act in their own interests without fear of coercion.

Americans need to be sensitive to instances in which others try to "use" the United States to further their own narrow interests or to avoid living up to their own responsibilities. We need to resist any such efforts that may be made to do that against China. And indeed we have seen many examples where Washington has rebuffed such efforts, including by Taiwan in the past.

The United States has not always acted toward Taiwan as Beijing wished, but I cannot think of a time since the first historic steps taken by Mao Zedong, Zhou Enlai, Richard Nixon, and Henry Kissinger in the late 1960s when the United States has ignored Chinese feelings about Taiwan or about U.S. policy. The leaders of that generation understood fully not only that the United States and China could not afford to be enemies, but that the potential for cooperative Sino-American relations was enormous. And they understood the complications caused by the situation vis-à-vis Taiwan. They wisely decided that even if they could not resolve those issues, they could manage them.

The challenge to do so, and to do so effectively, remains one for our current leaders to meet, and undoubtedly it will be one that tests the skills and vision of their successors as well. It will not be easy for the very reasons we have been discussing. But I have every confidence that they will succeed.

With thanks for this frank and constructive exchange and best regards,

Alan

REGIONAL SECURITY ROLES
AND CHALLENGES

WU XINBO
Fudan University

MICHAEL GREEN
Georgetown University

Framing questions: *How does China perceive the challenges to peace and stability in its neighborhood? What are its goals for foreign policy in the region and its vision of its own role? What are U.S. interests in the Asia-Pacific and Washington's vision of its current and future role? Are these visions compatible? What are the biggest irritants in the relationship when it comes to regional issues? To what degree can China and the United States work cooperatively to address common regional challenges like North Korea's nuclear program? How should conflicting territorial claims in the East and South China Seas be addressed? What roles should regional and international organizations, laws, and norms play?*

• • •

Dear Mike,

Whether you are a realist or a liberal, a discussion of Chinese and American security policies in the Asia-Pacific region has to entail, first and foremost, an analysis of each country's respective national interests in the region. Let me start with offering my understanding of China's regional interests. First, in terms of security, China desires a peaceful and stable regional security environment, including stability along its periphery, safety of its sea lanes of communications, denuclearization of the Korean peninsula, and peaceful resolution of disputes over territorial sovereignty and maritime rights and interests with its neighbors on land (i.e., with India) and at sea (i.e., with Japan in the East China Sea, and with Vietnam, the Philippines, Malaysia, and Brunei in the South China Sea). Second are developmental interests. Most of China's major trading partners are concentrated in the Asia-Pacific region, where China also draws the majority of its foreign direct investment. Sustainable development of China's economy requires the continued expansion of its economic and trade ties with the region as well as the promotion of liberalization and the facilitation of trade and investment. Third, in terms of political interests, China hopes to help establish a regional order in East Asia featuring the coexistence of different political systems, mutual political trust among nations, equal participation in regional affairs, and cooperation for mutual benefit.

If you look at the world map, you will realize that China lives with more neighbors than any other country in the world, and it has to confront a complicated and fluid security environment. Today, Beijing perceives the following challenges to peace and stability in its neighborhood: (1) unstable situations from the Korean peninsula to Central and South Asia; (2) sovereignty and maritime disputes with its neighbors; (3) rising influence of the "three evils," that is, extremism, separatism, and radicalism in Central Asia; and (4) last but not least, U.S. diplomatic and security maneuvers aimed at counterbalancing a rising China, such as expanding U.S. security ties with some of China's neighbors as well as putting its hands in South China Sea disputes.

In my understanding, the first of China's foreign policy goals in the region is preserving peace and stability in the region, especially on the Korean peninsula. This explains why China provides a large amount of aid to the Democratic People's Republic of Korea (DPRK) so as to help maintain its domestic stability, why it hosted the six-party talks (attended by China, North and South Korea, Japan, Russia, and the United States) to address the North

Korean nuclear program, and why it works to prevent an accidental or intentional conflict between North and South Korea. China's second major foreign policy goal is to seek a peaceful solution to sovereignty and maritime disputes with its neighbors, and until those are settled, China prefers the maintenance of the status quo. For instance, China and India reached an agreement in the 1990s on the preservation of the status quo in the disputed areas in their common borders. Beijing also proposed in the 1980s to shelve disputes in the South China Sea and seek joint exploration of the natural resources therein. China's third goal is to promote cooperation in dealing with non-traditional security challenges, such as terrorism, piracy, drug smuggling, illegal immigrants, and so on. A fourth goal is promoting economic cooperation with regional members both bilaterally and multilaterally. For instance, China is now the largest trading partner to many of its neighbors, including Japan, South and North Korea, India, Vietnam, Indonesia, and others. After kicking off the China–ASEAN (Association of Southeast Asian Nations) free trade agreement (FTA) in 2011, Beijing is now working to promote a China-South Korea FTA and a China–Japan–South Korea FTA.

Needless to say, as China's comprehensive national power grows, so does its role in regional affairs. Over the last decade, Beijing has come to develop a clearer view of its regional role: an active proponent and actor for regional cooperation, a significant contributor to regional security, and a provider of regional public goods in economic and security areas.

From a Chinese perspective, the United States' interests in the Asia-Pacific region also cover security, economic, and political areas. With respect to security, the United States seeks to enhance its own security as well as that of its allies, to ensure freedom of maritime navigation, to contain the proliferation of weapons of mass destruction (WMD), and to cope with terrorism. Washington also wants to preserve its superiority in military power and maintain a dominant position in regional security. In the economic field, the United States desires to expand its economic and trade ties with the region, particularly increasing its exports to the Asia-Pacific region. It also endeavors to prevent East Asia from forming a substantive economic bloc that excludes the United States. In the political sphere, Washington hopes to spread its political values and preserve its leadership role in regional affairs. Given the above national interests, Washington defines its current and future roles in the region as a leader in agenda setting and rule making, a balancer against rising powers, and a guarantor of regional security.

How does China feel about the United States' role in the region? Fully understanding the importance of the region to U.S. national interests and the indispensible role that the United States plays in regional affairs, China reiterates that it welcomes the United States "as an Asia-Pacific nation that contributes to the peace, stability and prosperity in the region."[1] However, China doesn't like the United States' self-proclaimed leadership, which compromises the aspirations of other regional members. Beijing also suspects that Washington's intended role of balancer serves only to check a rising China, undermining its legitimate national interests in the region.

Based on the above analysis, it is obvious that China and the United States have major common interests in the Asia-Pacific region. Both sides hope to preserve peace and stability in the region and have shared interests in combating terrorism, preventing proliferation of WMD, and ensuring freedom of maritime navigation. Both Beijing and Washington wish to promote economic growth as well as advance the liberalization of trade and investment in the Asia-Pacific region. Both countries also favor the building and improvement of an open, inclusive, and win-win regional framework of cooperation.

However, differences and contradictions in regional affairs also exist between the two countries and may even grow over time. Beijing feels that Washington is pursuing a strategy of counterbalance vis-à-vis a rising China, by strengthening its military presence in the western Pacific, expanding and deepening security ties with regional members, and fanning the flames of dispute in the South China Sea, among other ways. China also perceives the Obama administration's efforts to establish the Trans-Pacific Partnership trade agreement (TPP) as intended to obstruct the development of East Asian cooperation. Moreover, Beijing views Washington's attempt to play a leadership role in regional affairs as seeking a dominant position in a fast-changing region where the United States should be a partner rather than a hegemon.

As you may agree, whether China and the United States can interact constructively in the Asia-Pacific region will be the key to the management of relations between a rising power (China) and the lonely hegemon (the United States). This relationship will have a determining effect on whether the goal of building "a more stable, peaceful, and prosperous Asia-Pacific region for the 21st century," agreed upon by both Chinese and U.S. leaders,[2] can be achieved.

In my opinion, it is time for China and the United States to try to reach an understanding on the evolving regional architecture through candid dialogue. A consensus on the regional architecture will help build mutual trust between the two countries and lay the necessary foundation for them to cooperate on regional affairs. It will also provide a useful framework for the handling of individual regional issues. Moreover, a Sino-American consensus will send a reassuring message to other regional members that the two tigers can really get along with each other on the same mountain.

As we know, the current regional architecture is largely a U.S.-centered Cold War structure, especially on the security front. However, since the end of the Cold War, a series of important developments such as the unfolding of East Asian cooperation, the rise of China, and the activism of some regional members in Asia-Pacific affairs, have combined to impact the U.S.-centered architecture. The prospective architecture in the Asia-Pacific region should feature more equal relations between the two sides of the Pacific and a more preeminent role for East Asian countries, including China, in regional affairs. Such a structure should also repudiate the old power politics approaches to relations among regional members, such as balance of power, military blocs, use of force, and should advocate for such new norms as cooperative security, common security, non-use of force in solving disputes among countries, and so on. Only by so doing can the region avoid the division and confrontation witnessed in the past.

For the foreseeable future, the Korean peninsula issue remains a major challenge to regional peace and stability and also stands as a litmus test for effective Sino-American cooperation in regional affairs. Effective Sino-American cooperation on the Korean issue has to start with a shared understanding of the nature of the challenge. While the U.S. side has emphasized the seriousness of the North Korean (DPRK) nuclear issue, the Chinese side is concerned with at least three dimensions of the Korean problem: the stability of North Korea, peace and reconciliation between North and South Korea (Republic of Korea, or ROK), and the denuclearization of the peninsula. From a Chinese perspective, a more realistic roadmap to the Korean problem is as follows: stability of the DPRK → improvement of relations between the DPRK and the U.S. as well as reconciliation between the two Koreas → establishment of a permanent peace mechanism on the peninsula → denuclearization of the DPRK.[3]

Looking into the future, China and the United States can cooperate on the Korean issue in the following ways: support DPRK economic development so as to improve its people's welfare and facilitate its efforts to seek external economic cooperation; diffuse military provocations and conflicts between North and South; encourage the DPRK to improve relations with South Korea, the United States, and Japan; and push the agenda of DPRK denuclearization and non-proliferation of WMD. Meanwhile, China is unlikely to offer cooperation when the United States tries to destabilize the DPRK or exert military pressure on it.

Territorial disputes are another critical issue in regional security. For example, for decades, China and Japan had decided to shelve the issue of the territorial dispute over the Diaoyu Islands (called the Senkakus in Japan) in the East China Sea.

Then, in the fall of 2012, Japan stirred up the dispute by deciding to purchase the islands, thus nationalizing them. China viewed this as a major move to change the status quo and reacted strongly. Tension rose between the two countries. The United States intervened diplomatically to prevent the escalation of the crisis, which both Beijing and Tokyo welcomed. However, Washington's statement that the U.S.–Japan security alliance applies to the

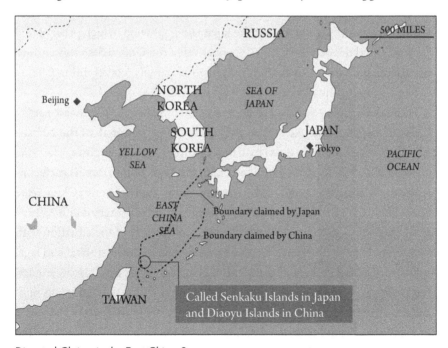

Disputed Claims in the East China Sea.

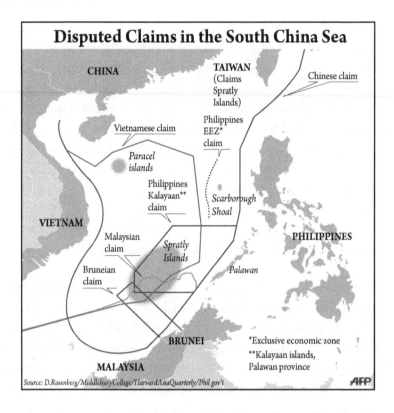

Disputed Claims in the South China Sea

CHINA

TAIWAN
(Claims
Spratly
Islands)

Chinese claim

Vietnamese claim

Philippines
EEZ*
claim

*Paracel
islands*

Philippines
Kalayaan**
claim

*Scarborough
Shoal*

VIETNAM

Malaysian
claim

*Spratly
Islands*

PHILIPPINES

Bruneian
claim

Palawan

BRUNEI

MALAYSIA

*Exclusive economic zone
**Kalayaan islands,
Palawan province

Source: D.Rosenberg/MiddleburyCollege/HarvardAsiaQuarterly/Phil gov't

AFP

islands only serves to encourage the Japanese right wing, which precipitated the crisis, and deepen the Chinese concern that the United States intends to use the dispute for its own strategic purpose, namely, constraining China's expanding maritime activities in the Western Pacific.

The South China Sea issue is another major challenge. The major part of the issue is the conflicting sovereignty claims over part or all of the Nansha Islands (or the Spratly Islands) by China, Vietnam, the Philippines, Malaysia, and Brunei, while four out of the five claimants (except for Brunei) each control some islands, islets, and reefs in the area. Although the South China issue is less likely than the Korean problem to ignite a major military conflict, there is no easy solution to the dispute given the complexity of the situation with sovereignty claims by related parties based on conflicting historical and legal rights, and actual control of parts of the Nansha Islands by China, Vietnam, the Philippines, and Malaysia. What makes the situation even more complicated is America's pursuit of its geopolitical interests in this part of the world —using the dispute to counter China's naval development in South China Sea and to preserve U.S. maritime dominance there. As one scholar noted, "[s]ince around 2010, the sea has started to become linked with wider strategic issues relating to China's naval strategy and America's forward presence in the area. This makes the disputes dangerous and a reason for concern, particularly as the United States has reaffirmed its interest in the Asia-Pacific and strengthened security relations with the ASEAN claimants in the dispute."[4]

In my opinion, the final solution to the dispute has to draw from a comprehensive consideration of historical and legal rights, as well as the status quo in South China Sea. As there is no easy way to settle the dispute, it will require political wisdom of related parties and good political relations among them. China, the most powerful of the claimants, should set a good example in dealing with the dispute. China should further clarify its sovereignty claims over the Nansha Islands, refrain from using force to solve the problem, and conduct flexible and creative diplomacy. Beijing should also resort to multilateral efforts to develop agreements and arrangements conducive to the management and solution of the disputes. Even if a multilateral approach does not ultimately work, it can still demonstrate China's willingness to find a peaceful and reasonable solution.

Since the summer of 2010, the United States has adopted a hands-on approach to the South China Sea issue. However, the United States' role should be to help calm down the situation in the South China Sea and facilitate a peaceful solution to the dispute. Washington should resist the temptation to turn the South China Sea into a battlefield for Sino-American strategic rivalry. Washington also has to be careful in extending support to the Philippines based on its alliance relations because Manila may regard such support as a blank check that it can use at will during South China Sea disputes.

That's all for now, I look forward to your comments.

Sincerely,

Xinbo

• • •

Dear Xinbo,

Your letter is characteristically cogent and precise. I agree that we need to begin by assessing each of our nation's interests in the Asia-Pacific region. That approach makes for better analysis and for more sustainable confidence-building measures going forward. Your description of China's interests in Asia strikes me as accurate, and I think you also capture the essence of U.S. foreign policy interests, though I will have some small dis- agreements and elaboration in my letter on that front. Within the contem- porary U.S. foreign policy debate, I am more conservative realist than liberal idealist, but I think I can fairly present the mainstream views on Asia strat- egy that have framed U.S. foreign policy for Republican and Democratic administrations since the end of the Cold War. In fact, I think that there are certain enduring U.S. interests in the region that date from at least the last century, and it is worthwhile to begin with these.

Broadly speaking, U.S. objectives in the Asia-Pacific region have flowed from our nation's global interests in maintaining an open and liberal inter- national order that protects the American people, promotes their economic well-being, and advances their democratic values. American grand strategists from John Quincy Adams to Alfred Thayer Mahan and Nicholas Spykman have stressed that the greatest threat to these interests in Asia would be the rise of a hostile hegemonic power from within the region. Uncertainties about how China will use its growing power trigger this historic instinct in American strategic culture. Most foreign policy elites in the United States would agree that the rise of China is one of the biggest geostrategic conun- drums we face as a nation today.

However, three important caveats are necessary. First, there is no main- stream support in the United States today for a policy of containing China. Instead, U.S. foreign policy strategy has focused since the 1990s on a com- bination of engagement and balancing. The engagement leg of the strategy has continued over eight administrations since Richard Nixon's historic visit to China in 1972 and is reinforced by powerful economic interests and cultural connections. The balancing leg of the strategy emerged in the mid-1990s as senior officials in the Clinton administration and allies across Asia grew concerned that engagement alone would not be sufficient to ensure win-win outcomes as Chinese power and influence expanded. U.S. balancing efforts have focused primarily on shoring up relations with key maritime allies and partners and ensuring that states within the region are not easily intimidated by growing Chinese power. While there is an inherently competitive dimension to this strategy—mirrored by Beijing's own pursuit of increased influence in the region—it is not a zero-sum game comparable to U.S.–Soviet interactions during the Cold War. The United States has a stake in China's successful development and faces no impairment of interests when China has good relations with its neighbors.

Second, maintaining a favorable strategic equilibrium in Asia is not the only U.S. foreign policy priority. The United States faces global challenges such as terrorism, proliferation, and climate change that necessitate cooperation among the leading powers in the world, particularly with China. The Obama administration entered office hopeful that recognition of these shared interests would transform U.S.–China relations. That did not happen because Beijing did not view the solutions in the same way as Washington and because the underlying competition in U.S.–China relations is structural and not just attitudinal. Nevertheless, the United States and China need each others' help to address these common global challenges and this factor should help bound the competitive dimension of relations within the Asia-Pacific region.

Third, the United States wants to see greater regional capacity to manage challenges ranging from North Korean proliferation to large-scale natural disasters. The goal of U.S. foreign policy strategy is therefore not to contain Chinese influence in Asia, but rather to find ways to encourage China to become a net exporter of security to the region. Official Washington appears to have grown more pessimistic about that prospect in the wake of China's often passive response to North Korean (DPRK) provocations and growing collisions with neighboring states over disputed maritime claims. The major debate now is about whether these disappointments are the result of internal Chinese political paralysis or a more deliberate strategy to tilt the region toward a Sino-centric system. Views in China about U.S. intentions in the region appear to have similarly deteriorated over the past two years.

It may be possible to reverse this negative trend, but only if we first take a candid look at our respective approaches to regional problems as you have done in your letter. Let me specifically address your observations on three subjects: North Korea, the South China Sea, and the emerging regional architecture.

I was struck by your roadmap for solving the Korean problem. I would describe your sequencing (stability of the DPRK → improvement of U.S. and ROK relations with Pyongyang → establishment of a permanent peace mechanism → the denuclearization of the DPRK) as an approach that *increases* risk to the United States and the region, though it may be more attractive initially to Pyongyang. I say this because we know from experience that the DPRK will not leave its nuclear and missile programs idle, even as we sign superficial peace agreements or temporarily freeze one part of their capability. The North began working on its uranium enrichment program in the late 1990s at the height of U.S. engagement (as Secretary of State Madeleine Albright was in Pyongyang, in fact) and was weaponizing its harvested plutonium over the same period. Technically, the enriched uranium program is much more difficult to verify than the plutonium program at Yongbyon, and the North could use the uranium program to develop one or two weapons a year in secret as we go through the first three phases of your roadmap. Moreover, it is unlikely that Pyongyang will behave once it has established a larger weapons stockpile. The North has historically used its weapons capabilities to manufacture tension and crises in pursuit of further concessions. That cycle is even more dangerous in the wake of Pyongyang's 2003 threat to proliferate horizontally and subsequent evidence that Syria's El Kibar reactor was built with North Korean help before the Israelis bombed it in September 2007. The North Koreans will not let us buy stability, no matter how much China is willing to pay; they will only rent it and then charge a higher price later when their capacity to threaten us increases.

I understand why China would view a focus on stability and confidence-building with the DPRK as preferable to pressure, but I think that preference is based on faulty assumptions about the sources of North Korean belligerent behavior. More importantly, I do not think that the United States, Japan, or the ROK is likely to take a similar view. As the North Korean threat increases, and becomes more direct, the United States will have no choice but to continue taking steps with allies to strengthen joint missile defenses. Meanwhile, the divergence in U.S. and Chinese views toward North Korea could negatively impact overall strategic relations between Washington and Beijing. Perhaps the best way to begin reversing that trend would be for Beijing to take concrete steps to implement previous UN Security Council sanctions on the DPRK (which is an obligation under the UN Charter) and for experts on both sides to engage in deeper and more candid discussions on the sources of North Korean behavior and regime stability.

When it comes to the Senkaku/Diaoyu Islands, the United States does not take a position with respect to Japanese and Chinese claims of sovereignty. However, Washington has long recognized that Japan retains administrative control over the islands and thus Article V (the defense of Japan clause) of the 1960 U.S.–Japan Mutual Security Treaty would apply should

Japan come under armed attack. Until recently, this was an academic question because Japanese and Chinese leaders endeavored to prevent their disagreement over the islands from affecting their otherwise mutually beneficial ties. As you note, Beijing believes that the Japanese government violated this modus vivendi by purchasing the islands from private Japanese landowners in 2012. The Japanese view is that Beijing first began violating the modus vivendi by significantly expanding military and paramilitary operations in the area and allowing or encouraging local commanders to use more intimidating rules of engagement vis-à-vis the Japanese Coast Guard and Maritime Self-Defense Force.

The prevailing view in Washington—though there is some debate among experts—is that Japan is correct in assessing that China's intention has been to contest and weaken Japanese administrative control of the islands. U.S. policy makers have observed this pattern with concern in Beijing's disputes with the Philippines and Vietnam in the South China Sea as well, which I will discuss next. That is why in 2012 the U.S. Congress passed a resolution and Secretary of State Clinton subsequently issued a statement opposing any effort by Beijing to change the status quo on the Senkaku/Diaoyu Islands issue through coercion.

Going forward, the United States will remain neutral on the question of sovereignty, but cannot remain neutral with respect to coercion of a key ally. At the same time, U.S. policy makers are struggling to find ways to discourage escalation by either side. From Beijing's perspective, American reassurance to Japan should be preferable to a policy that would abandon Japan and force consideration by Tokyo of unilateral measures that might increase tensions even further. In any case, this dispute has become a geostrategic rather than just an emotional or political problem (though it is those things as well). It will probably take years of serious dialogue and confidence building between Tokyo and Beijing before there can be any prospect of a lasting diplomatic breakthrough. In the meantime, the issue will require delicate handling and candid discussions between U.S. and Chinese leaders.

Unfortunately, the South China Sea disputes have also emerged as a problematic situation in which Washington and Beijing appear to be working at cross-purposes. You note in your letter that Washington is "using the dispute as a way to counter China's naval development in the South China Sea and preserve U.S. maritime dominance there." There is truth to that observation in that the United States was responding to regional alarm at China's apparent escalation of the problem. There has been an exponential increase in operations by People's Liberation Army (PLA) Navy and other Chinese maritime services in the South China Sea over the past year, against which the Philippines can barely muster two old U.S. Coast Guard cutters, and other claimants like Vietnam and Brunei are significantly outgunned. The U.S. goal is not to privilege one claim over another, but rather to ensure that coercion is set aside in favor of diplomatic negotiations that put smaller parties on a fair footing with China. More importantly, this is the role that most of the ASEAN member-states have urged Washington to play.

While many of your colleagues have warned us that Manila or Hanoi may be tricking the United States into confrontation with Beijing, I think we should give our Southeast Asian counterparts more credit for their skillful calibration of relations with the big powers. Remember that in 1997–1998 the United States was too heavy handed in the Asian financial crisis and ASEAN states imposed an influence cost on us by initiating East Asian-only institutions like the Chiang Mai Initiative with Japan and China. This time, China overplayed its hand militarily and diplomatically, and key ASEAN states are imposing an influence cost on China by tightening security relations with the United States and other maritime powers such as Japan, Australia, and India. At the end of the day, however, none of these smaller states want to be caught in a Sino-American confrontation or to give a blank check to Washington. They want us there, but not forcing them to choose sides. Perhaps if we each recognize how the other has benefited from our respective overreaching, we might be able to shift our focus to projects of common interest such as counternarcotics or even some coordination of development assistance to poorer countries in the region.

I think you are right about the importance of regional architecture to overall stability in the Asia-Pacific region, though as a realist I tend to believe that the institutions will reflect the underlying power relations and shape them only at the margins. I notice that you describe the United States as a "lonely" power and China as the "rising" power and argue that regional architecture requires "more equal relations between the two sides of the Pacific and a more preeminent role by East Asian countries, including China, in regional affairs." The clear implication here is that there are two poles, one in East Asia centered on China and the other across the Pacific centered on the United States. I do not think this is an accurate reading of how regional actors view China, the United States or the norms that should define an East Asian Community. For example, Center for Strategic and International Studies (CSIS) polling of strategic elites in the region indicates robust support for an institutional architecture that reinforces democratic norms, including free and fair elections, rule of law, and human rights. On the other hand, the CSIS poll reveals that some developing countries like Indonesia and India that are most enthusiastic about advancing democratic norms are also the most reluctant to give up the principle of non-interference in internal affairs advanced by Beijing.[5]

In short, Asian architecture is fluid and confused. States are choosing to join any institutional arrangements they can to maximize their relative influence. In some cases, states caucus together based on common values (in the U.S.–Japan–Australia Trilateral Security Dialogue or the Shanghai Cooperation Organization, for example), while in other cases they seek to build on economic ties (like the China–Japan–ROK Trilateral Secretariat, TPP, or APEC, for example); or to tackle shared challenges (like the six-party talks). We are unlikely to rationalize this hodgepodge of institutions and forums into one collective security architecture as long as regime types and threat perception are so varied across the region. Nor is the region likely to fall into two competing blocs given multiple overlapping interests. In fact, there may be virtue in the competition of different caucuses. In trade theory there is a concept of "competitive liberalization" in which battling bilateral free trade agreements drive down overall barriers to trade. The same could hold true for the security architecture in Asia, if states are driven to deliver security and transparency as the price of admission.

It is also important to put TPP in context. TPP actually began as an effort by Singapore, Chile, Brunei, and New Zealand to increase their own influence vis-à-vis larger economies in APEC. It worked. The United States latched on to TPP as an additional pillar with the U.S.–Korea Free Trade Agreement (KORUS) to build toward trans-Pacific free trade architecture. The eventual U.S. goal is a free trade area with all APEC member states, including China, but that does not prevent interim agreements with China that improve the environment for trade and investment. And if the United States is too slow in this process, then arrangements like the China–Korea–Japan FTA could put pressure on us to pick up the process of liberalization. The point is to reduce barriers to trade and investment, not to create new ones.

Let me conclude by highlighting that your list of Chinese strategic interests in Asia generally overlaps with U.S. interests, particularly with respect to secure sea lanes, denuclearization of the Korean peninsula, and peaceful resolution of territorial disputes. Moreover, despite some over-inflated rhetoric about "pivoting" or "rebalancing" to Asia, the United States is actually holding its military presence in the region fairly steady while drawing down in Europe and the Middle East. China's actions in 2010–2011 have led a number of states in Asia to align more closely with the United States, but those steps have been designed to restore perceived weaknesses in the strategic equilibrium and not to contain or limit anyone's economic or political ties with China—nor would the United States seek that outcome. The fact is that the other major states in this region also get a vote on U.S.-China relations. If China continues pressing aggressively on claims in the South or East China Seas, then major states in the region will place an even higher premium on U.S. alliances and an American presence. If the United States presses these countries to support containment or confrontation with China (which I do not believe we are), then they will resist. In other words, if we are each attentive and sensitive to our relationships in the region, then our bilateral ties will likely improve.

The United States and China are not in a Cold War in Asia, or even close to it. On the other hand, there is a pronounced increase in Sino-American strategic competition within the region. We cannot wish that away with idealistic visions of regional architecture or by pretending that balance-of-power is irrelevant. What we can each do is ensure that each side explains its respective interests; that we each calibrate where possible consistent with those interests; and that we continually seek new areas of common effort. And by all means, let us continue the dialogue started with your letter and with our previous Fudan–Georgetown conferences on Asia policy of recent years.

Best,
Mike

• • •

Dear Mike,

Thanks for your response, which provides a useful, mainstream perspective of U.S. strategy in Asia. For better mutual understanding between China and the United States, I believe it is important that each side speaks candidly about what its own policy intentions are, how it perceives the intentions and behavior of the other side, and where the other side gets it wrong.

Although U.S. national interests in Asia are rooted in U.S. history as you have noted, they have also evolved over time in response to changing U.S. power, aspirations, and regional circumstances. For instance, until recently, a major objective of U.S. Asia-Pacific policy was to prevent others (Japan before the Second World War and the Soviet Union during the Cold War) from dominating the region. However, since the end of the Cold War, the United States has taken for granted its hegemonic position in the region and preserving this position has become the centerpiece of its regional strategy. As a result, Washington sometimes tends to view China's rising power and influence in the region in a zero-sum way. I am less sure than you are that "there is no mainstream support in the United States today for a policy of containing China."

Just look at how some officials within the Obama administration advised several of our neighbors not to "over-rely" on China. This contradicts your statement that "[t]he United States has a stake in China's successful development and faces no impairment of interests when China has good relations with its neighbors." In my observation, the United States does not want to see China's neighbors draw too close to China as this will undermine the United States' influence in the region. When you wrote that "we should give our Southeast counterparts more credit for their skillful calibration of relations with the big powers," you are actually praising their efforts to balance a rising China by forging closer ties with the United States, Japan, and India.

On the South China Sea issue, you attributed more active U.S. involvement in recent years to China's behavior as well as to invitations from some ASEAN states. However, if you look at what Vietnam and the Philippines have been doing over the last ten years or so to consolidate their sovereignty claims in this region, it is not difficult to conclude that China has been largely responding to their actions rather than initiating a change to the status quo. Furthermore, it was Beijing who first proposed shelving the disputes while seeking joint development in the South China Sea. Also, even though Vietnam and the Philippines did push the United States to adopt a hands-on approach to the issue, I believe Washington took action primarily out of a calculation of its own political and security interests in the area. A mutually reinforcing effect has taken hold here: Manila and Hanoi pushed Washington to intervene to check China, while Washington's active involvement also served to encourage both Manila and Hanoi to push the envelope further.

On the Korean peninsula issue, I understand the U.S. concern over North Korea's nuclear program and the inclination to set the nuclear issue at the core of the entire Korean peninsula problem. However, China not only has broader concerns about the peninsula than the United States does (as I described in my earlier letter), but it also prefers a different approach to the nuclear issue. China believes that the DPRK seeks nuclear capability for defensive purposes. After all, Pyongyang began its nuclear program out of desperation in the 1990s when its two former major allies—the Soviet Union and China—moved to normalize relations with the ROK in the early 1990s. Therefore, unless its security concerns are adequately addressed, the DPRK is unlikely to give up its nuclear ambition. This is the reasoning behind the roadmap I proposed in my earlier letter.

To some extent, the difference between our respective approaches to the North Korean nuclear issue is like one between Chinese and Western medicines: while the latter prefers directly addressing the disease, the former prefers addressing the cause of the disease. In the case of North Korea, I believe the Chinese approach is going to be more effective in the long run, while China may need to adjust its tactics from time to time. Having said that, Beijing does share Washington's concern over Pyongyang's possible nuclear proliferation, and both sides should strengthen their cooperation in this regard while looking for ways to advance DPRK's denuclearization. Broadly, Beijing and Washington should also exchange views over what opportunities the DPRK's young leader Kim Jong-un may present to peace and stability on the peninsula.

With regard to Asia-Pacific regional architecture, I agree with you that it is "fluid and confused," yet the general trend is clear: East Asian countries are playing an increasingly important and active role vis-à-vis the United States in regional institutions. Gone are the days of a U.S.-centered architecture in which Washington establishes the institutions and sets the rules and agenda for East Asian countries. As we have seen over the last two decades, East Asian countries have been taking more initiative to promote regional cooperation among themselves, building cooperation mechanisms and setting the norms and rules. Because of robust economic growth and a rapidly developing sense of regionalism, East Asia has gained more clout and confidence in interactions with the United States. Most East Asian countries still view the United States as indispensible to regional affairs, and they have admitted the United States into some new institutions, such as the East Asia Summit, but regard Washington as a partner, not as a leader. Even though the Obama administration has pledged to exercise a leadership role in shaping a trans-Pacific architecture, it is unlikely that the United States can maintain its influence on regional affairs as strongly as it did in the 1990s.

You misunderstood me when you drew the implication from my first letter that in regional architecture "there are two poles—one in East Asia centered on China and the other across the Pacific centered on the United States." This is exactly the scenario China wants to avoid. Ever since more intensive East Asian cooperation began in the late 1990s, China has invariably supported ASEAN's leadership role, because Beijing fully understands the complexity of regional politics and does not want to compete for the driver's seat with Japan and ASEAN. As China rises, it seeks to embed itself in a more integrated and interdependent East Asia, rather than putting East Asia in its shadow and creating a Sino-centric order. In fact, the East Asia model of cooperation differs from the European Union and North American models. In East Asia, cooperation is led by a bloc of small and medium countries in Southeast Asia, while the European Union is driven by the two large, twin engines of France and Germany, and North America is dominated by the United States. As a result, when Washington claims a leadership role in trans-Pacific cooperation, it not only arouses concern in China, but also challenges the ambition of ASEAN.

I agree with you that "there is a pronounced increase in Sino–American strategic competition within the region." Yet, I don't agree with you that "[w]e cannot wish that away with idealistic visions of regional architecture or by pretending that balance-of-power is irrelevant." To prevent Sino-American competition from escalating into confrontation and conflict, both countries need to adopt new thinking and new policies while rejecting ideas and policy instruments that belong to the past. Frankly speaking, China is doing a better job than the United States in this regard. For instance, in spite of China's rising power, Beijing has not been tempted to revive a self-centered regional order that long existed in a previous era or to drive the U.S. out of the region as Japan attempted to do before the Second World War. Instead, China has been making efforts to promote a cooperative, integrated, and open East Asia while also supporting Asia-Pacific cooperation, mainly in the context of APEC.

The United States, in turn, should adopt an enlightened view of the evolving regional order characterized by a rising China, a more confident and proactive East Asia, and a less dominant United States. After all, no regional order is permanent, be it a Sino-centric or a U.S.-dominated one. Meanwhile, Washington should also resist the temptation to deal with new challenges using old techniques, including creating a favorable strategic equilibrium in Asia, playing balance-of-power politics, as well as consolidating and expanding military alliances. Those instruments were useful in dealing with the Soviet Union during the Cold War, but a rising China is not the Soviet Union, and the politics of the Asia-Pacific region today is very different from that in the Cold War years.

Given their respective power and influence, interactions between China and the United States in the Asia-Pacific region will shape not only their bilateral ties, but also the regional and global strategic landscape. Bearing this in mind, China recently has been advocating for forging a new model of major power relationship with the United States and creating healthy and constructive interactions between both countries. These efforts have received a favorable response from the Obama administration. To realize the goal of a new model of relationship between a rising and an established power, both sides need to explore practically and learn intellectually. A major part of learning is to maintain enduring, candid, and constructive dialogue between academic and policy communities in both countries. As scholars, we should guide policy makers and practitioners through our forward-looking, progressive, and, yes, sometimes even idealistic thinking. Without a positive vision, the world will not improve and evolve. I hope our exchanges now and in the future will contribute to this process.

Sincerely,

Xinbo

• • •

Dear Xinbo,

Thank you for your response. Let me first assure you that while I lean closer to conservative realism than liberal idealism, I remain an optimist about the future of U.S.–China relations. We cannot wish away competition, but with candid dialogue on areas of disagreement and deliberate focus on areas of common interest, we will have a good chance of managing the strategic competition that has crept into the bilateral relationship in recent years.

I would like to conclude our correspondence by focusing on three topics contained in your last letter: containment, North Korea, and ASEAN. You expressed skepticism at my assertion that there is no mainstream support in the United States today for a policy of containing China. I know that you are hardly alone among Chinese scholars and officials in holding this view. Yet "containment" has a specific meaning in diplomatic history and international relations that does not accurately describe U.S. policy today. As you know, containment was a doctrine developed during the Cold War to ensure that the Soviet Union could not become economically powerful enough to weaken the West or overthrow pro-Western governments. Under the containment doctrine, the United States and the West imposed crippling technology and trade restrictions on Moscow. As a result, U.S. trade with the Soviet Union reached no higher than 1% of total U.S. trade throughout the Cold War. In contrast, China is the United States' second-largest trading partner after Canada, representing about 14% of total U.S. trade. Moreover, the Cold War strategy of containment was enforced through collective security arrangements against the Soviet Union that no U.S. ally or partner in Asia is interested in reproducing vis-à-vis China today—even if the United States were. Nor does the American public think that containment is the right strategy. In a recent Chicago Council on Global Affairs survey, the American public was asked if the United States should "actively work to limit the growth of China's power"—the ultimate definition of containment—and only 28% of the respondents answered "yes." Sixty-nine percent of respondents favored instead pursuing "friendly cooperation and engagement" with China.[6]

Anonymous quotations from U.S. officials that Asian countries should not "over-rely" on China strike me as superfluous, since it is obvious from the behavior of states like Vietnam and the Philippines that they have no intention of over-relying on China. The striking feature of international relations in Asia today is that a range of middle powers are seeking the right strategic equilibrium in which they avoid over-reliance on either China or the United States. However, judging from public opinion polls in the region taken by groups like the Pew Foundation, the Lowy Institute in Australia, or the Asan Institute in Korea, the region's middle powers worry significantly more about China's intentions now than they do about the United States.[7]

Watching these trends, officials in Washington have to be careful about two things. First, they should not make the mistake of thinking that these middle powers want to choose sides between the United States and China; and second, they should be careful—as you note—not to become entrapped in the territorial ambitions of other states when our primary concern is stability and freedom of navigation and not the questions of sovereignty. If these territorial issues were being peacefully arbitrated in diplomatic settings without the coercive dimension of China's growing maritime power, the United States would have few interests beyond ensuring that our energy companies had an opportunity to participate in the lucrative joint ventures that would result. The current impasse on these disputes is not all China's fault, but China's response is creating uncertainty in the region that the United States cannot ignore. This is particularly true in the East China Sea, where the United States cannot remain neutral on potential threats or pressure against our ally Japan, even if we are strictly neutral on the question of territorial claims. That said, the overwhelming preference of officials and experts in Washington is that these disputes return to a purely diplomatic track among the claimants based on established international law and without the manipulation of nationalistic sentiment by any side.

Anyone reading our exchanges on North Korea would conclude that we are talking past each other, which unfortunately often reflects the state of our government-to-government dialogue on this issue. When we began the six-party talks process in the Bush administration, there was a sense that U.S. and Chinese efforts on North Korea were beginning to converge. Pyongyang's subsequent decision to sabotage our diplomatic efforts with nuclear tests in 2006 and 2009 and then conventional military attacks on South Korea in 2010 caused U.S. and Chinese positions to diverge. Where Beijing wanted immediately to return to the original six-party process, Washington became skeptical that North Korea would ever negotiate denuclearization in good faith. Perhaps at some level Chinese officials and scholars share that same skepticism about the North's intentions, but not to the point that they are willing to increase pressure on Pyongyang.

You note that the key to solving the nuclear problem is for the United States to address the North's security concerns. At some point, any diplomatic agreement requires security assurances. The fundamental problem in this case is that Pyongyang has defined the United States' so-called "hostile policy" so elastically and comprehensively, that the bar is impossibly high and leaves constant room for Pyongyang to claim U.S. violations and escalate tensions as it has so often before. I have had official and unofficial exchanges with North Korean counterparts where the resolution of the United States' "hostile policy" is defined to include: an end to U.S. nuclear umbrellas in Asia, an immediate and unconditional end to all international sanctions on the North, an end to any criticism of the regime, and acceptance of the North as a fellow nuclear weapons state. These are non-starters, particularly if the resulting agreement fails to completely and verifiably eliminate the North's nuclear weapons capability. Moreover, the North has not pursued nuclear weapons solely because of the external security threat of the United States. The major threat to regime survival in the North is its lack of legitimacy internally and vis-à-vis the South, and these factors also drive the quest for nuclear weapons status. And I suspect even concern about China is behind the regime's actions.

We need to weave a new process of cooperation between the United States and China on North Korea. We are not convincing each other of our respective assessments of the situation in the wake of Pyongyang's sabotage of the six-party process. Perhaps we need to think about an alternative approach—one that is less ambitious in scope, but that takes elements from both our strategies. This approach might include increased Chinese implementation of existing UN Security Council sanctions and a joint formula for restarting engagement of the six-party talks. While this might not solve the intractable North Korean nuclear problem, it would demonstrate to Pyongyang that its provocation cannot easily divide Beijing and Washington. It might also create a better atmosphere for long-overdue bilateral and multilateral discussions on how we assess the future of the Kim Jong-un regime, which was an excellent suggestion in your last letter. There is no reason why a desperate problem like North Korea cannot be treated with both Chinese and Western medicine.

You noted in your letter how important ASEAN-centrality is to stable international relations in the region. American officials are also coming to this view, which is why Hillary Clinton had the best attendance record at the ASEAN Regional Forum (ARF) of any U.S. secretary of state and why President Obama decided to join the East Asia Summit (something President Bush was prepared to do, but thought should be left for his successor to decide). It therefore came as a shock to ASEAN member states and Washington that Beijing blocked consensus on a joint statement in Phnom Penh at the 2012 ARF, the first time the forum had failed to issue a joint statement, ever. The reality is that neither Beijing nor Washington are going to make concessions on our core interests in a multilateral consensus-based forum like the ARF, but we should each respect ASEAN efforts to address issues—like the South China Sea in this case—that are sources of concern. We both have an interest in making certain that ASEAN is a cohesive group that builds greater integration and confidence in the region

All of this leads to your suggestion that the United States and China seek to forge a new type of major power relationship, a theme that President Xi Jinping has emphasized. This will not mean a "G-2" in which the United States and China co-manage the global economy, since I see only limited interest in such an arrangement in Washington and virtually none in China. Nor do I think the region or most experts in Washington would be attracted to a bipolar condominium in which the United States and China co-manage the major security issues in Asia and relegate other nations to second-tier status.

I suspect that no matter how we label U.S.–China relations, the coming decade will see a combination of cooperation on some key issues amidst continued if not growing bilateral competition for strategic influence. The key will be to construct patterns of official interaction that help to mini-mize the competition and maximize the cooperation. We have no shortage of channels for dialogue between Washington and Beijing. Some of them, like the Strategic and Economic Dialogue, have become almost grandiose in their scale. However, since the locus of Sino-American strategic competition is in Asia, perhaps it is time to develop a more discrete and discreet bilateral strategic dialogue on how we are each approaching problems in the region. This would be neither a G-2 on global issues nor a bipolar condominium to manage regional issues at the expense of other countries. Instead, it would allow senior officials to have the kind of candid exchange you and I have had in these essays, and to identify new areas where the United States and China would benefit from common approaches to problems. We might assist with ceasefires and economic development in Burma/Myanmar, for example; or coordinate development assistance for more effective delivery and enhanced good governance; or even quietly discuss trends in North Korea.

These all happen to be areas of perceived Sino-American strategic compe-tition that could be reconceived as areas of tactical cooperation; eventually leading to new thinking about our overall strategic relations going forward. Building mutual trust will not come from new labels alone; we will also have to put effort into these problems one by one.

Best,

Mike

CONCLUSION

JAMES B. STEINBERG

Over the preceding 220 pages, readers of this book have been treated to a kind of 21st-century, geostrategic equivalent of the 18th-century epistolary novel. The vibrant exchanges are filled with expressions of affection and commitment, along with a familiar litany of complaints, grievances—and even an occasional accusation of betrayal. Unlike many of its literary predecessors, however, the volume ends with the outcome in doubt and no certainty that virtue will triumph in the end—though no one can doubt that all of the authors are determined to use their intellect and their influence to achieve a favorable result.

The authors all share a conviction that managing Sino-American relations is one of the most consequential challenges of our time—a sentiment that has been embraced by the leaders of both nations. In each chapter they lay out clearly the enormous gains to be had from cooperation, and the incalculable risks for all concerned (and not just the United States and China) from conflict. Issue by issue they identify the broad range of shared interests—from combatting common threats like terrorism and proliferation of WMD; to mitigating climate change, enhancing global public health, and promoting sound economic development; to maintaining a vigorous and open global trading system.

Yet despite the strenuous efforts—and obvious good will of the writers—important gaps remain. On economic policy, Barry Naughton shares the views of many Americans in questioning the intentions of China's exchange rate policy and China's unbalanced growth model, while Yao Yang argues that these assertions are simply an American attempt to scapegoat China for the flaws in the U.S. economic system, while ignoring what he claims is the equivalent currency manipulation by the Federal Reserve (through quantitative easing). On human rights, Andy Nathan challenges China's human rights practices as a violation of its own commitments (both in its constitution and through its international undertakings) while Zhou Qi accuses the United States of practicing double standards at home and abroad. On international cooperation, Nina Hachigian laments China's tendency to link engagement on areas of common interest to disputes over issues like Taiwan, while Yuan Peng asks why China should be expected to cooperate with the United States when "Americans still view Chinese corporations as the devil due to an outdated, Cold War mindset." Wu Xinbo claims that the United States is "fanning the flames of dispute in the South China Sea" and pursuing the Trans-Pacific Partnership trade negotiations "to obstruct the development of East Asian cooperation." On maritime issues, each side challenges the other's interpretation of the application of the Law of the Sea to military operations in the exclusive economic zones (EEZs).

Nowhere is the gap more obvious—or of greater concern—than on security policy. It comes as little surprise—but no comfort—that the chapter where the differences emerge most starkly is the exchange between Christopher Twomey and Xu Hui. Twomey challenges his Chinese colleague to justify China's military modernization in light of China's improving security environment over the past decades—only to be countered by Xu Hui: "If [your] logic stands, than I am afraid to say that the United States should have given up its military transformation a long time ago ... If China's motives for military modernization are to be questioned, than what explains America's motivation to seek absolute military superiority?"

This exchange illustrates a common thread running through the volume— uncertainties and anxieties about the underlying motives and strategies of the two protagonists—a concern framed here in the exchange between Ken Lieberthal and Wang Jisi and in their earlier writings,[1] but present across all of the chapters. For example, in their spirited debate on human rights and democracy, Zhou Qi argues that the U.S. concern for human rights is at its heart an effort to change the Chinese system. She "suggests that values, ideology and political systems are, in the end, key causes of strategic suspicion." On Taiwan, Jia Qingguo voices the suspicion that the United States sells arms to Taiwan "with the evil intention of splitting Taiwan from China forever."

Several Chinese contributors (Wang Shuo, Wu Xinbo, and Xu Hui) attribute much of the difficulty to the perception in China that the United States is pursuing a policy of containment, thinly disguised in the Obama administration's "rebalance." Mike Green vigorously disputes this notion and notes (correctly in my view) that such a policy would be unsustainable even if that were the United States' intention (which, as Mike argues, it manifestly is not). Their suspicions are mirrored by the American writers who see signs that China seeks to dominate the region and bully its weaker neighbors—a claim rejected by Yuan Peng, who claims that "China...has no intention of challenging American dominance either globally or in the Asia-Pacific area."

This book highlights the complex mixture of factors that lead to tensions in the Sino-American relations. These range from the structural challenges associated with the emergence of new powers (including the irony of a Chinese contributor—Wang Shuo—quoting Thucydides!) to differences in values and political systems.

Both Chinese and American contributors point to domestic factors as an important element in deepening mutual mistrust and suspicion and making it harder for leaders to forge common ground. They identify a number of factors that constrain the actions of leaders—including the nature of the decision-making processes in each country and the roles of interest groups and the military.

These concerns should not lightly be dismissed. The past 20 years have seen disappointment in both countries that the relationship has not progressed to the level that many hoped. Despite the extraordinary intensity of the engagement between the two sides, both informed and casual observers see signs of trouble—a potential spiral (to use the process identified by both Wang Shuo and Christopher Twomey) that, left untended, could see a deterioration in the relationship that might, in the worst case, actually lead to conflict. A relationship that started out on such an optimistic note on both sides at the beginning of the Obama administration has faced tensions on a myriad of issues ranging from Taiwan and Tibet to the Copenhagen climate change summit, North Korea, cyber-intrusions, and the proper role of multilateral institutions in the South China Sea.

But such a pessimistic outcome is not inevitable, and the authors here offer a number of useful and concrete suggestions for how to arrest this tendency. From cooperation on clean energy (Qi Ye) to collaborating with each other to enhance corporate social responsibility in developing countries (Zha Daojiong), these pragmatic steps (to use Kelly Sims Gallagher's phrase) can not only achieve important benefits themselves, but can demonstrate to skeptical publics that the two sides do in fact share interests and can successfully work together.

But as important as these steps may be, more will be needed. No matter how effectively we work together on issues of common interest, unless we address the fundamental sources of mistrust in the relationship, all our good work is likely to come to naught. While Nina Hachigian usefully counsels us to try to compartmentalize our differences, tensions in one sphere will inevitably spill over to the relationship as a whole.

To dispel this mistrust will take more than high-level declarations, however sincerely intended—the ritual assertions on the U.S. side that we welcome China's rise, on China's side that it welcomes the United States as an Asia-Pacific power. As Yuan Peng rightly observes, actions speak louder than words. For this reason, I've argued for the need for "strategic reassurance"—concrete steps that explicitly address each other's sources of misgiving—especially, but not exclusively on matters of security.[2] We must strive for ways to accommodate each other's concerns where we can do so without sacrificing our own "core interests." The Strategic Security Dialogue (SSD) inaugurated during the past two years is an effort to tackle these difficult but crucial sources of tension—but it needs to move beyond dialogue to real achievements.

This leads to a second conclusion—that we must be ambitious about the possibilities of the relationship but also mindful of the constraints. Wang Shou offers an insightful model when he observes that "U.S.–China relations have moved between a *limiting* line and a *supporting* line" (my emphasis). The supporting line is grounded in mutual interdependence, the limiting line includes the structural values and domestic political considerations I've identified above. Through the efforts of both sides, I believe that both the supporting line and the limiting line can be raised to a new level.

This will take the involvement not just of leaders, but the broader public as well. Wang Jisi worries that the "the general public and large parts of the elites...on both sides cannot be expected to understand the whole picture of the China–U.S. relationship...." However difficult this task, we have no choice but to try, because, as policy practitioners in both countries know, without the support of the broader public the forces pulling us apart may overwhelm those that draw us closer. This volume is an important contribution to that goal. Through its candid exploration of the sources of the barriers to agreement as well as its hopeful efforts to identify common ground, it will help both policy makers and the engaged public become better aware of the challenges and opportunities this "most important relationship" faces.

NOTES

INTRODUCTION

1. For International Monetary Fund (IMF) data on China's GDP, see http://www. imf.org/external/pubs/ft/weo/2013/01/weodata/index.aspx

CHAPTER 1: AN OVERVIEW OF THE U.S.-CHINA RELATIONSHIP

1. U.S. Department of Commerce International Trade Administration Office of Travel and Tourism Industries, "2011 U.S. Resident Travel to Asia," July 2012, available at http://tinet.ita.doc.gov/outreachpages/download_data_table/2011-US-to-Asia.pdf; U.S. Department of Commerce International Trade Administration Office of Travel and Tourism Industries, "2011 Market Profile: China," May 2012, available at http://tinet.ita.doc.gov/outreachpages/download_data_table/2011_China_Market_Profile.pdf
2. Since President Nixon's trip to China in 1972.
3. I provided details in an essay written then: Kenneth Lieberthal, "Domestic Forces and Sino-U.S. Relations," in *Living With China: U.S.–China Relations in the Twenty-First Century*, ed. Ezra Vogel (New York: W.W. Norton, 1997), pp. 254–76.
4. Albeit on the assumption that at some point the United States may have to respond to a massive surprise attack by the Chinese military.
5. Martin Jacques, *When China Rules The World: The End of the Western World and the Birth of a New Global Order* (London: Penguin Press, 2009).
6. China has officially stated that it does not endorse a G-2 system that makes decisions for the world but prefers a multipolar world. The Obama administration has not supported the notion either.
7. Publicity Department was previously translated as Propaganda Department.

CHAPTER 3: POLITICAL SYSTEMS, RIGHTS AND VALUES

1. Joshua Muravchik, *Exporting Democracy, Fulfilling America's Destiny* (Washington, D.C.: American Enterprise Institute, 1991), p. 3.
2. See Michael H. Hunt, *Ideology and U.S. Foreign Policy* (New Haven, Conn., and London: Yale University Press, 1987).
3. Susan Mendus, "Human Rights in Political Theory," *Political Studies*, 43 (Special Issue 1995), Politics and Human Rights, p. 13.
4. Jack Donnelly, "Human Rights and Asian Values: A Defense of 'Western' Universalism," in *The East Asian Challenge for Human Rights*, ed. Joanne R. Bauer and Daniel A. Bell (New York: Cambridge University Press, 1999), p. 80.
5. Tu Weiming, "Implications of the Rise of 'Confucian' East Asia," *Multiple Modernities, Journal of the American Academy of Arts and Sciences*, 129, no. 1 (Winter 2000) of the Proceedings of the American Academy of Arts and Sciences (Cambridge, Mass.: American Academy of Arts and Sciences, 2000), pp. 199–200.
6. Yu Keping, *Democracy Is a Good Thing: Essays on Politics, Society and Culture in Contemporary China* (Washington, D.C.: Brookings Institution Press, 2009), p. 3.
7. Ibid., pp. 3–5.
8. Li Junru, "*Zhongguo Nenggou Shixing Shenmeyangde Minzhu?*" (What Kind of Democracy Can China Adopt?") *Beijing Daily*, April 14, 2006.
9. Li Junru, "*Lun Renmin Zhengxie Yu Xieshang Minzhu*" ("On People's Political Consultation and Consultative Democracy"), October 22, 2009, *Remin Zhengxiebao* (*People's Consultation Newspaper*), available at http://cppcc.people.com.cn/GB/71578/10237355.html
10. "*Zhongguode Minzhu Zhengzhi Qile Shenme Zuoyong?*" ("What Kind of Role Does Chinese Democratic Politics Play?") July 24, 2011, quoting an article by Qiu Shi, available at http://zhidao.baidu.com/question/297116868.html<http://baidu.com/question/297116868.html>
11. "*Zhongguo He Meiguo Minzhu Zhidu De Chayi Biaoxianzai Naxie Fangmian?*" ("What Are the Differences between Chinese and American Democracy?") May 5, 2012, available at http://zhidao.baidu.com/question/419597042.html
12. These are not isolated cases. Many more are less well known. Ni Yulan, a housing rights activist, was beaten in prison in 2002 so she can no longer walk, was forced out of her home, and charged with fraud for resisting eviction. A young graphic designer, Sun Zhigang, was beaten to death in a government detention center in 2003. Fu Xiancai, a peasant advocate who tried to defend fellow villagers displaced by the Three Gorges Dam, was paralyzed in a beating in 2006 that local police characterized as "a fall." Gao Zhisheng, a lawyer, disappeared in 2010 after trying to protect the rights of Falun Gong religious practitioners; at first the government said they had no idea where he was, then they announced that he was "where he should be," which turned out to be prison, where he was allegedly tortured. Xue Jinbo, a village leader from the southern village of Wukan, was beaten to death in police custody in 2011 for protesting corrupt land transfers. Li Wangyang, an activist who was left frail, blind, and deaf after two long jail terms served for criticizing the government, was found dead by hanging in a guarded hospital room in 2012, which the police implausibly labeled a suicide. The list could go on and on.

13. Zhao Ziyang, *Prisoner of the State: The Secret Journal of Premier Zhao Ziyang*, trans. and ed. Bao Pu, Renee Chiang, and Adi Ignatius (New York: Simon & Schuster, 2009).

14. Andrew J. Nathan and Andrew Scobell, *China's Search for Security* (New York: Columbia University Press, 2012), esp. Ch. 13.

15. Among international conventions on human rights, only two are designated as "covenants," the International Covenant on Civil and Political Rights (ICCPR) and the International Covenant on Economic, Social and Cultural Rights (ICESCR), to indicate that they are fundamental conventions on human rights.

16. You might argue that because of the Chinese government's censorship, the Chinese populace is not informed about these. But what I want to emphasize is, whether you believe it or not, a great number of Chinese people are able to access the information, especially Chinese intellectuals.

17 Erik Eckholm, "In China, So Many Liberties, So Little Freedom," *The New York Times*, January 3, 1999.

18. See A. Glenn Mover Jr., *Human Rights and American Foreign Policy, the Carter and Reagan Experiences* (New York: Greenwood Press, 1987).

19. Jeane Kirkpatrick, "Dictatorship and Double Standards," *Commentary*, November 1979, p. 44.

20. Michael E. Hunt, "China's Foreign Relations in Historical Perspective," in *China's Foreign Relations in 1980s*, ed. Harry Harding (New Haven: Yale University Press, 1984), p. 41.

21. For an excellent summary, see Aryeh Neier, *The International Human Rights Movement: A History* (Princeton: Princeton University Press, 2012). I have also written about this process, for example in "China and International Human Rights: Tiananmen's Paradoxical Impact," ed. Jean-Philippe Béja, *The Impact of China's 1989 Tiananmen Massacre* (London: Routledge, 2010), pp. 206–220.

22. For examples of Human Rights Watch reports criticizing the U.S., see reports available at http://www.hrw.org/en/united-states/us-program and http://www.hrw.org/en/united-states/us-foreign-policy

CHAPTER 4: THE MEDIA

1. Gary King, Jennifer Pan, and Molly Roberts, "How Censorship in China Allows Government Criticism but Silences Collective Expression," *American Political Science Review* 107, no. 2 (May 2013), pp. 1–18, available at http://j.mp/LdVXqN

CHAPTER 5: GLOBAL ROLES AND RESPONSIBILITIES

1. Hillary Rodham Clinton, Remarks at the U.S. Institute of Peace China Conference, March 7, 2012, available at http://www.state.gov/secretary/rm/2012/03/185402.htm

2. Hillary Rodham Clinton, Remarks on United States Foreign Policy, September 8, 2010, available at http://www.state.gov/secretary/rm/2010/09/146917.htm

3. Hillary Rodham Clinton, A Conversation with Secretaries Hillary Clinton and Leon Panetta, August 16, 2011, available at http://m.state.gov/md170611.htm

4. For details about how the Obama administration is encouraging other nations to act, see Nina Hachigian and David Shorr, "The Responsibility Doctrine," *The Washington Quarterly*, 36, no. 1 (Winter 2013), pp. 73–91, available at https://csis. org/publication/twq-responsibility-doctrine-winter-2013

5. The U.S.-China Study Group on G-20 Reform report is available at http://www. americanprogress.org/issues/china/report/2013/02/13/52548/us-china-study-group-on-g-20-reform-final-report/

CHAPTER 6: CLIMATE AND CLEAN ENERGY

1. U.S. Energy Information Administration, International Energy Statistics, U.S. Department of Energy, Washington, D.C., available at http://www.eia.gov/environment/data.cfm#intl

2. Malte Meinshausen, Nicolai Meinshausen, William Hare, Sarah C. B. Raper, Katja Frieler, Reto Knutti, David J. Frame, and Myles R. Allen, "Greenhouse-Gas Emission Targets for Limiting Global Warming to 2°C," *Nature* 458 (2009), pp. 1158–1163.

3. William Chandler, "Breaking the Suicide Pact: U.S.-China Cooperation on Climate Change," Policy Brief 57 (Washington, D.C.: Carnegie Endowment, 2008).

4. In 2005, the Chinese National Offshore Oil Corporation (CNOOC) withdrew its $18.5 billion bid to acquire Unocal Oil Company because of political opposition in the United States. Huawei, the third-largest mobile technology provider in the world has been thwarted from numerous efforts to invest in U.S. firms, including 3Com, 3Leaf, and Sprint by the Committee on Foreign Investment in the United States (CFIUS).

5. David M. Marchick, "Fostering Greater Chinese Investment in the United States," Policy Innovation Memorandum No. 13, Council on Foreign Relations, February 2012.

6. Todd Stern, "Remarks at Dartmouth College," Hanover, NH, Aug. 2, 2012, available at http://www.state.gov/e/oes/rls/remarks/2012/196004.htm

7. Some have pointed out the difficulty in getting the U.S. Congress to ratify the Kyoto Protocol regardless of the President's position. This was true even long before President George W. Bush took office. According to President Clinton, Members of Congress had already made up their mind even before Vice President Gore got off his airplane from the negotiations in Kyoto in 1997. See the U.S. Senate 95-0 Byrd–Hagel resolution in 1997.

8. Originally credited to the Gospel of Luke in the Bible. Even though the United States is religiously pluralistic, this Judeo-Christian principle resonates widely in the United States.

CHAPTER 7: GLOBAL INVESTMENT AND DEVELOPMENT

1. James K. Jackson, "U.S. Direct Investment Abroad: Trends and Current Issues," Congressional Research Service (February 2011), 2.

2. "China encourages private capital in mining industry," *Xinhua*, February 10, 2012, available at http://English.peopledaily.com.cn/90778/7725443.html

3. Li Jia, "South Africa Ambassador: China, Africa Good Partners," *People's Daily Online*, January 26, 2011, available at http://english.people.com.cn/90001/90778/7273341.html

4. Lindsey Hilsum, "We Love China," *Granta* 92 (Winter 2005).

5. Zha Daojiong, "All Roads Lead to Myanmar," *PacNet*, no. 6A (January 25, 2012).

6. USAID, Agency Performance Report 1995, p. 1, available at http://pdf.usaid.gov/pdf_docs/PNABY343.pdf

7. Dambisa Moyo, "Beijing, a Boon for Africa," *The New York Times*, June 27, 2012, p. A27.

8. Yu Bin and Lu Jiangyong, "Foreign Direct Investment, Processing Trade, and the Sophistication of China's Exports," *China Economic Review*, 20, no. 3 (September 2009), pp. 425–439.

9. Yuhuan Ling, "41 Chinese Arrested in Ghana," *Global Times*, August 27, 2012, available at http://www.global times.cn/content/729236.shtml

10. Wenping He, "More Soft Power Needed in Africa," *China Daily*, February 27, 2012.

11. Barry Bearak, "Zambia Uneasily Balances Chinese Investment and Workers' Resentment," *The New York Times*, November 20, 2010.

12 Rafael Marques de Morais, "Growing Wealth, Shrinking Democracy," *The New York Times*, August 29, 2012.

13. Julie Jiang and Jonathan Sinton, *Overseas Investments by Chinese National Oil Companies: Assessing the Drivers and Impacts*, Information Paper, International Energy Agency, February 2011.

14. Judith M. Dean, Mary E. Lovely, and Hua Wang, "Are Foreign Investors Attracted to Weak Environmental Regulations? Evaluating the Evidence from China," *Journal of Development Economics*, 90, no. 1 (September 2009), pp. 1–13.

15. Xianbing Liu, Can Wang, Tomohiro Shishime, and Tetsuro Fujitsuka, "Environmental Activisms of Firm's Neighboring Residents: An Empirical Study in China," *Journal of Cleaner Production*, 18, nos 10–11 (July 2010), pp. 1001–1008.

16. "New Zealand and China Collaborate on World First in Development," available at http://www.aid.govt.nz/media-and-publications/development-stories/september-2012/new-zealand-and-china-collaborate-world-fi

CHAPTER 8: MILITARY DEVELOPMENTS

1. For comparative discussions of China's budget data, see George J. Gilboy and Eric Heginbotham, *Chinese and Indian Strategic Behavior: Growing Power and Alarm* (New York: Cambridge University Press, 2012), pp. 100–106.

2. Keith Crane, Roger Cliff, Evan S. Medeiros, James C. Mulvenon, and William H. Overholt, *Modernizing China's Military: Opportunities and Constraints* (MG-260, Santa Monica, CA: RAND Corporation, 2005).

3. The U.S. figure includes Defense Department budgets ($688b), nuclear weapons ($19b), veterans' benefits ($130b), and so on, as the "compiled" estimates of Chinese

spending attempt to capture. See Office of Management and Budget, Historical Table 3.2, available at http://www.whitehouse.gov/omb/budget/Historicals

4. U.S. figures include Department of Defense baseline budget, war spending for Iraq and Afghanistan, and non-Department of Defense expenditures such as Energy Department spending on nuclear weapons. Chinese official figures are adjusted to include payments to the People's Armed Police, retirement benefits, subsidies to defense industry, and R&D, among other expenditures. Although PPP adjustments are not made, the overall numbers are very consistent with sector specific PPP adjust figures as calculated in George J. Gilboy and Eric Heginbotham, *Chinese and Indian Strategic Behavior: Growing Power and Alarm* (New York: Cambridge University Press, 2012). SIPRI is a respected, non-American, non-Chinese assessment with a specific methodology that it applies rigorously across time to all countries.

5. Indeed, the newest Pentagon annual report on China's military development exemplifies exactly this, as does Japan's white paper on defense: Office of the Secretary of Defense, "Military and Security Developments Involving the People's Republic of China: Annual Report to Congress" (Washington, D.C.: Department of Defense, April 2013), 36–37, 51; and Ministry of Defense, *Defense of Japan 2012*, Tokyo, Japan, 35–36.

6. *Report to Congress on Foreign Economic Collection and Industrial Espionage*, 2009–2011, available at http://www.dni.gov

7. David E. Sanger and Nicole Perlroth, "Hackers From China Resume Attacks on U.S. Targets," *The New York Times*, May 19, 2013.

8. Brian Weeden, "Dancing in the Dark: The Orbital Rendezvous of SJ-12 and SJ-06F," *The Space Review*, August 20, 2010, available at http://www.thespacereview.com/article/1689/1

9. Linda Jakobson and Dean Knox, *New Foreign Policy Actors in China*, SIPRI Policy Paper No. 26, SIPRI, Stockholm, Sweden, September 2010, available at http://books.sipri.org/files/PP/SIPRIPP26.pdf

10. General Norton A. Schwartz and Admiral Jonathan W. Greenert, "Air-Sea Battle: Promoting Stability in an Era of Uncertainty," *The American Interest*, February 20, 2012, available at http://www.the-american-interest.com/article.cfm?piece=1212

11. Joint Communiqué of the People's Republic of China and the United States of America, August 17, 1982, available at http://www.china-embassy.org/eng/zmgx/doc/ctc/t946664.htm

12. United Nations Convention on the Law of the Sea, p. 44, available at http://www.un.org/Depts/los/convention_agreements/texts/unclos/unclos_e.pdf

13. Liu Qun, Liu Jinyu. "A Rational Look at China's Defense Expenditure Increase in 2011," *China National Defense Economy*, January 2011.

14. Angus Maddison, *Chinese Economic Performance in the Long Run*, 2d ed. (Paris: Organisation for Economic Cooperaton and Development, 2007), p. 44, available at http://browse.oecdbookshop.org/oecd/pdfs/product/4107091e.pdf

15. International Institute for Strategic Studies (IISS), *The Military Balance in 2012*, available at http://www.iiss.org/publications/military-balance/

16. *China's National Defense in 2010 White Paper*, p. 18, available at http://news.xinhuanet.com/english2010/china/2011-03/31/c_13806851_19.htm

17. Charles Krauthammer, "Beyond the Cold War," *New Republic*, December 19, 1988, p. 18.

18. Samuel P. Huntington, *Who Are We? The Challenges to America's National Identity* (New York: Simon & Schuster, 2004), pp. 178–220.

19 Joint Communiqué of the United States of America and the People's Republic of China, August 17, 1982.

20. This might be an appropriate time to remind you that I am expressing my own views as a scholar, and not any official U.S. government position.

21. For the best discussions, see Raul Pedrozo, "Preserving Navigational Rights and Freedoms: The Right to Conduct Military Activities in China's Exclusive Economic Zone," *Chinese Journal of International Law* 9, no. 1 (2010), pp. 9–29; Haiwen Zhange, "Is It Safeguarding the Freedom of Navigation or Maritime Hegemony of the United States?—Comments on Raul Pedrozo's Article on Military Activities in the EEZ," *Chinese Journal of International Law* 9, no. 1 (2010), pp. 31–47; *Military Activities in the EEZ: A U.S.-China Dialogue on Security and International Law in the Maritime Commons*, ed. Peter Dutton (Newport, R.I.: United States Department of Defense, 2011); Raul Pedrozo, "Responding to Ms. Zhang's Talking Points on the EEZ," *Chinese Journal of International Law* 10, no. 1 (2011), pp. 207–223.

22. On both this point, and the next, see Raul Pedrozo, "Coastal State Jurisdiction Over Marine Data Collection in the Exclusive Economic Zone," in Dutton, op. cit., 2011, pp. 31–33 and related notes.

23. See "APT1: Exposing One of China's Cyber Espionage Units," Mandiant Intelligence Center Report, February 18, 2013, available at http://www.mandiant.com/apt1; and Ellen Nakashima, "Report on 'Operation Shady RAT' Identifies Widespread Cyber-spying," *The Washington Post*, August 2, 2011.

24. Scott Shane and Andrew W. Lehren, "WikiLeaks Archive—Cables Uncloak U.S. Diplomacy," *The New York Times*, November 28, 2010.

25. See *Report to Congress on Foreign Economic Collection and Industrial Espionage, 2009–2011*, available at http://www.dni.gov

26. Michael Riley and Dune Lawrence, "Hackers Linked to China's Army Seen from EU to D.C.," *Bloomberg*, July 26, 2012, available at http://www.bloomberg.com/news/2012-07-26/china-hackers-hit-eu-point-man-and-d-c-with-byzantine-candor.html. See also "Merkel's China Visit Marred by Hacking Allegations," *Speigel Online*, August 27, 2007.

27. David Sanger, "Obama Ordered Wave of Cyberattacks Against Iran," *The New York Times*, June 1, 2012.

28. Nicole Perlroth, "Electronic Security a Worry in An Age of Digital Espionage," *The New York Times*, February 10, 2012.

29. John Pomfret, "U.S. Takes a Tougher Tone with China," *The Washington Post*, July 30, 2010.

30. Andres Kohut, "The World Says China Will Overtake America: But Not Many Are Cheering," *The Wall Street Journal*, July 14, 2011, available at http://www.pewglobal.org/2011/07/13/china-seen-overtaking-us-as-global-superpower

31. In the same way that China doesn't trust U.S. statements that our missile defense capabilities aren't aimed at China.

32. Allen S. Whiting, "China's Use of Force, 1950-96, and Taiwan," *International Security* 26, no. 2 (2001): 103–131; Roger Cliff, *"Entering the Dragon's Lair: Chinese Antiaccess Strategies and Their Implications for the United States"* (MG-524, Santa Monica, CA: RAND Corporation, 2007).

33. Lyle Goldstein, *"Not Congruent but Quite Complementary: U.S. and Chinese Approaches to Nontraditional Security,"* China Maritime Study 9 (Newport, R.I.: Naval War College, 2012).

34. Zhang Haiwen, Deputy Director of China Institute for Marine Affairs, State Oceanic Administration, People's Republic of China.

35. Views expressed in his presentation of Gil Duvall, Chair of Cyber Integration and Information Operations with U.S. National Defense University iCollege, at JIDD March 2012 in Jakarta, Indonesia.

36. Xinhua, "China Defense Ministry Refutes Cyber Attack Allegations," February 20, 2013, available at http://news.xinhuanet.com/english/china/2013-02/20/c_132180777.htm

37. Xinhua, "Attacks Originating from U.S. Rank First Among Overseas Hackings in China: FM," February 20, 2013, available at http://news.xinhuanet.com/english/china/2013-02/20/c_132180786.htm

38. Ibid.

39. Xinhua, "China Defense Ministry Refutes Cyber Attack Allegations," February 20, 2013, available at http://news.xinhuanet.com/english/china/2013-02/20/c_132180777.htm

40. Xinhua, "Attacks Originating from U.S. Rank First Among Overseas Hackings in China: FM," February 20, 2013, available at http://news.xinhuanet.com/english/china/2013-02/20/c_132180786.htm

41. Naomi McMillen, "Fiftieth Anniversary of the 1962 Sino-Indian Border War," An Interview with Arun Sahgal October 30, 2012, National Bureau of Asian Research, available at http://www.nbr.org/research/activity.aspx?id=290

42. Harry Booty, "To What Extent was the 1979 Sino-Vietnamese Border War About Cambodia?" E-International Relations, available at http://www.e-ir.info/2012/09/21/to-what-extent-was-the-1979-sino-vietnamese-border-war-about-the-situation-in-cambodia/. For more on the persecution of Chinese residents of Vietnam before the border clash of 1979, see material by Western and Hong Kong scholars posted at these two Web sites (in Chinese): http://view.news.qq.com/a/20130921/002348.htm and http://www.yzw19.com/junshihuimou/2010/1106/4589_2.html

43. Michael Kiselycznyk and Phillip C. Saunders, *Assessing Chinese Military Transparency,* Institute for National Strategic Studies, National Defense University, June 2010, available at www.dtic.mil/cgi-bin/GetTRDoc?AD=ADA546679.

44. James J. Marquardt, *Transparency and American Primacy in World Politics,* (Surrey and Burlington: Ashgate, 2011).

45. Alastair Iain Johnston, "Is China a Status Quo Power?," *International Security,* 27, no. 4 (Spring 2003), pp. 5–56. Nicholas Taylor, "China as a Status Quo or Revisionist Power? Implications for Australia," *Security Challenges,* 3, no. 1 (February 2007), available at www.securitychallenges.org.au/ArticlePDFs/vo3no1Taylor.pdf

CHAPTER 9: TAIWAN AND TIBET

1. Election Study Center, National Chengchi University, "Changes in the Unification-Independence Stances of Taiwanese as Tracked in Surveys, 1994–2012.12," available at http://esc.nccu.edu.tw/english/modules/tinyd2/content/tonduID.htm

CHAPTER 10: REGIONAL SECURITY

1. See, for instance, "China-U.S. Joint Statement," November 17, 2009, Beijing, available at http://www.fmprc.gov.cn/eng/wjb/zzjg/bmdyzs/xwlb/t629497.htm; "China-U.S. Joint Statement," January 19, 2011, Washington, D.C., available at http://www.fmprc.gov.cn/eng/wjdt/2649/t788173.htm
2. "China-U.S. Joint Statement," January 19, 2011, Washington, D.C.
3. For a detailed discussion of the issue, please see, Wu Xinbo, "China and the United States: Core Interests, Common Interests, and Partnership," *Special Report* 277, June 2011, United States Institute of Peace, available at http://www.usip.org/publications/china-and-the-united-states
4. Leszek Buszynski, "The South China Sea: Oil, Maritime Claims, and U.S.-China Strategic Rivalry," *The Washington Quarterly* 35, no. 2 (Spring 2012), p. 140.
5. Bates Gill, Michael Green, Nicholas Szechenyi, and Kiyoto Tsuji, *Strategic Views on Asian Regionalism* (Center for Strategic and International Studies, 2009), available at http://csis.org/files/media/csis/pubs/090217_gill_stratviews_web.pdf
6. Dina Smeltz, *Foreign Policy in the New Millenium* (The Chicago Council on Global Affairs, 2012), p. 36, available at http://www.thechicagocouncil.org/UserFiles/File/Task%20Force%20Reports/2012_CCS_Report.pdf
7. A 2011 Pew Global Attitudes poll showed that majorities in most countries polled saw rising Chinese military power as a bad thing. Pew Research Center, "China Seen Overtaking U.S. as Global Superpower," July 13, 2011, p. 7, available at http://www.pewglobal.org/files/2011/07/Pew-Global-Attitudes-Balance-of-Power-U.S.-Image-Report-FINAL-July-13-2011.pdf. See also Fergus Hanson, *The Lowy Institute Poll 2011*, available at http://lowyinstitute.cachefly.net/files/pub-files/Lowy_Poll_2011_WEB.pdf; and Asan Institute polling in Korea, available at http://asaninst.org/eng/03_publications/report_detail.php?seq=1559&ipage=1&nums=0&ca=0

CONCLUSION

1. Kenneth Lieberthal and Wang Jisi, *Addressing U.S.-China Strategic Distrust* John L. Thornton Center Monograph Series (Washington, D.C.: Brookings, 2012).
2. See James B. Steinberg, "China's Arrival: The Long March to Global Power," keynote address at the Center for a New American Security, Washington, D.C., September 24, 2009, available at http://www.cnas.org/files/documents/publications/CNAS%20China's%20Arrival_Final%20Report.pdf

EDITOR AND AUTHORS

ABOUT THE EDITOR

Nina Hachigian is a Senior Fellow at the Center for American Progress where she focuses on U.S. foreign policy and U.S. relationships with major powers, particularly China. Earlier, she served as the director of the Center for Asia Pacific Policy at the RAND Corporation. From 1998 to 1999, Hachigian was on the staff of the National Security Council in the White House. She is a founding and current member of the U.S. Department of State's Foreign Affairs Policy Board.

Based in Los Angeles, Hachigian is the co-author of *The Next American Century: How the U.S. Can Thrive as Other Powers Rise* (Simon & Schuster, 2008), which was translated into Chinese. She has published dozens of reports, journal articles, and columns. Recent reports on U.S.–China relations include *Managing Insecurities Across the Pacific* (Center for American Progress, 2012) and *Conduct Befitting a Great Power: Responsibility and Sovereignty in U.S.–China Relations* (Center for American Progress, 2011). She has been a guest on numerous television, radio, and Internet news programs. Hachigian received her B.S. from Yale University, *magna cum laude*, and her J.D. from Stanford Law School, with distinction.

ABOUT THE AUTHORS

Elizabeth Economy

Dr. Economy is the C.V. Starr Senior Fellow and Director of Asia Studies at the Council on Foreign Relations and is an expert on U.S.–China relations and Chinese environmental and global investment policy. She is currently completing a book about China's resource quest, *By All Means Necessary*, with Michael Levi (forthcoming, Oxford University Press, 2014), and is the award-winning author of *The River Runs Black: The Environmental Challenges to China's Future* (Cornell University Press, 2004, 2d ed., 2010), which has been translated into both Chinese and Japanese. She has consulted with U.S. government agencies and taught at several universities, most recently Columbia University. She also serves as the Vice-Chair of the World Economic Forum's Global Agenda Council on the Future of China. Dr. Economy received her B.A. with Honors from Swarthmore College, her A.M. from Stanford University, and her Ph.D. from the University of Michigan.

Kelly Sims Gallagher

Dr. Gallagher is Associate Professor of Energy and Environmental Policy at The Fletcher School, Tufts University, where she also directs the Center for International Environment and Resource Policy. She is also a Senior Research Associate of the Belfer Center for Science and International Affairs at Harvard University. She is an expert on energy and climate policy in both the United States and China, with a focus on the role of policy in spurring the development and deployment of cleaner and more efficient energy technologies. Her most recent books include *The Globalization of Clean Energy Technology: Lessons from China* (MIT Press, 2014) and *China Shifts Gears: Automakers, Oil, Pollution, and Development* (MIT Press, 2006). A Truman Scholar, she has a M.A.L.D. and Ph.D. in international affairs from Tufts, and an A.B. from Occidental College.

Michael Green

Dr. Green is an associate professor of international relations at Georgetown University and Senior Vice President for Asia and Japan Chair at the Center for Strategic and International Studies (CSIS). He previously served as a Special Assistant to President George W. Bush for national security affairs and Senior Director for Asian Affairs at the National Security Council. He is a prolific author and his current research and writing is focused on Asian regional architecture, Japanese politics, U.S. foreign policy history, the Korean peninsula, Tibet, Burma, and U.S.–India relations. He is fluent in Japanese and spent over five years in Japan working as a staff member for the National Diet, as a journalist for Japanese and American newspapers, and as a consultant for U.S. business. He graduated from Kenyon College with highest honors in history in 1983 and received his M.A. from Johns Hopkins SAIS in 1987 and his Ph.D. in 1994.

Jia Qingguo

Dr. Jia is Professor and Associate Dean of the School of International Studies at Peking University. He is also the Vice President of the Chinese American Studies Association and board member of the China National Taiwan Studies Association. He is a member of the Standing Committee and the Foreign Affairs Committee of the CPPCC National Committee and a member of the Standing Committee of the China Democratic League. He serves on the editorial board of several established domestic and international academic journals. Dr. Jia served as a research fellow at the Brookings Institution twice and has taught at several American universities including the University of Vermont, the University of California at San Diego, and Cornell University. He has published extensively on relations, between the Chinese mainland and Taiwan, U.S.–China relations and Chinese foreign policy. He received his Ph.D. from Cornell University in 1988.

Kenneth G. Lieberthal

Dr. Lieberthal is Senior Fellow in Foreign Policy, Global Economy, and Development at the John L. Thornton China Center at the Brookings Institution. He was a professor at the University of Michigan from 1983 to 2009. He has authored or edited 24 books and monographs and over 70 articles, mostly dealing with China. He also served as Special Assistant to the President for National Security Affairs and Senior Director for Asia on the National Security Council 1998–2000. He graduated from Dartmouth College and received his M.A. and Ph.D. from Columbia University.

Andrew J. Nathan

Dr. Nathan is the Class of 1919 Professor of Political Science at Columbia University. His most recent books are *Will China Democratize?* coedited with Larry Diamond and Marc Plattner (Johns Hopkins University Press, 2013) and *China's Search for Security,* coauthored with Andrew Scobell (Columbia University Press, 2012). He is actively involved in Chinese human rights issues as a member of the boards of Human Rights in China, the National Endowment for Democracy, and Freedom House. He is the regular Asia book reviewer for *Foreign Affairs.* At Columbia he has served as director of the Weatherhead East Asian Institute, chair of the Department of Political Science, chair of the Executive Committee of the Faculty of Arts and Sciences, chair of the administrative committee of the Institute for the Study of Human Rights, and chair of the Morningside Institutional Review Board (IRB). Dr. Nathan received his degrees from Harvard University: a B.A. in history, an M.A. in East Asian regional studies, and a Ph.D. in political science.

Barry Naughton
Dr. Naughton is Professor of Chinese Economy and the Sokwanlok Chair of Chinese International Affairs at the School of International Relations and Pacific Studies at the University of California, San Diego. His book *The Chinese Economy: Transitions and Growth* (MIT Press, 2007) is an authoritative introduction to the Chinese economy, translated into Chinese and Korean. His research and writings focus on issues relating to technology and trade and China's transition to a market economy. Naughton's first book, *Growing Out of the Plan: Chinese Economic Reform, 1978–1993* (Cambridge University Press, 1996) was widely lauded and awarded the Ohira Memorial Prize. He received a B.A. from University of Washington in Chinese language and literature, an M.A. in international relations from Yale University and a Ph.D. in economics from Yale University.

Qi Ye
Dr. Qi Ye is the Cheung Kong Professor of Environmental Policy at the School of Public Policy and Management at Tsinghua University and the Director of the Climate Policy Institute there. He advises governments, NGOs, and international organizations on climate change, clean energy, and environmental policy issues. He is also the principal investigator and editor of the Annual Review of Low Carbon Development in China. His most recent book is *Environmental Governance in China* (Shanghai Joint Publishing Co., 2009). He has conducted research at the University of California, San Diego, and Cornell University and taught ecosystem modeling and management at University of California, Berkeley. He received a joint Ph.D. in

Environmental Science from the State University of New York's College of Environmental Science and Forestry and Syracuse University.

Alan D. Romberg

Alan Romberg is the Director of the East Asia Program at the Stimson Center. Prior to joining to Stimson, he had a distinguished career working on Asian issues in the State Department as well as at the Council on Foreign Relations. He was the principal deputy director of the State Department's Policy Planning Staff and Principal Deputy Assistant Secretary of State for Public Affairs and Deputy Spokesman as well as Director of the Office of Japanese Affairs, member of the Policy Planning Staff for East Asia, and staff member for China at the National Security Council. He was stationed overseas in Hong Kong and Taiwan as part of his State Department service. Mr. Romberg holds a B.A. from the Woodrow Wilson School of Public and International Affairs at Princeton University and an M.A. from Harvard University. He has written widely on U.S. policy toward East Asia, in particular the PRC, Taiwan, Korea, and Japan.

Susan Shirk

Dr. Shirk is the chair of the 21st Century China Program and Ho Miu Lam Professor of China and Pacific Relations at the School of International Relations and Pacific Studies (IR/PS) at UC San Diego. She served as the Deputy Assistant Secretary of State for East Asia and Pacific Affairs under President Bill Clinton and is the author and editor of several books, including *Changing Media, Changing China* (Oxford University Press, 2010) and *China: Fragile Superpower* (Oxford University Press, 2007). Dr. Shirk received a B.A. in political science from Mount Holyoke College, an M.A. in Asian studies from the University of California, Berkeley, and a Ph.D. in political science from the Massachusetts Institute of Technology.

James B. Steinberg

James Steinberg is Dean of the Maxwell School of Citizenship and Public Affairs at Syracuse University, and University Professor of Social Science, International Affairs, and Law. Prior to becoming Dean, he was Deputy Secretary of State, serving as the principal deputy to Secretary Clinton. From 2005–2008, Steinberg was Dean of the Lyndon B. Johnson School of Public Affairs. Previously, he was Vice President and Director of Foreign Policy Studies at the Brookings Institution. Steinberg served as deputy national security advisor to President Clinton from 1996 to 2000. During that period he also served as the President's personal representative to the 1998 and 1999 G-8 Summits. Steinberg is the co-author of *Strategic Reassurance and Resolve: Managing the U.S.-China Relationship in the 21st Century* (Princeton University Press, forthcoming) as well as *Difficult Transitions: Foreign Policy Troubles at the Outset of Presidential Power* (Brookings, 2008) with Kurt Campbell.

Christopher P. Twomey

Dr. Twomey is an associate professor in the Department of National Security Affairs at the Naval Postgraduate School, where he focuses on Chinese foreign policy and East Asian security. He works with the Departments of Defense and State on a range of strategic and Asian security issues and recently authored *The Military Lens: Doctrinal Differences and Deterrence Failure in Sino-American Relations* (Cornell University Press, 2010). Dr. Twomey received his B.A. and Masters of Pacific International Affairs from the University of California, San Diego, and his Ph.D. in Political Science from the Massachusetts Institute of Technology.

Wang Jisi

Professor Wang is Dean of the School of International Studies at Peking University. For the past 30 years, Professor Wang's role as a leading Chinese scholar on the United States and his frequent involvement in high-level track II diplomacy initiatives has made him one of the most influential figures in U.S.-China relations. He is a founding member of the Pacific Council on International Policy and has taught at a variety of colleges, including the University of Michigan and Claremont McKenna College. He is currently a Global Scholar of Princeton University. Professor Wang studied at Peking University, where he received his M.A.

Wang Shuo

Wang Shuo is the Managing Editor of Caixin Media, a Beijing-based media group providing financial and business news. Before that, he was the Managing Editor of *Caijing* magazine from 1998 to 2009. The World Economic Forum recently named him a "Young Global Leader." Wang Shuo has a degree in Philosophy from Renmin University of China, an M.A. in Philosophy from Peking University, an Executive MBA from the joint program of Fordham University and Peking University, and an M.A. in International Public Policy from Johns Hopkins University.

Wu Xinbo

Dr. Wu is a professor and director at the Center for American Studies and the executive dean of the Institute of the International Studies at Fudan University. He has authored several books on China–U.S. relations and U.S. Asia-Pacific policy, including *The New Landscape in Sino-U.S. Relations in the Early 21st Century* (Fudan University Press, 2011) and *Turbulent Water: U.S. Asia-Pacific Security Strategy in the Post-Cold War Era* (Fudan University Press, 2006). He has previously worked at the United States Institute of Peace, the Brookings Institution and the Stimson Center. Dr. Wu studied at Fudan University, where he received his Ph.D.

Xu Hui

Senior Colonel Xu Hui is a professor and Deputy Commandant of the College of Defense Studies (CDS) at the National Defense University (NDU) of the People's Liberation Army in Beijing. He also serves as a Deputy Secretary General of the Chinese Association of World Military Studies, an executive member of the Board of the Chinese Association of American Studies, and the Editor in Chief of CDS's *Defense Forum* magazine. His scholarly interests include military strategy of the United States and China, Sino-American relations, Asia-Pacific Security, and crisis management. His latest publications include *Crisis Management: Theory and Case Studies* (NDU, 2011) and *National Security and Defense Policies of Foreign Countries in the 21st Century* (NDU, 2010) Sr Col. Xu studied in a military academy, the Army Commanding School, and the National Defense University of China successively, and received his Ph.D. from the Chinese Academy of Social Sciences.

Yao Yang

Dr. Yao is a professor and the Director of the China Center for Economic Research and the Dean of the National School of Development at Beijing University. He focuses primarily on economic transition and development in China. In addition to his current position, Dr. Yao served as a consultant for the World Bank and taught at several universities in China, the United States, and Japan. He is the author or editor of several books, including *China's Economic Reform and Growth* (Routledge, 2010), *Economic Reform and Institutional Innovation* (Gale Asia/Cengage Learning, 2009), *Globalization and Economic Growth in China* (World Scientific, 2006), *Ownership Transformation in China* (World Bank, 2005), and *China's Private Enterprise* (Asia Pacific Press, 2001). Dr. Yao studied at Beijing University and the University of Wisconsin at Madison, where he received his Ph.D.

Yuan Peng

Dr. Yuan is the Vice President of the China Institutes of Contemporary International Relations. He focuses on Sino-American relations and East Asian security studies. He has edited several books, including *American and Chinese Accommodation in the Asia-Pacific Region: The U.S., China and Third Parties* (Shishi Chubanshe, 2013), *China-U.S. Relations: A Strategic Analysis* (Shishi Chubanshe, 2005), and *American Think Tanks and Their Attitudes Towards China* (Shishi Chubanshe, 2003). He served as research fellow at the Brookings Institution from 2003–2004 and visiting scholar at the Atlantic Council from 1999–2000. Dr. Yuan studied at East China Normal University and Northeast Normal University, where he received his Ph.D.

Zha Daojiong

Dr. Zha is a professor of international political economy at Peking University, where he specializes in Chinese investment strategy as well as energy, food, and water issues. He is the author and editor of several books, including *Managing Regional Energy Vulnerabilities in East Asia* (Routledge, 2013), *Building a Neighborly Community: Post Cold War China, Japan, and Southeast Asia* (Manchester University Press, 2006), and *The International Political Economy of China's Oil Supply Security* (Contemporary World Affairs Press, 2005). Prior to his tenure at Peking University, he taught at the University of Macao, the International University of Japan, and Remin University of China. Dr. Zha studied at the University of Hawaii, where he received his Ph.D.

Zhou Qi

Dr. Zhou is the Director of the Research Department of American Politics and a senior researcher and full professor at the Institute of American Studies in the Chinese Academy of Social Sciences (CASS). Dr. Zhou has authored ten books, including *American Energy Security Policy* and *Foreign Policy Strategy* (China Social Sciences, 2012), *American Foreign Policies on Human Rights* (Shanghai People's Publishing House, 2001), and over 60 academic articles. Her books *American Foreign Policies on Human Rights* and *Ideology and American Foreign Policy* won the Chinese Academy of Social Sciences Prize for Excellence in Scientific Research. In 1992 the Chinese National Education Commission named Dr. Zhou one of "100 Distinguished Associate Professors." She has twice been a visiting scholar at Harvard University and was the Frank M. Johnson Visiting Professor at Pomona College. Dr. Zhou studied at Fudan University and Johns Hopkins University's SAIS, where she received her Ph.D.

INDEX